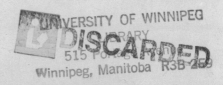

CHAUCER AND
THE POETS

CHAUCER AND THE POETS

AN ESSAY ON
Troilus and Criseyde

WINTHROP WETHERBEE

Cornell University Press

ITHACA AND LONDON

First published in 1984 by Cornell University Press.
Published in the United Kingdom by
Cornell University Press, Ltd., London.

International Standard Book Number 0–8014–1684–1
Library of Congress Catalog Card Number 84–7080
Printed in the United States of America
Librarians: Library of Congress cataloging information
appears on the last page of the book.

To My Best Friend, Andrea

Contents

Preface

This book argues that Chaucer's *Troilus* is a major statement about poetic tradition. Chaucer, who was remarkable in his early and profound appreciation of the achievement of Dante, shared Dante's sense of the special excellence of the classical Latin poets, Vergil, Ovid, and Statius. Like Dante, he recognized that classical poetry presented an authoritative view of human experience which earlier medieval poets had assimilated only partially and with an imperfect awareness of the dynamic role the Latin poets could play in the development of a classical tradition of Christian poetry. The *Troilus* is, of course, one of the great medieval statements on love, deeply indebted to Boethius and the *Roman de la Rose*, and it owes an obvious debt as well to the tradition of the *romans d'antiquité*, but it adopts a new perspective on these medieval affinities. Chaucer places his medieval version of a pagan love story in a context of allusions to classical epic which deepen and complicate its meaning, making the story a significant foil to the religious perspective that surfaces in the final stanzas of the poem.

Too little work has been done on Chaucer's poetics. There is still a persistent tendency to assume that he viewed "poetry" as synonymous with "courtly poetry," an assumption that I hope my discussion of the literary context of the *Troilus* may help to correct. The relations of different literary modes, in particular the opposition between courtly "making" and classically oriented "poetry," seem to me a central concern in Chaucer's work. I have tried to provide a concrete illustration of how this opposition functions in the *Troilus,* tracing the poet-narrator's evolution from a writer of romance who views his material in the idealizing light of the courtly love tradition to a disciple of the *poetae,* capable of realizing the tragic and finally the spiritual implications of his story.

In assessing Chaucer's debt to the classical poets and Dante I have tried to show that his engagement with them was a literary one—the engagement of an individual talent with its tradition—that he read them as poets, and that their influence was as complex as that of any major poet on another. These would not be controversial assumptions if we were talking about Milton, but the case of a medieval poet presents special problems. Having been shown to our profit the importance of commentary, gloss, and mythographical compendium in accounting for medieval notions about classical poetry, we tend to substitute such tools for the texts of the poets themselves, forgetting that these texts were read as well as annotated. Fulgentius and John of Garland have proved more efficient than direct recourse to the *Aeneid* or the *Metamorphoses* as a way of "cracking" medieval allusions to Vergil and Ovid; and while the cold finger of moral pedantry sometimes touches the spirits of practitioners of this method, it clearly reflects certain medieval habits of reading. There is a risk, however, of confusing the categories and purposes of teachers and glossators with those of poets. Without questioning Chaucer's knowledge of the commentators, I have tried to show that there is a significant difference between his use of them and his direct recourse to the poets themselves and that his reading of Ovid and Statius acknowledges interplays of theme and context which the commentaries, with their very different purposes, often ignore. It is finally the texts themselves, "the forme of olde clerkis speche," that meant most to Chaucer, as to Dante. In exploring the relation of these texts to the *Troilus* I have tried to locate and explicate what Chaucer, at those moments when he felt himself to have made contact with it, called poetry.

A great many friends and friendly institutions have helped me see this project through. Most of the reading and much of the writing were done with the benefit of fellowships from the John Simon Guggenheim Memorial Foundation and Cornell University's wonderfully hospitable Society for the Humanities. Friends who gave generously of their time to read and criticize portions of my manuscript include Stephen Barney, James Chandler, Carolyn Dinshaw, Judy Ferster, Nicholas Havely, Mark Lambert, Shirley Lukitsch, Michael Murrin, Lee Patterson, Allen Shoaf, and Michael Twomey. Jay Schleusener, in addition to reading most of the manuscript, spent several long afternoons of conversation helping me work out my ideas at an early stage, and Caron Cioffi, Rory Holscher, Rozalyn Levin, and Linda Lomperis have offered many helpful criticisms and suggestions along the way. Sherron Knopp produced a remarkably thorough and probing report for Cornell University Press and pointed the way to a number of important revisions. Finally, Allison Dodge, who edited for the Press what I had foolishly imagined was my final draft, made yet more valuable suggestions about organization and persuaded me to purge a great deal of gratuitous academese. I have not followed all my friends' suggestions, even when they were right, but they are largely responsible for whatever coherence this essay may possess.

Portions of two articles are incorporated at various points in the book: "The Descent from Bliss: *Troilus* III, 1310–1582," first published in *Chaucer's 'Troilus': Essays in Criticism*, ed. Stephen A. Barney (Hamden, Conn., 1980), pp. 297–317, and "'Per te poeta fui, per te cristiano': Dante, Statius, and the Narrator of Chaucer's *Troilus*," which appeared in *Vernacular Poetics in the Middle Ages*, ed. Lois Ebin (Kalamazoo, Mich., 1984), pp. 153–76. I am grateful to Medieval Institute Publications of Western Michigan University for permission to reprint material from the latter article.

WINTHROP WETHERBEE

Chicago, Illinois

A Note on Texts

All quotations from the *Troilus* are from the edition of R. K. Root, *The Book of Troilus and Criseyde* (Princeton University Press, Princeton, N.J., 1926). For Vergil I have used the Oxford Classical Texts edition of R. A. B. Mynors (Oxford University Press, Oxford, 1969); for Ovid, the Budé edition of the *Metamorphoses*, ed. Georges Lafaye, 3 vols. (Les Belles Lettres, Paris, 1928–30); for Statius, the Teubner edition of the *Thebaid*, ed. Alfred Klotz, rev. Thomas C. Klinnert (Teubner Leipzig, 1973); for the *Roman de la Rose*, the Classiques français du moyen âge edition of Félix Lecoy, 3 vols. (Champion, Paris, 1965–70); for Dante's *Commedia*, the edition of Charles S. Singleton, 6 vols. (Princeton University Press, Princeton, N.J., 1970–75); for Boccaccio, the Scrittori d'Italia edition of the *Filostrato*, ed. Vincenzo Pernicone (Scrittori d'Italia Bari, 1937). Translations are my own, except those from the *Commedia*, for which I have used the version of Singleton, and those from the *Filostrato*, most of which are taken from N. R. Havely, *Chaucer's Boccaccio* (D. S. Brewer, Woodbridge, Suffolk, 1980).

W. W.

CHAUCER AND
THE POETS

Introduction

As the narrator of Chaucer's *Troilus* seeks to conclude his poem, he is anxious to preserve the decorum of his courtly love story yet increasingly aware that there is more to be said than its conventional limits will allow him to express. The question what human love is and means arises with a new urgency as the moment for separating from Troilus draws nearer, and the final portions of the poem are largely concerned with finding the appropriate mode for dealing with this question. It is a problem with which Chaucer wrestled a good deal in the course of his poetic career. The richest of his early poems, the *Parliament of Fowls,* is largely about how traditional allegorical forms engage and fail to engage the question of the place of human love in the order of the universe. The unfinished *Anelida and Arcite* and the *Complaint of Mars* are early symptoms of a lifelong concern with expressing in poetry the relationship between love and history. But the poem that comes closest to the *Troilus* in addressing the problematic relations of love and poetry is the *House of Fame,* which deals not only with the problem of finding a form but with the nature of literary tradition.

The *House of Fame* dramatizes the delusions and uncertainties that hinder a courtly love poet's attempt to reconcile his commitment to love with a desire to write poetry of a higher order— more philosophical, more Dantean, more classical. The poem thus raises precisely the problem that the narrator of the *Troilus* confronts when he seeks to place his love story in its proper

relation to the achievement of earlier poets, a status higher than
that attained by his previous exercises in courtly "making" yet
deferentially "subject" to the authority of the great poets of
antiquity.[1] More than any other of Chaucer's works the *House of
Fame* is a poem about poetic tradition. A brief review of its complex and cerebral allegory can help us understand what was at
stake for Chaucer when he sought to come to terms with the
great poetry of the past—a task inseparable from that of finding
an adequately serious way of talking about love and one that
becomes the central concern of the final stanzas of the *Troilus*.

   In the *House of Fame*, too, the task of engaging with tradition is
central, but it is left wholly unaccomplished, and indeed most of
the poem is devoted to illustrating the necessity for undertaking
it. Despite the elaborate framework of the traditional celestial
journey, the narrator's strenuous touting of his vision in the
Proem, and the Dantean invocations to the several books, the
quest undertaken in the *House of Fame* is radically disoriented.
From beginning to end of his threefold vision, the dreamer-
narrator does not know what he wants to learn or what he
should expect to learn at the House of Fame. He is presented as
having concerned himself with love in theory and with the
courtly ritual of literary service to the god of love, to the point of
losing touch with the world around him. The eagle who carries
him to the House of Fame promises him "tydynges / Of Loves
folk yf they be glade," which we may presumably understand to
mean enlightenment as to the larger implications of his preoccupation with love, but he never receives the tidings themselves
or any further information as to their nature.

   The dreamer's problem is illustrated in the first book of the

---

1. The opposition between "making" and "poetry" is important for my argument. "Making" seems to have meant to Chaucer the production of literary work
that meets the demand of one's own society to be edified, pleased, and refreshed
on its own terms. This criterion fits the *Troilus* to the extent that we see it as
programmed by courtly convention and concerned with promoting courtly values. "Poetry" meant the work of *poetae*, the classical poets and Dante (see also
note 3 below). On the importance of this opposition for Chaucer see Glending
Olson, "Making and Poetry in the Age of Chaucer," *Comparative Literature* 31
(1979): 272–90; Anne Middleton, "Chaucer's 'New Men' and the Good of Literature in the *Canterbury Tales*," in *Literature and Society*, ed. Edward W. Said,
Selected Papers from the English Institute, n.s. 3 (Baltimore, Md., 1980), pp.
15–56.

poem, in which he reports and responds to the story of the *Aeneid* as set forth on the walls of Venus's temple of glass. The centerpiece of the story is an account of Aeneas's relations with Dido, and at the point of his abandonment of her, the Vergilian narrative comes to a standstill while we are given an Ovidian view of the heroine's wrath and sorrow, punctuated with references to other abandoned heroines. The dreamer is overcome with "pity" again and again as Dido acts out her tragedy and is noticeably distracted as he sums up the remaining eight books of Vergil's epic in thirty-odd lines.

The pity that Dido's Ovidian passion inspires in the dreamer, hindering and then dissipating his ability to apprehend the larger framework of destiny and renunciation which the Vergilian narrative expresses, is the index to a kind of alienation, a lack of moral orientation, which, though treated with a good deal of humor in the ensuing books of the poem, constitutes its serious theme. It is the poem's counterpart to the passionate involvement with the lovers which makes it impossible for the narrator of the *Troilus* to achieve a perspective on his love story through most of the poem, and its implications for the dreamer of the *House of Fame* are forcefully illustrated by the ensuing action. The dreamer emerges from Venus's temple to find himself in a desert inhabited by no natural thing. He is shocked into prayer, but his prayer is answered only with the bizarre visions of Books 2 and 3, his journey through the heavens and his tour of the House of Fame itself.

In one aspect the celestial journey is a dramatization of the dreamer's sense of his capacity for serious poetry. There are energy and exuberance in his recognition that he too has joined Macrobius, Martianus Capella, and Alain de Lille in recording the wonders of the spheres, and a sureness in his recognition of the rank and achievements of the major and minor poets who have adorned Fame's palace. What he cannot do, however, is reconcile his own ostensible purpose, the pursuit of love-tidings, with the emulation of any of these great models. He can find no adequate vehicle for the inspiration he feels, no way of ordering what he sees, and thus he is borne along from one spectacle to another, seemingly subject to forces beyond his control. At the climax of his journey he is on the point of receiving the long-sought tidings and simultaneously aware of the approach of a figure of "gret auctorite" who will presumably comment on them, but the poem breaks off before either of these elements can be incorporated into his vision.

Though the chronological relation of the *House of Fame* and the *Troilus* is uncertain, I think we may see them as reflecting two stages in the poet's progress. The narrator of the *House of Fame*, after a long service to Cupid and the French courtly tradition, has become vaguely aware of the limitations of this tradition and has decided to explore the possibility of a larger poetic undertaking, though he cannot free himself from his courtly preoccupations to the point of being able to see the new enterprise clearly. But in the *Troilus* we can trace the evolution of a poet who begins as a courtly maker, a servant of love's servants, enters into a sustained engagement with the classical tradition, and emerges at last as a Christian poet with a voice and perspective of his own. In the last hundred lines of the *Troilus* the abortive enterprise of the *House of Fame* is finally accomplished. The narrator who had begun his poem by willfully insisting on the gladness of love is forced at last to come to terms with Troilus's unhappy end. His development has proceeded by fits and starts, and he experiences its final stages as a series of crises,[2] but he emerges with a newfound sense of purpose that enables him to resolve the story and establish its relation to poetic tradition, consider its moral significance *sub specie aeternitatis*, and, in a final half-dozen stanzas, give expression to those spiritual implications of his theme which his earlier overinvolvement with the love story had concealed from him. In this last stage he achieves a perspective on poetry itself. He sees the perilously attractive rituals and values of both courtly romance and classical epic for what they are, and though the violence of his exorcizing of their delusive power hints at the survival of unresolved tensions in his attitude, he knows what he is doing in a way that the narrator of the *House of Fame* never does.

There is one further link to be noted between the two poems

2. On the emotional tone of the closing portion of the *Troilus*, see E. T. Donaldson, "The Ending of the *Troilus*," in his *Speaking of Chaucer* (New York, 1970), pp. 84–101; repr. in *Chaucer's 'Troilus': Essays in Criticism*, ed. Stephen A. Barney (Hamden, Conn., 1980), pp. 115–30.

before we go on to consider further the role of tradition in the *Troilus*. Chaucer is the first major poet outside Italy whose work reflects an appreciation of the importance of Dante, and in both the *Troilus* and the *House of Fame* the catalyst of the poetic enterprise, what inspires the poet-narrator to seek to reconcile his courtly allegiances with larger ambitions, is the example of Dante's *Commedia*. The *House of Fame*, with its tripartite structure, its elaborate use of dreams and invocations, and its self-scrutinizing artist-hero, seems to reflect the excitement of an initial encounter with the *Commedia*. For Chaucer Dante is not only a model but a standard by which the quality and seriousness of his own future work may be measured, and we will see him testing his finest work by this standard in the *Troilus*. But the Dantean borrowings in the *House of Fame* are at once audacious and self-mocking. When the narrator compares his journey to the visionary pilgrimages of biblical and classical figures and begins each book with a clear echo of the opening of the *Paradiso*, we are asked to recognize the incongruity of such grand gestures with the poem's prevailing tone and the indecisiveness of the dreamer's quest. In the *Troilus* Dante has become an informing and sustaining presence, and the perspective he provides is one the poet-narrator finally comes to share. Though many of the *Troilus's* borrowings are parodic, recalling Dantean moments of enlightenment to comment on the confused or unworthy motives of the narrator and his characters, the effect is not to reduce Chaucer's poetic world to a caricature, but to confirm the psychological depth of his rendering of the universe of paganism. The *Commedia* has become part of the classical tradition as the Chaucer of the *Troilus* has grown to understand it, and in the concluding stanzas of the poem Chaucer proclaims the continuity of purpose in the two poets' engagement with the forms and themes of ancient poetry.

One of the most remarkable features of Chaucer's response to Dante was his recognition of the profound level at which Dante had engaged the Latin epic poets. He shares with Dante a strong sense of the differences in outlook that separate the Christian poet from pagan models, but like Dante he also views these models as *poetae* in a special sense, possessed of an authority and power that he saw medieval poetry as having attained only in the work of Dante himself.[3] Like Dante, Chaucer seeks to give full expression to the pagan character of his classical material, and he allows his narrator to share to a surprising degree the limited historical and spiritual perspective of his pagan characters. The *Troilus* is finally a Christian poem, but it is a Christian poem on a pagan subject in a special sense for which Dante provides the only real precedent. The story it tells is viewed sometimes as a rapturous celebration of human love ending with a reluctant palinode, sometimes as a demonstration of the inevitable disappointment of blind earthly desire. And no doubt it is both of these, but it is also something more. For the narrator, who chooses to retell a story set in the pagan past, and whose response to it is grounded from the outset in a close identification with the lovers and their pagan values, the story is an experience he also lives through. The *Troilus* includes its pagan world largely as the *Commedia* includes the *Inferno,* and its Christian perspective dawns only after the narrator has lived through the full range of his characters' fortunes and shared the constraints of their world view. As with Dante's encounters in the *Inferno* and *Purgatorio* or the earthly phase of his love for Beatrice, it is through a sympathetic sharing of the errors and aspirations of his characters that Chaucer's narrator gains the knowledge that enables him, finally and at great emotional cost, to withdraw himself from the world of the poem and view the love of Troilus from a Christian perspective. Only then can his poetry realize its full expressive power, as Dante's *poesì* becomes a vehicle for recording his own spiritual progress only after he has emerged from the "dead air" of the underworld.

But the *Troilus* inevitably has a good deal in common with the poetry of its own place and time, and its distinctive, Dantean

3. Chaucer uses the terms "poet" and "poetry" sparingly and almost always with reference to classical literature. Aside from one or two general references in the *House of Fame,* the only exceptions occur in citations of Dante by the Monk and the Wife of Bath and in the Clerk's famous encomium of Petrarch. Since the Clerk probably thinks of Petrarch as writing in Latin, Dante would seem to be the sole vernacular writer to whom Chaucer concedes the title of poet. See the valuable excursus of J. S. P. Tatlock, "The Epilogue of Chaucer's 'Troilus,'" *Modern Philology* 18 (1920–21): 630–32, n. 8; Thomas J. Garbáty, "Troilus V, 1786–92 and V, 1807–27: An Example of Poetic Process," *Chaucer Review* 11 (1976–77): 300–301; Olson, "Making and Poetry in the Age of Chaucer," pp. 288–90; Middleton, "Chaucer's 'New Men,'" pp. 24–39, 53–54, n. 15.

qualities emerge more clearly when its debt to the medieval traditions of romance and courtly love are acknowledged. Like the *Commedia* itself, the *Troilus* is in many respects a thoroughly medieval poem, a making new of the *Roman de la Rose*. Chaucer's sense of the continuing vitality of the courtly tradition is clear when we see him following the Boccaccio of the *Filocolo* and *Filostrato* in appropriating Dante's rhetoric and imagery to a new, "realistic" treatment of courtly love. And while Chaucer follows Dante at his most significantly innovative in the depth of his engagement with classical poetry, there is much in the *Troilus* to remind us that he was also heir to the tradition of medieval romance, which presented the ancient themes in a significantly altered form. In the twelfth-century *romans d'antiquité* and their many offspring, the stories of Troy and Thebes and the heroes associated with them are vested with the trappings of chivalry and retold in a way that tends to blur cultural and historical contrasts. There is a marked tendency to soften oppositions between pagan and Christian values, to evade the purely tragic, and above all to give a new prominence to the theme of love.[4] The acknowledged obligation to adhere to the broad outlines of classical legendary history in these *romans* is balanced by the interpolation of love stories involving virtually all the major characters and a strong emphasis on the complex relationship between love and heroism.

The naiveté of the best of these works is finely calculated, but a tendency to sentimentalize and distort the classical stories in the process of adapting them is an ever-present danger and one to which Chaucer may well seem to have succumbed. Most of what is un-epic in the *Troilus* could be explained as a concession to the romance tradition of remaking the classical past, and it is clear that Chaucer's whole enterprise is largely dependent on it. His Troilus owes his good character, his beauty, his comparability with Hector, and the heroism of his last battles not to Homeric tradition as transmitted by the Latin poets, but to

4. See Jean-Charles Payen, "Structure et sens du Roman de Thebes," *Moyen Age* 76 (1970): 493–513; Daniel Poirion, "De l' 'Énéide' a l' 'Eneas': Mythologie et moralisation," *Cahiers de civilization médiévale* 19 (1976): 213–29; Renata Blumenfeld-Kosinski, "Old French Narrative Genres: Towards the Definition of the *Roman Antique*," *Romance Philology* 35 (1981–82): 242–49.

Dares Phrygius. Troilus's love of Criseyde is the invention of Benoit de Sainte-Maure.

It is also important to remember that these medieval versions of classical legend were accorded the status of history in Chaucer's time. To the extent that the *Troilus* is a product of this tradition it can be seen as possessing the practical political value of other medieval retellings of the story of Troy, works through which noble houses sought to legitimize their own status in terms of "descent from an omnipotent past."[5] Chaucer's use of medieval material about Troy to transform Boccaccio's version of his Trojan love story, from which historical detail has been largely eliminated, might be seen as intended precisely to restore the story of Troilus to a place within this medieval historical tradition.[6]

Chaucer was, of course, seriously interested in history and its exemplary bearing, and the *Troilus* in its own way speaks powerfully to the concerns of a court audience. But the historical significance of its exemplary narrative derives from an authenticating relation to the classical poetic tradition—from literary history rather than from historicity in the Troy-book sense. When the narrator of the *Troilus*, commending his book to the world, declares it "subject" to the standard of the great poets— Homer, Vergil, and the rest—he is at the same time implicitly setting himself apart from the historiographic tradition of Benoit and Guido, who had undertaken to correct the Homeric-Vergilian version of the story of Troy, and is tipping the balance back again, toward poetic rather than "historical" truth.[7] The real source of continuity in the *Troilus* is the continuity of theme and vision that Chaucer recognized among the works of the great *poetae,* a complementarity of poetic worlds that he respects scrupulously in "subjecting" his own work to theirs. He makes no such daring gesture as Dante does in including himself with

5. Lee W. Patterson, "The Historiography of Romance and the Alliterative *Morte Arthure," Journal of Medieval and Renaissance Studies* 13 (1980): 2.

6. See Patterson, p. 9; C. David Benson, *The History of Troy in Middle English Literature* (Woodbridge, Suffolk, 1980), pp. 134–43; A. J. Minnis, *Chaucer and Pagan Antiquity* (Woodbridge, Suffolk, 1982), pp. 88–90.

7. See the conclusion of Guido's *Historia Destructionis Troiae,* ed. Nathaniel E. Griffin (Cambridge, Mass., 1936), p. 276, in which he declares that he has written because of his concern over the "deficiencies" of Vergil, Ovid, and Homer in expressing "the truth of the fate of Troy."

Vergil and Ovid among the *bella scola* of Homer (*Inferno* 4. 94–102), instead defining for himself a humbler relation to these models. But the standard they provide is rigorous, and as for Dante, they provide him with a perspective that enables him to adapt the attenuated classicism of the romances to his own larger purpose.

In effect Chaucer uses allusion to the classical *poetae* to comment on the effects of the "medievalizing" of classical story. His consistent use of the *poetae* as a standard of authenticity is complemented by his use of material from the romance tradition, with its more limited historical validity, to express the more limited world view of the pagan characters in the *Troilus*. He makes clear at a number of points that the knowledge of classical myth and legend displayed by his Trojans has been mediated by the romance tradition, with its blurrings of outline and shifts of emphasis. At critical junctures he compounds their confusion by providing them with classical lore derived from neither classical authors nor the medieval romances, but from the mythographical compendia, marginal glosses, and summaries that accompanied the classical texts in the medieval schools and often served as substitutes for them. Like the romances, these ancillary writings often provide incomplete or ambiguous versions of the classical material they transmit. Chaucer's alleged "auctour," Lollius, born of an artful misreading of Horace, may be seen as an emblem for his use of such compendia.

The effect of Chaucer's imposition of what amounts to a medievalized perspective on his characters is largely to sentimentalize their view of their world and its past, and the intrusion of what we may call the tradition of Lollius tends to fragment it. It is often only the tragic or destructive aspects of mythic history that they recall, rather than those that might suggest continuity or give some grounds for optimism about human life. Again and again their recollection of a myth or legend will break off before recalling the crucial feature, the transformation or heroic act that gives the story its fullest meaning. They know of the chaos wrought by an Oedipus or Meleager, but show no awareness of the redemptive function of such heroes as Theseus or Hercules. They know of stories in which metamorphosis is used as punishment or provides a partial release from guilt or grief or fear, but they seem never to have heard those in which transformation is the reward of heroism or *pietas*. They can see the beginnings of continuity and meaning. For example, they make tentative connections between their situation and the story of Thebes; Troilus discerns the shape of an old story in his sufferings at the hands of Cupid; and he later suspects that the boar of his dream has been "shewed hym in figure" (5. 583–85, 1448). But they cannot read these materials clearly or interpret them accurately. Their view of the past is confused and deceptive, and to the extent that their vision of history possesses any coherence at all, it is bleak and fatalistic.

The ambiguity and inconsistency of the characters' view of history is strikingly summed up in Cassandre's long gloss on Troilus's boar dream. Their confusion is shared to a great extent by the narrator, whose sense of the historical aspect of his task is extremely uncertain during most of the poem. His few direct references to the Troy-book tradition are curiously offhand, alluding only to aspects of the "Troian gestes," the war itself and the city's fall, with which his own poem is not concerned (1. 141–47, 5. 1770–71). He is frequently unsure what perspective to adopt toward the love story proper, vacillating between a naive sense of intimacy with his characters and a strikingly modern awareness of the potentially distorting effect of distance in time, custom, and language on his perceptions and ours.

Even when unquestionably major events are directly engaged, there is apt to be a puzzling lack of emphasis on their historical significance. Thus in a passage that follows closely on Cassandre's enigmatic historical commentary on Troilus's dream, the narrator draws on Dante for a sonorous account of how Fortune oversees the transferal of dominion "fro folk in folk" (5. 1541–45) and then proceeds to illustrate the declining fortunes of Troy by recording the death of Hector. Reflections on the inevitability of fate and the specific circumstances of Hector's death (as reported by Benoit) are interspersed with a conventional appeal to "every manner wight / That haunteth armes" to lament the death of this noble knight (1555–57) and a brief reference to the "wo" occasioned by his death, a woe to which Benoit and Guido had devoted hundreds of lines. Beyond the juxtaposition of the hero and the city in successive stanzas, the

narrator offers no reflections on what Hector meant to Troy or
on the implications of his death. Instead we are shown the grief
of Troilus:

> That next hym was of worthynesse welle.
> And in this wo gan Troilus to dwelle,
> That, what for sorwe and love, and for unreste,
> Ful ofte a day he bad his herte breste.
>
>   [5. 1565–68]

As love and unrest displace mourning in Troilus's heart, Hector,
and with him all thought of the fate of Troy, disappear from the
poem. The window that had opened for a moment onto the
plane of history is closed again, and the narrator returns to the
narrative line of the *Filostrato*.

But while the medieval romance tradition is sufficiently present in the *Troilus* to reduce the dead Hector to a mere object of
conventional chivalric piety, Chaucer's treatment of Troilus
himself presents a striking contrast. It is clear that one of the
things he valued most highly in the *poetae* was their ability to link
the enactment of historical change with the most complex kinds
of human experience. He found in them a warrant for endow-
ing his hero with a human and spiritual identity that is always to
some extent at odds with his exemplary role as an embodiment
of the fate of Troy. To some extent this is no doubt a matter of
Chaucer's "novelistic" power: Criseyde, too, is individualized
enough to resist the sort of conventional moral categorizing that
"the story wol devyse." But Troilus's development involves
something far more complex. He seems almost to outgrow the
world of the poem, and the virtue that reveals itself in his response to love somehow survives his death, coming to a posthumous fulfillment in the experience of the narrator. Troilus
evolves through love to become a virtual pagan counterpart to
the lover-pilgrim of Dante's *Commedia*, and his progress is
marked by allusions to a range of figures whose experiences, as
described by Vergil, Ovid, and Statius, inform and enhance his
own. As the narrator comes at last to sense the full meaning of
Troilus's example and invites the young lovers in his audience to
bring the capacity for love they share with Troilus to a fuller

spiritual realization in their own lives, it becomes clear that
Chaucer saw his poem as a genuine extension of the classical
tradition, a vehicle for new insight into the human experience
rendered with such richness and depth in ancient poetry.

Dante, as I have suggested, provides the one real precedent
for this assimilation of the pagan past into Christian poetry, and
even Dante offers no equivalent to Chaucer's emphasis on the
continuity of experience which links his pagan hero with the
medieval reader. But the experience of the narrator of the
Troilus, whose intuitive sympathy draws old poets into collaboration in the generation of new meanings, is remarkably close to
the role Dante creates for Statius in his *Purgatorio*, in which the
poet who had sung of Thebes in the reign of Domitian appears
reborn as a Christian. Both Dante's Statius and Chaucer's narrator begin in darkness, Statius amid the shadows of paganism and
the narrator in the dark depths of his preoccupation with the
pains of love, and for both the development of a religious perspective on their poetic undertakings is inseparable from their
activity as poets. The growth of the Statius who dates his baptism
by a reference to his progress in the writing of the *Thebaid* (*Purgatorio* 22. 88–89) and who describes the stages of his spiritual
advancement in terms of a progressively clearer understanding
of Vergil parallels the evolution of Chaucer's narrator, who is
from the outset both deeply involved and perceptibly ill at ease
with conflicting poetic roles, but who comes at last to a sense of
the spiritual meaning of his poem that is inseparable from a
recognition of his debt to the great poets of the past.

In the following chapter I will show how the literary program
of the *Troilus* is implied by a pattern of allusion to the *poetae*
which first appears in the poem's opening lines and how the
narrator's developing perspective on love is linked to that of
Troilus by an allusive use of earlier medieval love poetry. Chapter 2 argues that Troilus's experience conforms to the classic
pattern of human love delineated in the *Roman de la Rose* and
finally transcends that pattern. Chapters 3, 4, and 5 survey the
ways in which the distinctive features of Troilus's role as lover-
hero are pointed up by allusion to Vergil, Ovid, Statius, and
Dante. Chapters 6 and 7 show how the broader implications to

which allusion calls attention are reflected in peculiarities of the poem's narrative and in certain consistent features of the behavior of Criseyde, the narrator, and Troilus. The final chapter concentrates on the convergence of allusion and narrative in the final stages of Troilus's career and traces the gradual subordination of his role to that of the narrator, who emerges from the world of the poem to become capable at last of seeing his story in a perspective that enables him to set his own work side by side with that of Dante.

[1]

The Narrator, Troilus,
and the Poetic Agenda

The importance of the classical tradition for the *Troilus* and the complexity of the poet's engagement with that tradition are evident from the opening lines of the poem. The narrator begins with a solemn and sweeping statement of his theme, defining the noble status of his hero and the outlines of his tragedy:

> The double sorwe of Troilus to tellen,
> That was the kyng Priamus sone of Troye,
> In lovynge how his aventures fellen
> Fro wo to wele, and after out of joie,
> My purpos is, or that I parte fro ye.
> [1. 1–5]

It is hard to know to what extent or in what sense Chaucer intended his opening lines to recall the opening of a classical epic. Their sheer sonority and the sureness and economy with which they trace the arc of Troilus's experience are impressive; but their very comprehensiveness tends to call attention to the shape of the story and its implicit moral, rather than set off any heroic attribute of Troilus himself. Moreover, a number of details conspire to offset whatever impression of epic grandeur the lines may seem to convey. The poet can hardly be said to leap *in medias res*, and indeed his opening is not far from the "Fortunam

Priami," which Horace cites as a classic example of how *not* to begin a poem.[1] The very resonance of the repetition in "Troilus" and "Troye" is anticlimactic[2] and interrupts the sweep of the poet's overview of his story. There is perhaps a further hinting at the not-quite-epic nature of his theme in the revelation that the adventures of the Trojan prince befell him "in lovynge" rather than in war. This hint is strengthened if we hear (as I will later suggest we should) an echo of Dante in the opening line: for when Dante's Vergil uses the formula of the "double sorrow" to sum up the theme of Statius's *Thebaid,* he associates it not with love but with "cruel arms."[3]

Whatever solemnity the opening of the poem manages to attain is further disrupted by the lines that follow the initial overview. All this I intend to tell, the narrator declares, "or that I parte fro ye." In this abrupt shift from the statement of high purpose to a direct address to his audience we are given a first hint of what we will come to see as the narrator's characteristic uneasiness with the weighty responsibilities of serious poetry, his need to descend from time to time and speak as a mere man in

---

1. *Ars poetica* 136–39:

> ne sic incipies, ut scriptor cyclicus olim:
> "fortunam Priami cantabo et nobile bellum."
> quid dignum tanto feret hic promissor hiatu?
> parturient montes, nascetur ridiculus mus.

> And do not begin, as did the cyclic poet of old, "I will sing the fortune of Priam and the noble war." What can this promiser deliver that will be worth such an opening? The mountains will labor, and a ridiculous mouse will be born.

Horace contrasts this beginning with the opening lines of the *Odyssey,* and then goes on to warn against beginning a poem on Diomedes by harking back to the death of Meleager (146), precisely what Chaucer's Cassandre does in explaining Troilus's dream of the boar (*Troilus* 5. 1464–1519).

2. Troy and its fate circumscribe the life and vision of Troilus. It is probably the point of Chaucer's sound play both to suggest this and to evoke the contrast of the opening lines of the *Aeneid,* which announce Aeneas's *departure* from Troy. Dante, too, has Vergil characterize his poem as the story of the just son of Anchises "che venne di Troia" (*Inf.* 1. 74), and for all three poets, leaving Troy is associated with the mainstream of history. Troilus by contrast is static, bound to the doomed city, a hero without a historical purpose.

3. *Purg.* 22. 55–56: ". . . le crude armi / de la doppia trestizia di Giocasta. . ." (". . . the cruel arms / of Jocasta's twofold sorrow. . .")

the reassuring presence of sympathetic listeners.[4] But after appealing to us with this touch of domesticating humility, the narrator shifts again, even more abruptly than before:

> Thesiphone, thow help me for tendite
> Thise woful vers, that wepen as I write.
>
> [1. 6–7]

The summoning of the Fury stands in jarring contrast to the human bond that the poet had established with his hearers in the previous line. In the wake of its disorienting effect, the poet's "weeping" verses seem similarly dislocated, not simply a projection of his own emotion like Boccaccio's *verso lagrimoso* (*Fil.* 1. 6), but as if charged with an energy of their own.

Shocking and puzzling in itself, the appeal to Tisiphone assumes an added complexity if we hear in it an allusion to the one precedent for it that earlier poetry provides. Again the allusion invokes Statius's *Thebaid*, this time directly: when Chaucer's narrator, in the "derknesse" of his private alienation from love, calls on the "cruel furie," his gesture bears an odd and striking resemblance to the prayer of the blinded Oedipus, who calls out from the "eternal night" of his self-damnation to summon this same "cruel goddess" Tisiphone, and by so doing sets in motion the plot of Statius's poem (*Theb.* 1. 56–87). At least as striking as the resemblance, however, is the contrast it suggests between the perspectives of the two poets, or their narrators, on the stories they are about to tell. Statius begins his work by claiming for himself the inspiration of the Muses, and traces Theban history back to the rape of Europa and the banishment of Cadmus before settling on the house of Oedipus and the war of the Seven against Thebes as his subject. It is only after he has given a summary of the war and dwelt briefly on the fates of the Argive heroes, revealing in the process a moral perspective on the violence to come and compassion for the human suffering it causes, that Oedipus appears, to invoke the Fury, pronounce a terrible

4. See Charles Dahlberg, "The Narrator's Frame for *Troilus*," *Chaucer Review* 15 (1980–81): 87. On the possible social significance of the narrator's expressions of diffidence see Richard F. Green, "Troilus and the Game of Love," *Chaucer Review* 13 (1978–79): 207–8.

curse on his twin sons, and give utterance to all that is impious and savage in the world of the *Thebaid*.

Statius will reveal himself to be deeply and at times almost helplessly involved with the dark forces that ravage the world of his poem. He takes pains to show how the demoralizing and spiritually enervating burden of Theban history affects both his characters and his own attitude toward them and threatens to undermine his resolve to affirm the value of piety and heroic virtue. But he clearly wants at the outset to assert his authorial distance from the horrors with which he must deal. The effect of Chaucer's summoning of the Fury is to eliminate any such distance, and with it much of the narrator's claim to a controlling perspective. He too begins with a brief overview of his material, but within the very opening stanza of the *Troilus* he is himself suddenly caught up in the world of the story and drawn, like Statius's Oedipus, into a new and strange kind of collaboration with fate and tragedy. The Fury, traditionally the avenging agent through whom the gods punish impiety and effect violent change in human life, has become a sort of Muse. It is hard to know how to deal with a poetic situation in which Tisiphone is invoked, not simply as a catalyst to the tragic action, but as the power from whom the poet himself professes to derive his inspiration.

We can hardly suppose the narrator capable of any such malign intention toward his lovers as that which leads Oedipus to incite Tisiphone against his progeny. Indeed as the story unfolds, his involvement with the forces that doom the lovers is as unwitting as their own. At the level of conscious intention, there would seem to be no reason for questioning the banal justification he offers for the summoning up of Tisiphone—that her "dreariness" is appropriate to his own sad mood and story. Set in contrast to the deliberate impiety of the embittered Oedipus, such a motivation suggests an innocence of intention worthy of "sely Troilus" himself. But however innocent the narrator's engagement with Tisiphone may be, the pressure she exerts is nonetheless real, and a fuller consideration of what she represents may help us understand the literary challenge Chaucer is taking on in the *Troilus*.

The Fury's role in the poem conforms to her function in epic tradition insofar as she reinforces in her collaborator a radically subjective and limited outlook on the coming action. Though the narrator of the *Troilus* is linked with his protagonists by a vicarious identification with their love rather than by hatred, his attachment to them has a desperate intensity such that at times the fulfillment of his own emotional need through their union becomes all-important to him. At such moments, that larger perspective that enables him to see the love as inevitably doomed and to regard the lovers with an enlightened charity becomes wholly inaccessible. In a similar way, to the extent that Oedipus's curse and Tisiphone's power define and govern the action of the *Thebaid,* that action is reduced to a conflict of private passions. Its historical dimension and anything that might anticipate the final redemptive intervention of Theseus are obscured as we watch the working out of this conflict and experience the narrator's near despair in the face of it. For both poets, then, Tisiphone is the symbol of an obsessive involvement with the tragic action which the narrators of both poems finally manage to transcend with great difficulty, but which dominates their vision during the unfolding of the action and threatens at times to overwhelm them. And in both cases the narrators' struggle to achieve a perspective on their material reflects a certain uneasiness in the poets themselves about their relation to a poetic tradition whose tragic vision is informed by no clear saving awareness of a spiritual goal.

But while there are deep affinities between Chaucer and Statius, the invocation of Tisiphone in the *Troilus* exhibits a combination of flamboyance and innocence that has no Statian equivalent, and the implied lack of control expresses Chaucer's sense of the special predicament of a medieval poet vis-à-vis the classical tradition. For Statius this is the only tradition, and if he falters in addressing it, he does so in the face of challenges and dangers clearly recognized. But Chaucer is working in the tradition of medieval romance as well as that of classical epic, and it is the peculiar dilemma of his narrator to be torn between a "romance" attachment to his characters' love and a reluctant awareness of the larger pattern of historical forces by which their love is unalterably governed. Invoking the Fury, yet at the same time attempting to restrict her function to commiseration and collab-

oration in his treatment of the love story, expresses this dilemma
and points up the narrator's utter inability to define his role in a
consistent way. His intention is to minister to the emotional
needs of lovers as a quasi priest. Through his story he will seek
to alleviate their inevitable sorrow by sympathizing with their
pain and offering them the hope of a future "solas." But despite
his priestly commitment he himself is chronically alienated from
the power he invokes, resigned to a vicarious identification with
the joys and sorrows of others. His will to affirm the reality and
value of the happiness that can be attained by lovers is continually threatened by an awareness that "peyne and wo" are the
lot of most lovers most of the time and that the danger of losing
what one loves is ever present. Foreknowledge of the outcome of
his story controls his emotions and leads him in his office as
priest to pray that the god of love, in his mercy,

> So graunte hem soone out of this world to pace,
> That ben despeired out of loves grace.
>
> [l. 41–42]

In dealing with this dark aspect of the narrator's self-presenta-
tion it is important to recognize that his rueful reflections on his
own "unlikeliness" as a lover are more than a comic touch or an
appeal to sentimentality: like Statius's Oedipus, though for very
different reasons, he is motivated in large part by deprivation.
The deep personal need that underlies his vicarious identification with Troilus and the willed optimism that enables him to
ignore the final implications of the story he is about to tell are
always in danger of giving way to frustration, envy, and bitterness. Like Pandarus, who is in this respect his surrogate within
the poem, and whose emotional involvement with the lovers we
can never wholly trust, the narrator has invested all his hope of
happiness in the love of Troilus and Criseyde, to the point at
which, during the consummation scene of Book 3, he can imagine trading his very soul for a moment of such bliss as he imagines them to know. And in proportion as he commits himself to a
vision of love as the supreme bliss, he is haunted by a sense of
the loss of love as a kind of hell. Hence his inner darkness, too, is
a function of his obsession. At this early stage, one effect of his

engagement with his "auctor," with literary tradition, and with history, is seemingly to exclude the spiritual as a valid category of response to the story he is telling. The intensity of his involvement, the sense in which he both possesses and is possessed by the lovers, imposes on his version of the story a foreshortening of spiritual perspective which complements Pandarus's emphasis on the finite end of sexual consummation. Together Pandarus and the narrator maneuver the lovers into an unwitting collaboration with the laws of change and the inevitabilities of history; the dire prophecy of the Proem and our awareness of the fate of Troy loom over the action.

The narrator becomes dimly aware at certain moments that his relation to his material is ambiguous. Thus he seeks to explain away our misgivings and his own by claiming to be at the mercy of his source, and hence of the sexual mores of a remote place and time, in rendering the action of the poem (2. 12–49). At times, too, he excuses possible discords in his language on the grounds of his ignorance of love (2. 19–21; 3. 1401–14). But he never fully recognizes the contradictory demands imposed on him by the different traditions with which he is working until the moralizing outbursts of the poem's concluding stanzas, where, as new awareness dawns, he seeks to exorcise the values of romance and classical poetry together. In the meantime the conventions that program his narration override his better judgment. As the story moves toward the "grete effect" at its center, he is increasingly willing to accept Pandarus's rationalizations and affirm the pseudo-religious assumptions of *courtoisie* as a seductive alternative to recognizing the true nature of his involvement with his material. Hence he is wholly unprepared when he is inevitably betrayed by these conventions. Once compelled to recognize their inadequacy to control the larger forces that are shaping the course of events in his poetic world, he is easily brought to the point of despair, and the Furies are invoked once again to express his capitulation:

> O ye Herynes, Nyghtes doughtren thre,
> That endeles compleynen evere in pyne,
> Megera, Alete, and ek Thesiphone,
> Thow cruel Mars ek, fader to Quyryne,
> This ilke ferthe book me helpeth fyne,

So that the losse of lyf and love yfeere
Of Troilus be fully shewed here.
                [4. 22–28]

The tradition with which the narrator is involved would seem to have no real place for a *pietas* capable of transcending the world view implied by the poem's machinery. The only outlets he discovers for response to the unhappy outcome of the love story are grief and moralism ("Swich is this world . . ."), and the only appropriate conclusion is the death of the hero. Read under the influence of Tisiphone and her sisters, the message of the story of Troilus is despairing, and the narrator's attachment to it is desperate.

There is nothing quite like the strange, lonely experience of the *Troilus* narrator in earlier medieval poetry, but the same complex relationship between erotic obsession and spiritual enervation may be seen powerfully dramatized in two closely related episodes in Dante's *Inferno*. Dante, too, is concerned with dramatizing the interaction of classical and medieval influences in the imagination of a poet whose vision of love has been conditioned both by romance and by a sentimentalized awareness of classical tragic themes. The two episodes I wish to examine, taken together, constitute a powerful analysis of the romance ethos and its effects. The first is the famous moment in *Inferno* 5 when the Pilgrim, overcome by pity at hearing the story of Paolo and Francesca and unable to distinguish his situation and feelings from theirs, lapses into unconsciousness. At the center of the story Francesca tells is the romance she and Paolo have been reading, the elaborate account of Lancelot's quasi-mystical awe in the presence of Guinevere, a story that programs the lovers' own behavior as the values implied by it program Dante's response. The seductive appeal of romance is clearly implicated here as well as in the lines that introduce the scene, a catalogue that begins with Semiramis, Dido, and Cleopatra, powerful embodiments of destructive desire, and then becomes increasingly "romanticized," until the hapless company of the lustful is transformed in Dante's mind into a courtly procession:

"... e vedi 'l grande Achille,
che con amore al fine combatteo.

Vedi Parìs, Tristano"; e più di mille
 ombre mostrommi e nominommi a dito,
 ch'amor di nostra vita dipartille.
Poscia ch'io ebbi il mio dottore udito
 nomar le donne antiche e' cavalieri,
 pietà mi giunse, e fui quasi smarrito.

"... and see the great Achilles, who fought at the last with
love. See Paris, Tristan," and more than a thousand shades
whom love had parted from our life he showed me, pointing
them out and naming them.
  When I heard my teacher name the ladies and the knights of
old, pity overcame me and I was as one bewildered. [*Inf.* 5.
65–72]

The relation between the Pilgrim's loss of perspective here
and his response to Paolo and Francesca is clear enough. The
love stories conjured up in *Inferno* 5 are projections of the Pilgrim's own imaginative desire, their larger meaning obscured by
his obsession with their erotic aspect to the point at which all the
protagonists are reduced to the status of the conventional
knights and ladies of courtly romance. The Pilgrim's bewilder-
ment here and the swoon to which he succumbs at the end of the
episode become more meaningful when set in relation to a second passage, much less frequently discussed, that provides a
kind of frame for the Paolo-Francesca episode. The passage I
have in mind describes the Pilgrim's first encounter with the
souls of the damned at the end of *Inferno* 3. The heart of the
passage for our purposes is the simile in which Dante describes
how these souls hurl themselves from the shore of Acheron at
the command of Charon, the boatman who is to ferry them to
the realm of the damned:

  Come d'autunno si levan le foglie
   l'una appresso de l'altra, fin che 'l ramo
   vede a la terra tutte le sue spoglie,
  similemente il mal seme d'Adamo
   gittansi di quel lito. . . .

  As the leaves fall away in Autumn, one after another, till the
  bough sees all its spoils upon the ground, so there the evil seed
  of Adam cast themselves from the shore. . . . [*Inf.* 3. 112–16]

We are told explicitly that the catalyst of the process described
here is the cruel words, the "parole crude" of "Caron demonio"
(100–102, 109). Vergil had used the adjective *cruda* to describe the
strange, demonic vitality of Charon in his old age (*Aen.* 6. 304), and
Dante's use of the Italian cognate seems intended to impute a
somewhat darker version of the same quality to Charon's speech.
The effect of Charon's words points up the importance of language
in the episode as a whole.[5] Throughout, the Pilgrim is responding
not only to what he sees, but also to the remembered words with
which Vergil had described the same scene:

> huc omnis turba ad ripas effusa ruebat,
>
>   . . . . .
>
> quam multa in siluis autumni frigore primo
> lapsa cadunt folia. . . .
>
> Here the whole throng of souls rushed forward toward the
> bank. . . : as many as the leaves which fall in the forest at the
> first chill of autumn. . . .   [*Aen.* 6. 305, 309–10]

There is a significant analogy between the effect of Charon's
words on the damned souls and the effect of Vergil's remembered words on the Pilgrim; he too is caught up as if by a demonic force, and the results may be seen in the alterations Dante
has introduced in appropriating the Vergilian image. For Dante
the central detail is not the leaves but the bough that "sees" them
as they lie on the earth; the leaves themselves, moreover, fall one
by one, "l'una appresso de l'altra." The unnaturalness of the two
details draws us away from the beauty of the image in itself and
points us toward its significance in the context of the *Inferno:* the
bough is the Pilgrim; the behavior of the leaves, as they fall in
sequence, mirrors the sequentiality of his imaginative and verbal
response to the controlling influence of Vergil's words. The simile thus becomes a powerful expression of Dante's sense of the
spiritual challenge involved in imitating a great poetic forebear.
So deeply has he felt the power of Vergil's language and imagery that he has momentarily assimilated also the deep sadness

5. In using the image of tree and leaves Dante is probably thinking not only
of Vergil but also of Horace's use of the same ultimately Homeric image to
compare the "generations" of leaves with the disappearance and recurrence of
words in poetic tradition (*Ars poetica* 60–61).

behind them. Thus the action of the "evil seed of Adam" represents not only the self-destructive impulse of damned souls but
the self-diminishing effect of Dante's identification with them
under Vergil's spell. The leaves, representing his own words, are
the "seed" that he spends in an ejaculation of vicarious participation in the scene he beholds. And the peril of thus succumbing
to the effect of Vergil's words—themselves finally "parole
crude"—is indicated by the terrible shock the Pilgrim undergoes
when he is forced to consider this potentially suicidal involvement in relation to the promise of his salvation implied by Charon's initial reaction to his presence in Hell (90–93, 127–36).
Totally disoriented by his self-indulgent response to the pathos
and bleak finality of the Vergilian moment, he has lost all sense
of his own moral and spiritual mission and let himself be drawn
to the brink of psychological chaos. The result is that he falls into
a swoon, "like one who is seized by sleep." When at the end of his
encounter with Francesca he falls again, "as a dead body falls,"
we are invited to see in the second fall a more insidious and
perilous version of the same moral and psychological failure, the
failure of a sensibility rendered incapable of recognizing the fact
of mortality and the self-betraying nature of human passion.[6]

Though Chaucer clearly studied both of these Dantean episodes carefully and recalls them at significant turning points in
the *Troilus,* what is most important for the moment is the similarity they point up between the situations of the narrators of
the two poems. Dante's story of the ill-fated love of Paolo and
Francesca is presented to the Pilgrim just as the story of Troilus
presents itself to Chaucer's narrator. Its language, like the
"weeping" verses of the *Troilus,* is suffused by a grief whose
source is somehow uncertain: Francesca's posture *imitates* genuine sorrow: she is "like one who weeps in speaking" (126). And
in both cases the effect on a spirit already made "tristo e pio" by
an obsession with unhappy love is overwhelming. But both poets
are careful to keep their narrators' emotional involvement in
perspective. As the Pilgrim's self-abandonment to *pietà* in the
circle of the lustful is only one aspect of the larger engagement

6. On the sense in which the encounter in Canto 5, like that in Canto 3,
constitutes a misreading of Vergil, and of the story of Dido in particular, see
Giuseppe Mazzotta, *Dante: Poet of the Desert* (Princeton, N.J., 1979), pp. 160–79.

with the world of the dead which is introduced by his encounter
with Charon and the *anime prave* of *Inferno* 3, so the fate of
Troilus "in lovynge" is only one part of the long, tragic story that
Chaucer's invocation of Tisiphone conjures up. Both poets, that
is to say, evoke the contexts of classical epic as a way of suggesting levels of more profound meaning which their narrators,
committed as they are to a "romance" view of their material, can
appreciate only dimly.

To suggest, as I have done, that the attitudes of both narrators
are influenced by their common experience of the idealizing
love-code of medieval poetry is not, of course, to deny that both
Dante and Chaucer were influenced in more positive ways by
the tradition of romance and *courtoisie*. The experiences delineated in the *Commedia* and the *Troilus* are conditioned by deep
and appreciative study of courtly models, the most important
being the *Roman de la Rose* of Guillaume de Lorris.[7] Both poets
were concerned with giving new expression to the element of
aspiration, what Dante calls the "good courage" at the heart of
courtly idealism, and each in his way can be said to have reconstituted the courtly tradition in his own terms.

It is important, too, to recognize that the narrator's conditioning by the romance tradition is not the sole reason for the uncertainty of his engagement with classical material. Like Dante,
Chaucer understood clearly that taking on the themes of classical poetry and assimilating the roles of the great *poetae* were
dangerous enterprises in themselves. Though he offers nothing
comparable to Dante's direct and sustained involvement with the
single figure of Vergil, his knowledge of classical poetry was as
extensive and profound as Dante's. He shared Dante's sense that
the vision of these poets had been tragically unfulfilled, a vision
circumscribed by darkness, ending only in the shadowy afterlife
of the underworld and the sorrow of those whom Dante's Vergil
calls "the ancient suffering spirits" (*Inf.* 1. 116). The last thing
we will learn of Troilus is that he has been assigned to the charge
of Mercury, whose office is to conduct the souls of the dead to

7. On Chaucer and the *Roman*, see ch. 2. On Dante and the *Roman*, see Luigi
Vanossi, *Dante e il "Roman de la Rose": Saggio sul "Fiore,"* Biblioteca dell' "Archi-
vum Romanicum," no. 144 (Firenze, 1979), pp. 332–49, and Gianfranco Con-
tini, *Un 'idea di Dante* (Torino, 1976), pp. 245–83, esp. pp. 258–61.

this last abode.[8] The opening invocation to Tisiphone offers us, in a single concentrated image, a clear sense of the psychological threat posed for the narrator himself by his acquiescence in the bleak finality of Troilus's fate. For Chaucer the telling of such a story means following his chosen *auctores* in the same way that Dante followed Vergil into the world of the dead. It is not too much to see Chaucer's narrator, too, descending imaginatively into hell when he conjures up Tisiphone in preparing to tell of a love that passes finally and irrevocably "out of joie." His sudden reduction to a "sorwful instrument," a faithful transmitter of the story's despairing message, is a version of the almost paralyzing despair that menaces Dante at the gate of the citadel of Dis, "the woeful city," in *Inferno* 9, where Tisiphone and her sisters demoralize not only the Pilgrim but Vergil himself.[9]

But it is important to remember that the narrator's vision is not totally or finally circumscribed by the forces that threaten to distort and subvert his outlook. Vulnerable as his position is, his intuitive human sympathy, what Dante would call his *pietà*,[10] somehow remains a constant element in his attitude toward the lovers. Though it threatens to overwhelm him with sorrow for their fate, it also gives him the capacity to attain at times a certain distance from his story. Thus toward the end of the Proem his attitude becomes informed for a moment by an instinctive charity; he withdraws from his intense emotional identification with the lovers and redefines his bond with them in what seem unmistakably religious terms:

> For so hope I my soule best avaunce,
> To preye for hem that loves servauntes be,
> And write hire wo, and lyve in charite,
>
> And for to have of hem compassioun,
> As though I were hire owne brother dere.
>   [1. 47–51]

8. On the problem of Troilus's ultimate fate see ch. 8, p. 234, note 6.

9. *Inferno* 9. 34–54. Chaucer seems to recall Dante's account at several points: with the "cruel furie sorwynge evere yn peyne" of *Tr.* 1. 9, cf. Dante's reference to the Furies as handmaids of Proserpine, the "queen of eternal lament" (*Inf.* 9. 44). Cf. *Tr.* 4. 22–24, with Root's note, and 4. 473–76, where Troilus looks forward to an afterlife of "endless complaint" in company with Proserpine.

10. In appropriating the term *pietà* I am thinking of the two quite different

These lines follow immediately on the long "bidding prayer" in which the narrator in his priestly role asks the happy lovers in his imagined audience to invoke the god of love on behalf of all his servants. The attitude expressed here is, as I have suggested, an instinctive one: the narrator proceeds "streyght to my matere" without further comment, and shows no clear awareness of the perspective on love that these lines imply.[11] But they nonetheless indicate that a simpler and more genuine piety, so fundamental as to be effectively unconscious, underlies the narrator's conscious attitude of devotion to the god of love and compassion for his servants. They thus foreshadow the more decisive distancing of the narrator from his subject matter which will take place in the final stanzas of the poem. There the seductive dangers of the story and its traditional vehicle will be exorcised once and for all, leaving behind a scintilla of essential human significance to which the poet can respond in full confidence.

The narrator's sense of purpose will have to undergo a long and complex evolution to attain this final perspective. As Dante, astray amid false images of good, is rescued by being made to experience imaginatively the fates of "the lost people," so Chaucer's narrator can be liberated from his perilous involvement with the fate of Troilus only by living it through to the end. Like Dante vicariously experiencing damnation on the shore of Acheron or swooning out of sorrow at the story of Paolo and Francesca, he will abandon all rational and spiritual perspective in his identification with the lovers, and the providential effect of his experience will take place almost wholly at an unconscious level. But as for Dante, so for Chaucer the imaginative experience constitutes an artistic as well as a spiritual process, a sym-

---

meanings assigned to it in *Convivio* 2. 10. 6, in which Dante distinguishes true *pietà*, a noble disposition of mind apt to receive "charitable emotions," from the mere *passion* of *pietà*, which consists in a potentially debilitating sorrow for the ills of others. The implications of this opposition for the poet of love are discussed by Roger Dragonetti, "L'épisode de Francesca dans le cadre de la convention courtoise," in his *Aux frontières du langage poétique*, Romanica Gandensia, no. 9 (Ghent, 1961), pp. 96–99. See also Mazzotta, *Dante: Poet of the Desert*, pp. 168–69.

11. D. W. Robertson, Jr., "Chaucerian Tragedy," *ELH* 19 (1952): 12–13, seems to confuse the narrator's point of view with Chaucer's own, reading these lines as making a clear distinction between the wrong love of the servants of Cupid and the right love which the speaker elects to follow himself. See also Robertson, *A Preface to Chaucer* (Princeton, 1962), p. 475, where Chaucer's "detachment" in these lines is contrasted with the personal involvement of Boccaccio in the story of the lovers.

bolic and practical exercise in the creation of high poetry. Both
poets attain a sense of profound affinity with the vision of the
greatest of the *antichi spiriti*, even as they are led to a rejection of
that vision.

At this point I would like to turn to a consideration of how the
narrator's engagement with poetic tradition is complemented by
the experience of Troilus, an experience in which the shaping
influence of earlier medieval thought and poetry on the theme
of love is omnipresent. In the world of the *Troilus* even Bayard
the talking horse is sufficiently a clerk to acknowledge the law
that keeps him between the traces, and to ease the burden of
submission with the consolation of philosophy (1. 218–24). It is
inevitable that Troilus, preparing to enter upon the life of a
lover, should have come to terms with broad areas of experience
whose laws are authoritatively defined, and seem at times to be
virtually imposed, by books. No poet has understood better than
Chaucer that falling in love is the most thoroughly conventional,
as well as the most natural and inevitable, of human experiences,
and the *Troilus* is one of the greatest treatments of this characteristic medieval concern. In its demonstration of the complex
ways in which the literary history of love informs the experience
of Troilus and Criseyde it becomes, as truly as the *Roman de la
Rose* itself, a poem "ou l'art d'Amors est tote enclose."

For the poets of the medieval courtly tradition art and love are
in collaboration from the first stirrings of erotic or aesthetic
feeling. Art at this primary level is articulation, a vocabulary and
a set of images in terms of which we first realize imaginatively
the condition of loving; it is extremely difficult to determine
whether love develops in response to some external phenomenon or whether it is one's own imaginative creation. Hence
the concern of so many medieval poets with the relationship of
love and poetry: the virtual identification, in the highly conventional courtly lyric, of the impulse to love with the impulse to
sing; the preoccupation of lovers in romance with the fore-
shadowings of their joys and sorrows in the stories of other
lovers; and Chaucer's presentation of the narrator of the *Troilus*
as "the sorwful instrument / That helpeth loveres, as I kan, to
pleyne" (1. 9–10).

Certainly Troilus's experience as lover is intimately bound up with poetry. From the moment he first takes purpose to pursue "loves craft," he seems to respond, spontaneously and intuitively, to the promptings of tradition, and his experience is presented again and again in terms of a sequence of roles borrowed from other poems. His first attempt to articulate the love he feels takes the form of a Petrarchan sonnet. He is compared allusively to Dante the Pilgrim, the lover of the *Roman de la Rose,* and a host of youthful victims of erotic violence in Ovid's *Metamorphoses.* Faced with the loss of Criseyde, he becomes Boethius's prisoner, helpless in contemplation of the seemingly inevitable workings of fate.

Pandarus, too, assumes a variety of conventional roles that complement those of Troilus. Most obviously he is the guide, cast variously as Dante's Vergil, the *Ami* of the *Roman,* and Boethius's Lady Philosophy. But he is also the artist, a fount of courtly rhetoric, and the architect from within of most of the plot of the love story. In certain of the poem's most memorable scenes he is a virtual god of love, the presiding genius whose will seems to draw the very elements into collaboration with his grand design. The complementarity between his role and that of Troilus defines the primary level on which the programmatic influence of literary tradition manifests itself in the poem. But as I will suggest in Chapter 2, the relation between Pandarus's art and Troilus's love involves a profound tension, and this tension is central to the experience of love the poem describes. Troilus's love seems preeminently the expression of his own pure feelings, his poetry that of the fool who sings what he discovers in his own heart; but his role is circumscribed by the artistry of Pandarus, who creates around him a continually evolving scenario, allowing full scope to Troilus's idealism while drawing him ever closer to the fatally compromising goal of consummation. Thus while Troilus undergoes the experience of the lover at the fountain, a pilgrim sustained by the Dantean "good courage," a visionary who discovers in love the "holy bond of thynges," Pandarus is ceaselessly engaged in a process of translation, creating an earthly counterpart to Troilus's imaginative vision in the light of his own earthbound imagination, an *ingenium* that reduces all courtly idealism to a repertory of erotic stratagems and will lead Troilus, Pandarus himself, and the poem's deeply engaged narrator to invest all their imaginative longings in a vision of sexual consummation as "blisse" which inevitably betrays them.

What happens to Troilus's vision of love under the influence of the literary program imposed upon him by Pandarus is illustrated in broader terms through the poem's allusions to the *poetae*. Beginning on the level of the narrative itself with Chaucer's subtle but thoroughgoing transformation of *Il Filostrato* and moving outward to the level at which the world of the *Troilus* comes into alignment with the cosmology and historical paradigms of Ovid, Statius, and finally Dante, we can trace a progressive enlargement of the implications of Troilus's experience and a growing involvement of his experience with that of the poem's narrator, to the point at which the narrator himself emerges at last as the figure in whom the poem's meaning is most fully realized. For the narrator, though he resists the implications of his own awareness through most of the poem, is finally in possession of a larger and truer vision of love than pagan Troilus or worldly Pandarus can ever know. Troilus is the aeolian harp on whom the complexities of love are registered, but it is the narrator, rather than Troilus himself, who comes at last to see the relation between the erotic and the spiritual in Troilus's love and who finally succeeds in discovering and affirming the nucleus of truth at the heart of the courtly ecstasy he has described. For the narrator to come to a clear understanding of this experience, he must come to terms with the literary tradition that shapes his own view of Troilus's love, provides him with the essential resources for articulating the meaning of what he sees, but at the same time threatens to inhibit his own vision by imposing on it alien and limited conceptions of love, fate, and human freedom.

The narrator's experience and that of Troilus converge most strikingly in Book 3 of the poem. In the magnificent hymn with which that book opens we can see not only the operation of the cosmic power to which both figures pay conscious homage, but also the higher love of which this natural force is a partial manifestation:

> O blisful light, of which the bemes clere
> Adorneth al the thridde hevene faire;
> O sonnes lief, O Joves doughter deere,

Plesaunce of love, O goodly debonaire,
In gentil hertes ay redy to repaire;
O verray cause of heele and of gladnesse,
Iheryed be thy myght and thi goodnesse.

In hevene and helle, in erthe and salte see,
Is felt thi myght, if that I wel descerne;
As man, brid, best, fisshe, herbe, and grene tree
The fele in tymes with vapour eterne.
God loveth, and to love wol nat werne;
And in this world no lyves creature,
Withouten love, is worth, or may endure.·

Ye Joves first to thilke effectes glade,
Thorugh which that thynges lyven alle and be,
Comeveden, and amoreux hem made
On mortal thyng, and as yow list, ay ye
Yeve hym in love ese or adversitee;
And in a thousand formes down hym sente
For love in erthe, and whom yow list, he hente.

                              [3. 1–21]

    These stanzas are a close imitation of Boccaccio's *Filostrato* 3.
74–76, in which their counterparts represent Troiolo's own response to the joys of love, but Chaucer has quietly adjusted the
passage to his own purposes and established a clear hierarchy
among the kinds of love it celebrates. Boccaccio from the outset
stresses the continuity between cosmic and sexual love; Chaucer
is acutely aware of this continuity, but refrains from developing
it until he has defined the power he invokes in unambiguously
religious terms. Like Boccaccio's, Chaucer's opening stanza celebrates love first as a planetary "light," then as a goddess, and
finally, in the language of Dante, as an active force in human
life. But where Boccaccio's Troiolo employs Dante's *stilnovo* diction in praise of erotic love, noting that the power he celebrates
is the source of his own "sweet sighs" (*Fil.* 3. 74. 6–7), Chaucer
remains on a level of Dantean exaltation. His association of love
with "gentil hertes" seems to echo the opening line of Guido
Guinizelli's famous *canzone* and perhaps the even more famous
revision of that line by Dante's Francesca, reflecting on the fatal

power of erotic love (*Inf.* 5. 100). But the "hele," "might," and "goodness" he attributes to love are closer to the saving grace, the power and goodness of Beatrice as invoked in Dante's final prayer (*Par.* 31. 79–84) than to the healing power (*salute*) which is the object of the sweet sighs of Boccaccio's Troiolo. Again, in the second stanza, in which Boccaccio places "the gods" together with man and all the other creatures subjected to the *eterno vapor* of love (75. 7), Chaucer points rather to the source of the "vapor": the benevolence of a single transcendent god whose love is a constant sustaining force in the universe.[12]

Only after defining love in the highest possible terms, poetic and theological, does Chaucer proceed to address the rampant Ovidian power that once inspired the metamorphoses of Jove.[13] Though he goes on to consider love at length on the earthly level and deals objectively with its power for good or ill in human life, he has established an allusive context in which good and ill mean far more than success or failure in the attainment of the "grace" that is the reward of Troiolo's gallantry. For Chaucer, too, courtesy is one of the benefits of love, but it is only a beginning:

> Algates hem that ye wol sette a-fire,
> They dreden shame, and vices they resigne;
> Ye don hem curteys be, fressh and benigne;
> And heighe or lowe, after a wight entendeth,
> The joies that he hath, youre myght it sendeth.
>
> [3. 24–28]

The "entente" that is first aroused by lust or aesthetic attraction can evolve into "gentilesse"; it can become, as it will for Troilus,

---

12. See P. M. Kean, *Chaucer and the Making of English Poetry* (London, 1972), 1: 199, n. 70.

13. Ida L. Gordon, *The Double Sorrow of Troilus* (Oxford, 1970), p. 32, claims that the entire hymn can be read in Christian terms, and that "the third stanza, for example, where Venus seems to be identified with the Holy Spirit, vivifying and impersonating the Love of God, can be read in just that way, if we think of Jove as Providence." But these remarks apply much better to Boccaccio's version of the third stanza than to Chaucer's, and they ignore Chaucer's careful delimitation of the functions of Jove from those of the higher power he invokes directly. Where Boccaccio's Giove, influenced by love, is "merciful to the offensive actions of us mortals" (*Fil.* 3. 76. 3–5), Chaucer's Jove is simply made "amoreux . . . / On mortal thyng"; where Boccaccio's goddess makes Jove visit pleasure, rather than deserved punishment, on mankind, Chaucer substitutes an eroticized power that visits "ese or adversitee" on Jove himself.

a sense of cosmic harmony. At its highest it is Dante's ecstatic contemplation of Beatrice, and it is one function of allusion in the hymn to remind us of the Dantean vision of a love that transcends and embraces the Ovidian world of natural force and human passion.

In its positive aspect, then, this hymn is one of the most powerful affirmations by a medieval poet of the meaning of human love. I think also that in Chaucer's allusions here we can see his fascination, at once reverent and speculative, with the imaginative and spiritual life of human beings, in whom love "upgroweth" to a capacity for experiencing its effects on all of the levels at which the hymn evokes it. He maintains a magisterial Boethian control over the rich imagery—cosmological, mythic, and religious—that conveys his sense of the hierarchy of love in the universe, but he also invites us to consider the evolution of our appreciation of this hierarchy. The history of religion itself becomes a bond between its Christian and pagan elements.

But the range of experience implied by the great hymn is, of course, far greater than Troilus, or the narrator insofar as his vision is identified with that of Troilus, can know. It provides the setting for Troilus's attempt to realize the full implications of love as he and the narrator invoke it; but eros, and the limit imposed on his spiritual horizon by history itself, will combine to betray his vision, and he will attain only a physical and imaginative *simulacrum* of the bliss he so briefly glimpses. The allusions in the great hymn, visionary and Dantean on the one hand, Ovidian and courtly on the other, evoke not only the spiritual and imaginative energy with which Troilus seeks to transcend his earthly situation, but also the forces of necessity and physical desire to which he succumbs. The irony of Troilus's rise and fall is best defined by reference to one last book, the most authoritative of all Chaucer's chosen texts in its formulation of the role of love in the universe, Boethius's *Consolation of Philosophy*.

The *Consolation* affirms love as the source of cosmic and social order, the power that preserves the bonds among the elements and among human beings and impels all creatures in their proper courses of behavior. The dialogue is punctuated by moments of epiphany when this universal power can be seen as expressing the will of a benevolent creator. Virtually all of these passages are drawn on at comparable moments in the *Troilus*. Troilus sees love for a vivid instant as a cosmic "charity," the "holy bond of thynges" (3. 1254, 1261), and later as the source of "holsom alliaunce" among humankind (3. 1746); the narrator hymns it as "the verray cause of heele and of gladnesse" (3. 6).

But Boethius makes plain that the relation of divine and cosmic love to human behavior is not simple, and their particular effects in human life often bear an uncertain or even contradictory relation to the larger design. There is a natural impulse toward survival, a love of oneself or *caritas sui*, which in its highest form is a desire for unity and a love of the good (*De consolatione philosophiae* 3, pr. 11. 30–41).[14] But this impulse is mediated by appetite and self-interest as well as idealism and instinctive virtue, and its power to direct our actions along virtuous paths is frequently at odds with the more narrowly self-determining impulse of the individual will. Moreover, the larger natural impulse is not invariably the more virtuous: nature and the will come into conflict not only when the will expresses itself in a self-indulgent way, or is driven to elect some rash course like suicide, but also when we choose to resist our natural attraction to food or sexual activity. Our relationship with the natural order is always subject to the pressure of contradictory feelings, and only rarely can we see our desires in any clear relation to the benevolent power in which they originate and to which they ultimately seek to reunite us.

In the absence of such vision, the natural "intention" that the divine love instills in us may well seem more tyrannical than benevolent, a power coercive and enslaving insofar as it directs the will toward those lesser goods that compromise reason in the interest of sustaining and continuing our natural existence. The *Consolation* makes it plain that the "laws" divine love imposes through the natural order may even be directly at odds with our pursuit of the greater good of self-realization. Thus Bayard himself, if he chose to question the authority of the "horses lawe" that condemns him to draw with his fellows (1. 223–24),

---

14. All references to the *Consolatio* are to the edition of Ludwig Bieler, Corpus Christianorum, vol. 94 (Turnhout, 1957). References to specific portions of the *metra* are by line, those to the *prosae* by sentence.

could quote Boethian scripture to his purpose. For Boethius, who has so much to say on the necessity and virtue of hierarchy, is also capable of seeing the resistance of animals to human governance as a striving to realize their true natures, comparable to the impulse by which humans seek "the good" (3, pr. 2, metr. 2).

But as Bayard is aware of the whip, so Boethius makes us aware that it is dangerous to resist love's law: the reins and lashes that subject beasts to human authority are analogous to the coercive power of *natura potens*, who "plies the reins" of creation itself (3, metr. 2. 1). Chaucer recalls this menacing aspect of the Boethian cosmic *amor* in Book 1 of the *Troilus* in the course of a homily on love's power which has as text the proposition that "may no man fordo the lawe of kynde" (238):

> Now sith it may nat goodly ben withstonde,
> And is a thing so vertuous in kynde,
> Refuseth nat to love for to be bonde;
> Syn as hym selven list he may yow bynde.
> The yerde is bet that bowen wole and wynde
> Than that that brest; and therfor I yow rede
> To folwen love that yow so wel kan lede.
>
> [1. 253–59]

Interspersed with the affirmation of love in these lines are three separate reminders of its inevitability. And the image of the pliant sapling recalls one of Boethius's more ominous images of the power of nature:

> Validis quondam uiribus acta
> pronum flectit uirga cacumen;
> hanc si curuans dextra remisit,
> recto spectat uertice caelum.

> When a sapling is bent with great strength, it bows its top downward to the ground; but if the hand which bends it lets it go, it draws erect and faces heaven. [3, metr. 2. 27–30]

The opposition between the tree bowed down by the strong hand and its original heavenward orientation recalls the condition of the Boethian prisoner himself, who had learned from Philosophy to direct his gaze on high, but who has been bowed down to earth by his misfortunes (*De cons.* 1, metr. 2). But here the coercive hand is not worldly fortune but the power of nature itself. The natural order, it would seem, can be as powerfully disruptive of human aspiration as any worldly accident, and the irony is underscored by the fact that the language of the passage just quoted echoes the famous final poem of Book 2 of the *Consolation*, on the ordering power of love.[15] Divine love, then, can manifest itself in radically opposing ways in human life, and in both the *Consolation* and the *Troilus* there is a persistent undertone of doubt: when human beings pursue happiness, it would seem, they are fated never to know with certainty whether they are fulfilling their role in the natural economy or recklessly deviating from it. Troilus's impulse toward full participation in the harmony of a universe whose elements are "married" by cosmic love draws him into a chain of events that lead inexorably to the moment when his only impulse will be to seek death in battle.

But if Troilus's own intuition of beauty and harmony is inescapably bound up with the "blynde lust" in which earthly love consists, the narrator and his audience can come to appreciate it at its full value from their surer spiritual vantage point. The process of breaking away from Troilus's earthbound desire and entering the realm of charity is inseparable from a recognition that the vehicle of this new insight into love has been "the forme of olde clerkes speche / In poetrie." The narrator's final vision is largely dependent on the sympathetic, even reverent assimilation of the flawed but profoundly humane vision of the great *poetae*. In the end, the poem's central concern is the narrator's discovery, and by implication Chaucer's, of what it means to be, first, a poet, and, second, a Christian poet.

15. With the effect introduced by the *si . . . remisit* of line 29, compare that introduced by *si . . . remiserit* in 2, metr. 8. 16.

[2]

Love Psychology: The *Troilus* and the *Roman de la Rose*

I
n the course of unfolding the story of the lovers and their narrator, the *Troilus* appropriates to its own design the greatest of earlier medieval poetry. Its allusive range extends from the minutiae of Ovidian love lore to the great confrontation at the summit of Dante's Purgatory, and for a brief moment Chaucer uses the language of Paradise to express the joy of love. But the *Troilus* is also firmly rooted in the courtly tradition. First and most obviously it is a reworking of an early work of Boccaccio, a reworking that, as C. S. Lewis long ago pointed out, involved adapting the narrative of the *Filostrato* to the paradigmatic love experience set forth in that *summa* of *courtoisie*, the *Roman de la Rose*.[1]

For Lewis this adaptation amounts to a "medievalizing" of Boccaccio's modern love story, and if the result is to make the story more realistic and richer in psychological insight and human appeal, it is because Chaucer has succeeded in restoring to the poem the values of the code of courtly love, a code that is truer, because more universal, than Boccaccio's "cynical Latin gallantries." I agree with Lewis that the *Troilus* draws far more extensively than the *Filostrato* on the courtly tradition, but I do

---

1. C. S. Lewis, "What Chaucer Really Did to 'Il Filostrato,'" *Essays and Studies* 17 (1932): 56–75; repr. in *Chaucer's 'Troilus': Essays in Criticism*, ed. Stephen A. Barney (Hamden, Conn., 1980), pp. 36–50. See also Lewis's *The Allegory of Love* (Oxford, 1936), pp. 176–79.

not find in it so straightforward an affirmation as he does of the courtly values he associates with Guillaume de Lorris. Lewis sees in the poem a love separated "only by the thinnest partition" from lawful wedded love.[2] It seems to me that Chaucer retains a good deal of Boccaccio's irony in treating the social status of the affair, and a good deal of Boccaccio's skepticism about human relations in general. While Lewis sees Chaucer drawing chiefly on Guillaume de Lorris in his use of the *Roman*, I would suggest that his debt to Jean de Meun is at least as great, and that the net effect of his synthesis of the *Filostrato* and the *Roman* is a psychological analysis of the experience of courtly love far more rigorous, and closer in spirit to both Jean de Meun and Boccaccio, than Lewis's interpretation will allow.

The *Filostrato*, if simpler than the *Troilus*, has proved hardly less difficult to characterize. It is clearly "modern" in its pragmatic view of the relations between the lovers and in the utter finitude of the value it claims for their love, and to an extent it flaunts this modernity: as Lewis observes, it is meant to be taken largely as "a new poem by Boccaccio." But this modernity has limits. The recent article arguing that the poem presents what Boccaccio regards as "the perfect affair," distinguished by "that very sensuousness which love paramours affords and marriage cannot,"[3] ignores the element of literary persona in the narrator's attitude and misses the strong hints of a very medieval skepticism about the crowning joy, the *ultimo valore*, attained by the lovers.

Charles Muscatine provides the best definition of the *Filostrato's* relation to the courtly tradition. It omits the element of *dangier* and the "semi-religious awe" with which love is treated in French courtly poetry and introduces "a sensuality, and a sauce of cynicism, a realistic knowingness" foreign to French and English *courtoisie* alike. Its emotional and moral range is narrow. Its relaxed narrative manner and its tendency toward realism never give way to a clearly comic perspective; the narrator maintains something like the traditional seriousness about the values of courtliness and the crowning importance of the lady's love. But

2. *The Allegory of Love*, pp. 196–97.
3. R. P. apRoberts, "Love in the *Filostrato*," *Chaucer Review* 7 (1972–73): 1.

this seriousness never approaches the tragic, as it will in Chaucer's version. We may hesitate to conclude with Muscatine that "the poem's ostensible moral is its actual one: 'Giovane donna è mobile,'" but it is hard to find solid evidence with which to refute him. However Chaucer read Boccaccio's work, it may well have seemed to him, as it is apt to seem to us when set side by side with the *Troilus*, a "youthful, urban, pagan, immoral poem."[4]

Certainly Chaucer goes to elaborate lengths in his own poem to insulate his characters and their story against any such dismissal. While Boccaccio's Troiolo is constantly aware of the fire of love within him and can declare that the pains of hell would be worth enduring for a single night with Criseida (*Fil.* 2. 88), Troilus is far more concerned with showing proper reverence to Criseyde and to love than with satisfying his own sexual desires—which he seems at times to be wholly unaware of. And while it is possible to see the net effect of Chaucer's treatment of Pandarus and Criseyde as a condemnation a good deal stronger than Boccaccio's, Chaucer complicates our view of their emotions and circumstances so that we cannot be simply cynical. The chief means to this end, and by far his most elaborate creation, is a narrator whose involvement with the story is far more complex than that of his counterpart in the *Filostrato*, who is virtually immune to any suspicion of his characters' motives, and whose retreats into euphemism and apology at crucial moments do a good deal to disarm possible condemnation of their behavior.

But while Chaucer is at pains to render his characters' behavior as fully as possible and while this "rounding" tends to offset categorical judgments, their dominant traits and the relations among them were already perceptible in Boccaccio's poem. This is particularly true of the relationship between Troilus and Pandarus. Though only Chaucer could have done justice to Troilus's unique combination of idealism and sexual innocence, Troiolo is in many respects only a slightly less naive version of Chaucer's hero, franker and more self-aware in his sexual desire, but also subject to a strong sense of love's dominion, which makes him

4. Charles Muscatine, *Chaucer and the French Tradition* (Berkeley, 1957), pp. 125–29.

doubt his worth in Criseida's eyes (1. 47–57). The Pandaro who can declare that "all women are at heart inclined to love" (2. 27. 1–2) is a younger, superficially more cynical and less sententious version of the Pandarus who cites "wise lered" in discoursing on the aptness of all mankind to feel the heat of love (*Tr.* 1. 976–79). Like Pandarus, moreover, he is markedly more aggressive and down to earth than his friend and meets Troiolo's needs with an energy peculiarly his own. Troiolo and Pandaro are both young; they speak more nearly the same language than their Chaucerian counterparts; and Troiolo is less in the dark about Pandaro's design on him. But we cannot suppose Troiolo any more capable than Troilus of the directness and skill with which Pandaro simply confronts Criseida after an exchange of letters has left her still unyielding and Troiolo burning with desire. Operating on the crudely pragmatic assumption that a widow is by definition amorous (2. 27. 7), Pandaro requires a bare seven stanzas to break his cousin's resistance; she confesses that her honor is "shattered and destroyed," and Pandaro moves quickly to questions of "when, how, and where" (2. 133–39). Again, Pandaro's first embassy to Criseida, his successful appeal to her *pietà*, and Troiolo's joy at the outcome of his mission (2. 63–80) are linked by a series of echoes of Dante which seem to parody the office of Vergil as defined in *Inferno* 2 and suggest that Boccaccio is at least partly aware of the potential thematic value of the Dante-Beatrice-Vergil relationship that Chaucer will develop in a much more elaborate way.[5]

Even Chaucer's complication of the role of the narrator does not effect so radical an adjustment of Boccaccio's point of view as may at first appear. Though he has no Maria d'Aquino to inspire him, his involvement with his story is no less intense than that of Boccaccio's passionate young man, and he never succeeds in wholly distancing himself from its appeal to his human feelings.[6] While incapable of cynicism, he manages by his evasions

5. With *Filostrato* 2. 63. 2 cf. *Purgatorio* 27. 130; with *Fil.* 2. 80. 1–4 cf. *Inferno* 2. 127–30; with *Fil.* 2. 135. 8 cf. *Purg.* 3. 78. See also the excellent notes to Nicholas Havely's translation of the *Filostrato* in *Chaucer's Boccaccio* (Woodbridge, Suffolk, 1980), pp. 197–205; and below, ch. 5.

6. On the narrator see Howard Schless, "Transformations: Chaucer's Use of Italian," in *Writers and Their Background: Geoffrey Chaucer*, ed. Derek Brewer (London, 1974), pp. 208–17. For a very different view see Robert C. Payne, *The Key of Remembrance* (New Haven, Conn., 1963), p. 177.

and contradictions, his frequent confusion, and his ill-starred attempts at hearty good humor, to point in spite of himself to just those features of the story that invite the sort of skepticism for which Boccaccio appeals more openly. And only in the final stages of the painful process by which he comes to terms with the unhappy outcome of his story and accepts its harsh lesson about the fate of lovers' "gladnesse" does he decisively leave behind the disappointment and futile anger of Boccaccio's narrator over the betrayal of Troiolo.

In short, though the *Troilus* is unquestionably a very different poem from the *Filostrato,* there are good grounds for supposing that Boccaccio, or at the very least a somewhat older Boccaccio, would have readily understood Chaucer's enterprise and found himself largely in sympathy with it. This is not to deny the importance of the changes Chaucer made in Boccaccio's poem, changes that deepen, ennoble, and finally transform its presentation of human love. It is important to recognize, though, that the irony with which Boccaccio often treats courtly idealism is present in Chaucer's poem as well and that this irony is all the more apparent because of Chaucer's alterations. Chaucer shows love not only ennobled but also exploited and betrayed; and in representing this betrayal he neither rejects nor wholly transcends Boccaccio's "cynical" view of the relations of his characters, but rather analyzes these relations and discovers in them implications at once richer and darker than Boccaccio's more simply worldly emphasis can reveal.

Just as Chaucer's adaptation preserves in a more complex form tensions and contradictions already present in the *Filostrato,* so his use of the *Roman de la Rose* shows him fully aware of the complex interplay between the two authors of the poem. Muscatine has shown that the one-sidedness of Lewis's version of the medievalization of Boccaccio is closely related to his view of the *Roman* itself. Lewis tends to play down the purposiveness and coherence of the work of Jean de Meun and its critique of the allegory of Guillaume de Lorris. What Chaucer really did, Muscatine suggests, was to medievalize the *Filostrato* in two directions, by balancing courtly and practical values in what amounts to an enlightened fourteenth-century synthesis of Guillaume de Lorris and Jean de Meun. The *courtoisie* of Guillaume, as embodied in Troilus, is not just perfect, but *too* perfect, and in a number of the narrator's innocent remarks on Troilus's behavior, as well as in Pandarus's frequent exasperation with him, we see Chaucer himself treating the excesses of the courtly code with gentle irony. But Jean's more practical view of life is subjected to similar ironic scrutiny, as in those moments when Pandarus's pragmatic and acquisitive temperament shows through his attempts to preserve courtly decorum. Pandarus is finally limited, as the vision of Jean de Meun is limited, by his inability to do full justice to the nobility and spirituality of the courtly ideal. In the end, the poem presents both views as being at once admirable and incomplete, in the light of a third, higher view, which sees "the imperfections inherent in any mode of life . . . wherein the end is earthly joy."[7]

Muscatine's reading of the relationships among the *Troilus,* the *Filostrato,* and the *Roman de la Rose* makes a valuable contribution by calling attention to the significant opposition between the viewpoints of Troilus and Pandarus. Like Muscatine I see this opposition as defining the poem's central concerns, but it seems to me to imply things both positive and negative about the two characters which his sense of a healthy and essentially worldly interplay between their two points of view will not admit. This problematic aspect of their relationship unquestionably owes a great deal to the *Roman de la Rose,* but Chaucer has gone beyond the *Roman* in his emphasis on the separateness of the imaginative worlds from which the attitudes of Troilus and Pandarus derive. Their opposition, moreover, serves not only to focus Chaucer's more probing critique of love in its earthly context, but also to make us aware of a potential spiritual meaning that Muscatine's view tends to obscure and that even Lewis recognizes only in a somewhat sentimentalized form.

At the beginning of the *Troilus,* in a speech that alludes directly to the *Roman de la Rose,* Pandarus attempts to find a positive meaning in the contrast between his own misfortunes as a lover and the happiness he hopes to attain for Troilus. Troilus has expressed skepticism about Pandarus's fitness as a guide: "Thou koudest nevere in love thi selven wisse: / How, devel, maistow brynge me to blisse?" (1. 522–23). Probed too deeply at

---

7. *Chaucer and the French Tradition,* pp. 130–32.

this stage such a question might expose the whole enterprise of
"love" as Pandarus conceives it, but he counters by proposing a
doctrine of contraries to illustrate the functional relation of his
role to Troilus's:

> A wheston is no kervyng instrument,
> But yit it maketh sharpe kervyng tolis;
> And there thou woost that I have aught myswent,
> Eschew thow that, for swich thyng to the scole is:
> Thus often wise men ben war by foolys.
> If thow do so, thi wit is wel bewared;
> By his contrarie is every thyng declared.
>
> For how myghte evere swetnesse han ben knowe
> To him that nevere tasted bitternesse?
> Ne no man may ben inly glad, I trowe,
> That nevere was in sorwe or som destresse;
> Ek whit by blak, by shame ek worthinesse,
> Ech set by other, more for other semeth,
> As men may se, and so the wyse it demeth.
>
> [1. 631–44]

Ostensibly these lines express no more than the practical notion
that experience teaches. In context, however, as part of Pandarus's strategy, the maxim becomes a way of diverting attention
from the potentially disturbing implications of the opposition
between Troilus's almost religious sense of love and Pandarus's
more practical concerns and anxieties, by emphasizing a dialecti-
cal relation between their points of view. The lines evoke a passage from the concluding scene of the *Roman*, in which the lover,
about to achieve the bizarre fulfillment of his quest for the Rose,
reviews his experience and offers the wisdom of it to other
would-be seducers: He who has tasted many dishes can tell the
bitter from the sweet; having experienced hardship we appreciate good fortune; by knowing honor we recognize shame;[8] dis-
comfort teaches the enjoyment of comfort. And the lover
concludes:

8. Note Pandarus's deft reversal of this pairing in line 642 of the passage just
quoted. In the *Roman* it is clearly stated: "ne qui ne set d'*aneur* que monte / ja ne
savra connoistre *honte*. . ." (He who does not know what *honor* means will not
know how to recognize *shame*. . .") (21535–36).

Ainsinc va des contreres choses,
les unes sunt des autres gloses;
et qui l'une an veust defenir,
de l'autre li doit souvenir,
ou ja, par nule antancion,
n'i metra diffinicion;
car qui des .ii. n'a connoissance,
ja n'i connoistra differance. . . .

Thus it is with contrary things: one is the gloss of the other.
And whoever wants to define one of them must keep the other
in mind, or he will never give it a definition by any amount of
mental effort. For he who does not have knowledge of both
things will never know the difference between them. . . .
[21543–50]

This view of experience, which Pandarus will reduce to the
proposition "by his contrarie is every thyng declared," informs
the *Roman* itself at several levels. It suggests most obviously the
contrast between the pain and privation the lover has endured
and the reward he is about to enjoy, but it bears as well on the
larger contrast between the ideal and the practical dimensions of
love as the *Roman* develops them. The lover as he speaks these
lines is about to conclude in an emphatically physical manner a
sexual quest that is "glossed" at several points by the imagery of
religious pilgrimage, most strikingly by the lover himself in a
passage that follows closely on the lines just quoted.[9] The tension between practical and ideal extends finally to the vast plane
of allegory, or mock allegory, on which the lover's facile Ovidian
cynicism and his involvement with the self-delusion of Narcissus
and the idolatry of Pygmalion are set in vivid contrast to, and at
the same time brought into secret collaboration with, Genius's
vision of sexual activity as a means to the recovery of Paradise.

In the *Troilus*, too, the common enterprise of Troilus and
Pandarus will be perceived by them in radically different ways,
Pandarus's words and actions providing a sustained and consistently reductive gloss on the idealism and intuitive spirituality
of Troilus. In seeking to substitute the facile optimism of his

9. *Roman* 21553–76; cf. 21316–22.

doctrine of contraries for the profound sense of inner contradiction expressed by Troilus in his Petrarchan *Canticus* a few stanzas earlier, Pandarus is substituting one view of reality for another.[10] It is emblematic of the extent to which they exist at cross purposes that at a point when Troilus is still very much the neophyte of Guillaume's poem, his love as yet untested by even the most tentative address to Criseyde's good will, her *Bel Acueil*, Pandarus should already be speaking in the worldy wise accents of the sexual pilgrim of Jean de Meun, whose earlier doubts and fears have been cast out by a suddenly emboldened physical desire.

A comparison that may help us appreciate more fully the scope of Pandarus's design on Troilus and its programmatic character is provided by the moment at the center of the *Roman* when the god of love, having summoned his barons to besiege the Castle of Jealousy where the Rose is immured, prophesies for them the glorious consequences of the campaign they are about to undertake. By helping young Guillaume de Lorris, they will help bring into being the poem that will recount Guillaume's success and thus pay tribute to love. But Guillaume will die before finishing his masterwork; only after forty years, when Jean de Meun completes the poem, will the implications of Guillaume's conception be realized (*Roman* 10465–574).

The way Jean's task is defined seems straightforward enough: he will "continue" Guillaume's narrative, completing it "if time and place permit," speaking on in Guillaume's voice "until he shall have plucked . . . the beautiful Rose." (10554–72). But the effect of this definition of Jean's role is to identify poet with lover to such an extent that the fulfillment of the one role is described wholly in terms of the other. In citing "time and place" as necessary conditions for the completion of the poem, he is appropriating an Ovidian formula that had become traditional for defining the conditions appropriate to sexual activity. His fitness for his task consists in his physical vigor and his hostility to Reason (10536–42), qualities the lover of the *Roman*

---

10. By l. 946–52, where he artfully misapplies the imagery of Ovid, *Remedia amoris* 45–46, Pandarus is speaking of his contraries even more confidently—almost in terms of simple cause (bad) and effect (good).

will triumphantly reaffirm at the moment of his final sexual
conquest (21560, 21730–31).

To appreciate the full significance of this passage as it bears
on the role of Pandarus, we must recognize its broader implications in its original context in the *Roman,* implications that bear
on the literary program of the *Troilus.* On one level it is a statement about poetic tradition: the god of love places Guillaume de
Lorris in the tradition of Catullus, Ovid, and other Latin love
poets (10477–500) and so accords him something like the status
of the *poetae* themselves. On this basis it has been suggested that
Jean de Meun should be regarded as the first vernacular writer
to sense the possibility of an authentic modern extension of the
classical tradition.[11]

But it is clear that Jean's reductive conclusion to the *Roman* has
a largely satirical purpose: he will set the progress of Guillaume's
lover against a backdrop of Ovidian and Vergilian history on the
grand scale, but his purpose is to point up the incongruity between a poetic universe founded on Guillaume's courtly values
and the world view of the true *poetae,* and to show that any
synthesis of the two is implausible. No doubt we should take
even this parodic and deliberately incoherent coupling of ancient and modern as evidence that Jean de Meun was seriously
concerned with the possibility of an authentic engagement with
the classical tradition, and to that extent his poem constitutes a
significant first step toward the emergence of a vernacular *poeta.*
But it is only a first step, and Jean offers no clear indication of
the way toward a more complete assimilation of classical poetry.

The subversive irony that underlies Jean's juxtaposition of
courtly and classical models has, as I have suggested, an important programmatic significance for the *Troilus.* It is one of the
challenges Chaucer's narrator must meet in the course of his
evolution from the perspective of a poet of romance to that of a
poet writing in conscious subjection to the tradition of the classical authors. But this challenge manifests itself largely on the
level of the narrative itself, and Jean's exploitation of Guillaume

11. Karl D. Uitti, "From *Clerc* to *Poète*: The Relevance of the *Romance of the
Rose* to Machaut's World," in *Machaut's World: Science and Art in the Fourteenth
Century,* ed. Madeleine P. Cosman and Bruce Chandler, Annals of the New York
Academy of Sciences, vol. 314 (New York, 1978), pp. 209–16.

finds its truest equivalent in the complex role of Pandarus as ✳
author-from-within of the story of the *Troilus*. Like Jean, Pandarus takes over the story in a way that leaves the narrator
virtually as powerless as the dead Guillaume to alter the course
of events. Like Jean's poet-lover, he can bring his creation to full
realization only by finding "a tyme therto, and a place" (1. 1064),
and his own "entente" impinges on and threatens to dominate
that of Troilus to the point at which it becomes unclear whose
desires are being served. Not only does he bring the lovers to the
necessary heights of desire by employing the full rhetorical and
psychological arsenal of the Ovidian *Ars amatoria* and the tradition of *fin amor*, but he manages to make time, place, the elements, and the crises of war and politics collaborate toward the
realization of the "great effect" that he and the narrator await
with equal enthusiasm. He is, as it were, the genius of the story
itself, the shaping power that defines the role of each of the
other characters and the motivating force that draws them into
collaboration with the conventions of love.[12] In the face of Pandarus's inventiveness, the narrator becomes a mere spectator, as
awed and reverent as Troilus at the realization of his hopes and
freed of the necessity to act out in his own person the interest he
shares with Pandarus in furthering the cause of Troilus's love.

But just as Pandarus embodies in an extreme form the manipulative power of Jean de Meun's poetic *persona*, Troilus's private
involvement with love is significantly more intense than that of
Guillaume's lover. While Pandarus pursues his elaborate design,
Troilus will continue to experience love on the visionary plane,
and his Dantean imaginative integrity will endow this love with a
significance beyond Pandarus's power to comprehend or wholly
subvert. So also Genius in the *Roman* adheres to his vision of the
beauties of Paradise even as his powers are being appropriated
by Venus and the god of love, who are identified with the ar-
tifice and materialism of the fallen world. But to establish this
opposition is to raise the question of how it is resolved. In the

12. The best treatment I have seen of this aspect of Pandarus's role is by
David Grossvogel, *Limits of the Novel* (Ithaca, N.Y., 1968), pp. 62–73, for whom
Pandarus is finally "the fictile power of romance, the contrivance of literary and
social forms trying, sometimes with comic frenzy, to coerce the human response
into artificial patterns" (p. 68). See also John M. Fyler, "The Fabrications of
Pandarus," *Modern Language Quarterly* 41 (1980): 115–30.

Roman, no doubt, we are to see the relationship between Genius's visionary enthusiasm and the exploitation of that enthusiasm by *Amors* as ultimately a cooperative one. If Genius is
mocked and in a sense seduced, his seduction nonetheless leads
to the conception of a child and hence the fulfillment of his own
declared view of the divine mission of mankind. To that extent
we may see the conclusion of the *Roman* as achieving in a very
tentative way the sort of balance between the literal and the
idealistic perspective which Muscatine finds in the *Troilus,* an
opposition that enhances the meaning of both perspectives and
at the same time qualifies it rigorously in the light of an implied
higher truth of which both *Amors* and Genius fall short.[13]

In the *Troilus,* the separation between the practical and the
idealistic points of view is maintained even more rigorously than
in the *Roman,* and the subversion of the latter does not lead to
even so tentatively positive an issue as the impregnation of the
Rose. Troilus remains, from beginning to end of his experience
of love, unaffected by any taint of the opportunism and half-
conscious blasphemy with which the lover of the *Roman* comes to
view his triumph, and the promise of his momentary vision of
love as a functional cosmic bond, uniting lovers under the pa-
tronage of Hymen (3. 1254–60), is left wholly unfulfilled.

It is equally clear that Troilus as well as Pandarus is implicated
by this failure. If he is like the Genius of the *Roman* in his radically innocent sense of sexual love as a participation in the divine
order, he seems incapable of giving physical expression to this
intuition, and it is Pandarus whose relentless pursuit of the "fyn"
of consummation represents the "genial" response to Troilus's
vision. There is, in fact, no single integrative principle that informs the view of love presented in the *Troilus,* nothing to correspond to the traditional function of the genius figure, and this
absence should warn us of the rigorously qualified value Chaucer assigns to sexual procreation as a bond between man and any
higher order. Whatever the case for an Alain de Lille or Jean de
Meun, Chaucer is consistent in developing only the psychologi-

13. One cannot, of course, affirm anything about the ending of the *Roman*
without being uneasily aware of Jean's powerful and somewhat unwieldy irony.
On the problems of interpreting his portion of the *Roman* see Stephen A. Barney, *Allegories of History, Allegories of Love* (Hamden, Conn., 1979), pp. 191–212.

cal and potentially spiritual implications of his sources, and there is no point in his poetry at which we can see him indulging in "naturalism."[14]

Psychologically, at least, Chaucer is very close to both Guil-laume de Lorris and Jean de Meun. Troilus's passive and largely solitary role carries to an extreme the isolation of the lover which develops in Guillaume's portion of the *Roman* and is maintained through nearly the whole of Jean's. Like Jean's lover, Troilus disappears from view for long intervals while Pandarus pursues his various stratagems. Like the lover in the *Roman*, he is lec-tured, maneuvered, and goaded into pursuing love on a level which he does not understand. He is distanced psychologically from this kind of love by innocence, by a deep-seated reluctance to compromise his ideal view of his lady's perfection with the least show of aggression or possessiveness toward her person, and perhaps most fundamentally by a profound sense of some-thing obscurely forbidding associated with love itself.

The most striking feature of Troilus's role as lover is his ex-traordinary passivity. From the moment Criseyde's image enters his heart, he is virtually powerless to act. Like the Dante of the *Vita nuova* he is subjected to love largely by the power of his own imagination, suspended in contemplation of an image too pure to elicit a response from his lower nature. His vital spirit seems to him to die (1. 306–7), and from this point to almost the very moment of physical consummation all of the "art" and ardor with which he pursues love, all of his imaginative and emotional energy, will tend to seek expression within the closed world of

14. The evident unimportance of the genius figure for Chaucer is even more striking in the *Parlement of Fowles* and the final episodes of the *Merchant's Tale*, in which he is obviously very conscious of both the *De planctu naturae* and the *Roman*. See David Aers, "The *Parliament of Fowls*: Authority, the Knower and the Known," *Chaucer Review* 16 (1981–82): 9–10. On the ambiguities in the treat-ment of sexuality in the *Parlement*, see Emerson Brown, Jr., "Priapus and the *Parlement of Fowles*," *Studies in Philology* 72 (1975): 258–74. That the *Troilus* draws on the tradition of "cosmic allegory" is argued by James Wimsatt, "Realism in *Troilus and Criseyde*," in *Essays on Troilus and Criseyde*, ed. Mary Salu (Woodbridge, Suffolk, 1979), pp. 48–55, though Wimsatt is somewhat equivocal about the contribution of this tradition to the poem. Donald Rowe, *O Love O Charite! Contraries Harmonized in Chaucer's 'Troilus'* (Carbondale, Ill., 1976), pp. 88–91, shows that Pandarus as well as Troilus assumes attributes of the genius figure, but seems to me to overstate the positive implications of this association. The limits of the Pandarus-Genius comparison are well defined by Ian Bishop, *Chaucer's Troilus and Criseyde: A Critical Study* (Bristol, England, 1981), pp. 37–38.

courtly idealism. Set against this idealistic tendency, the challenge of pursuing love on the earthly plane assumes an increasingly menacing aspect. Like the lover in the *Roman*, Troilus is utterly demoralized by the thought of *dangier*, the moral and psychological barrier presented to his own timid inexperience by the lady's imagined disdain. Confronted by this barrier, yet urged forward by strong but scarcely acknowledged desires, he feels love only as the convergence upon him of conflicting forces. The impulse to give expression to his feelings is reduced to the articulation of this conflict in passages like the *Canticus Troili*, in which rhetorical antitheses precisely define the contradictory emotions that hold him suspended in a state of powerlessness.

That the *Canticus* so closely imitates its Petrarchan model suggests that Troilus's experience is determined by his innocent responsiveness to a preconceived pattern of conventional behavior—an idea we may sense again in such gestures as Troilus's submission to the lordship of love, which immediately follows the *Canticus* (1. 422–24). Chaucer's divergences from Petrarch reinforce this view and at the same time suggest a "dark," potentially malign element in the love he describes, the first of many instances in the story in which Troilus's love is associated with disease. He stresses the apparently chronic nature of Troilus's infirmity (406, 418); eliminates even the tentative moral perspective of Petrarch's lover, who sees himself "so light of wisdom, so laden with error"; inserts into the very center of the song a reference to the curious diminishment of Troilus's vital powers (410); and ends with an added reference to death.

The *Canticus* thus marks the apogee of an emotional process that then descends toward the soliloquy that concludes this section of Book 1, leaving Troilus, with no hope of gaining Criseyde's favor, longing for death. The ebbing of his morale in this section recalls the long, slow descent toward despair and thoughts of death in Guillaume's portion of the *Roman*. The interruption of his lament by Pandarus is equivalent to the abrupt shift in the mood of the *Roman* effected by the intervention of Jean de Meun.[15]

15. The structure of Book 1 sets off with mathematical precision the programmatic character of Troilus's experience and the significance of Pandarus's intervention. The first quarter of the book ends at the precise moment (marked

The tendency of Troilus's emotions to turn in upon themselves rather than to cause him to actively pursue love is perhaps
the most consistent feature of his behavior in the early books of
the poem. From the moment he first begins "his hornes in to
shrinke" in response to his initial discovery of the beauty of
Criseyde (1. 300), his diffidence and sense of unworthiness are
such that every outward gesture of praise or appeal generates its
own reaction, the fear and threat of suffering. Thus when he is
first brought into close confrontation with Criseyde at the house
of Deiphobus, his immediate reaction is a helpless abrogation of
"lordshipe" and anything remotely resembling an aggressive
sexual role. The pattern of his behavior is set by his first words,
after Pandarus has ushered Criseyde into the "triste cloos"
where he lies waiting:

> "Ye, swete herte? allas, I may nat rise
> To knele, and do yow honour in some wyse."
>
> [3. 69–70]

The will to act expressed in "rise," followed at once by an instinctive self-abasement ("knele") and the profession of respect-
ful but vague and unfulfilled intentions, will be illustrated again
and again in Book 3. Here it leads into a literal acting out of the
same pattern. Troilus attempts to sit up, but is pushed back by
Criseyde's "hondes softe," and then thrown into instant and
utter confusion by her request for his protection. As he lan-
guishes, "neither quyk ne dede," his helplessness is such that he
cannot respond to Criseyde, as Chaucer remarks with a hint of
sexual unmanning, "Although men sholde smyten of his
hede."[16] When Troilus has sufficiently mastered his feelings so
that he is able to plead for "mercy," Criseyde is bewildered by his
lugubrious appeal, in which protestations of fidelity alternate
with assertions of his willingness to die. Challenged by Pandarus

---

by the almost onomatopoetic "stente") in which Troilus's eye first strikes
Criseyde and he is simultaneously stricken by the arrow of love (273). The
emotional process Troilus undergoes in the second quarter of the book reaches
its peak of intensity in the *Canticus Troili*, which is its numerical center (400–20).
The second half of the book begins with the entry of Pandarus (547ff.), and the
final quarter, rather less precisely, with Troilus's first positive gesture, an acknowledgment that something must be done (82off.).

16. The sexual implication of the image is reinforced by the somewhat cruder
use of it by Pandarus in 3. 1572–73.

to "help" Troilus, she can only answer that she does not know what he wants:

> "Now thanne thus," quod she, "I wolde hym preye
> To telle me the fyn of his entente;
> Yit wiste I nevere wel what that he mente."
>
> [3. 124–26]

Troilus's appeal is unintelligible because his intentions toward Criseyde have no clear "fyn": desire and the hope of reward are expressed tentatively only to be thrust aside by thoughts of punishment:

> "And I to han, right as yow list, comfort,
> Under youre yerde, egal to myn offence,
> As deth, if that I breke youre defence. . . ."
>
> [3. 136–38]

> "And with good herte, al holly youre talent
> Receyven wel, how sore that me smerte. . . ."
>
> [3. 145–46]

Troilus's feelings in such passages resemble those of the lover of the *Roman* at the moment when his initial overtures to that personification of the lady's good will called *Bel Acueil* have caused him to be rebuffed as uncourtly or *vilains;* there the accusation is followed immediately by the appearance of *Dangier,* the virtual incarnation of *vilanie,* whose coarse strength and grotesque appearance cause the lover to flee in terror and leave him

>   esbaïz,
> honteus et maz; si me repens
> dont onques dis ce que je pens.
> De ma folie me recors,
> si voi que livrez est mes cors
> a duel, a poine et a martire.
>
> [2936–41]

> dazed, shamed and downcast; I repented having said what I thought to do. I reflected on my folly, and I saw that my body had been subjected to injury, to pain and martyrdom.

In one aspect, no doubt, *Dangier* is a more forceful expression of the Rose-maiden's rejection of the lover, perhaps a manifestation of the pride or anger that provokes her.[17] But the vividness and menace of his description and his deeply demoralizing effect on the lover suggest that he represents something more than the lady's dismissive gesture in itself—the aspect, perhaps, in which her rejection seems to the lover to mirror his own inadequacy. It is tempting, indeed, to see his rough physicality and his repeatedly emphasized rudeness, or *vilanie*, as representing the challenge of aggressive sexuality itself, a demand for self-assertion in the face of which the lover withdraws in confusion, just as Troilus becomes confused and demoralized at the prospect of any too active address to Criseyde.[18]

However we locate the phenomenon of *Dangier*, it clearly contributes to the strongly reflexive tendency in the feelings of both Troilus and the hero of the *Roman*. It is also closely related to another common trait of the two lovers, their inability to conceive their quest in concrete sexual terms. Troilus's articulations of desire, when not wholly thwarted by his deep sense of unworthiness, are abstract; he frequently expresses willingness to "serve" his lady in "some wise" he cannot define. Essentially the same sensibility is mocked by Jean de Meun, in the well-known episode in which the lover and *Raison* fall out over the latter's uncourtly reference to *coilles* ("balls") in recalling Jupiter's castration of Saturn (6898–7174). In both cases a combination of genuine innocence, sexual timidity, and the deceptive euphemisms of courtly rhetoric creates a barrier, verbal and psychological, that prevents any open acknowledgment of the physical realities of the quest.

In Troilus's case both the blindness to sexual implication and the innocence that underlies it are developed to an extreme degree. Even after Pandarus has withdrawn from the center of the action, abandoning him to Criseyde's arms, Troilus's con-

17. See Lewis, *Allegory of Love*, pp. 123–24, and his appendix on the history of the word, pp. 364–66. Douglas Kelly, *Medieval Imagination* (Madison, Wis., 1978), pp. 88–91, discusses the relation of *Dangier* to other personifications in the *Roman*.

18. For the possibly reflexive aspect of *Dangier*, note (in addition to the *vilanie* stressed in 2899, 2904) the echo of *Dangier*'s turbulent feelings in the lover's at their second meeting (3724, 3749). The verb *esbair*, used of the lover's timidity in the face of *Dangier* at 2936, also describes Narcissus's reaction to his reflection at 1483; cf. 2752, 3356.

scious, reverent experience of love as a "grace," freely given and involving no action on his part, remains wholly insulated from any contamination by the workings of physical desire in him. But the most striking illustration of his imperviousness is the earlier scene in which Pandarus, after announcing that Troilus is now "in wey / To faren wel" in love (3. 247–48), acknowledges, less baldly than in the corresponding section of the *Filostrato* but still in plain terms, that he has compromised himself in pandering to Troilus's desires and has compromised his niece's honor in the process. Troilus's unfaltering response to Pandarus's confession is a refusal to acknowledge anything ignoble in his conduct, to extol it as an act of disinterested friendship, and to offer his own services in a similar role should Pandarus desire one of his sisters. To some commentators this moment seems the moral nadir of Troilus's career. He recognizes plainly enough that such a service as Pandarus has provided, done for money, would constitute a "bauderye" and deserve another name than "gentilesse" (395–99); hence, it would seem, he can hardly fail to recognize that there is something dishonoring to the lady in the arrangement itself, whatever motive may have inspired the go-between.

But Chaucer leaves ample room for the supposition that Troilus does indeed miss the point of Pandarus's speech. For one thing, Pandarus's confession, while plain enough as to his own role, becomes vague and euphemistic when it touches on the consequences of his actions. Where Boccaccio's Pandaro looks forward repeatedly to the moment "when you hold sweet Criseida in your arms" (*Fil.* 3. 6. 8; 3. 10. 1–3), Pandarus speaks only of a time when things will come to pass "right as thow wolt devyse" (336). Pandaro acknowledges having "corrupted the pure breast" of Criseida and "removed all shame from her heart" (3. 6. 3–4, 3. 9. 3–4). In Chaucer's version this becomes

> "For the have I my nece, of vices cleene,
> So fully maad thi gentilesse triste,
> That al shal ben right as thi selven liste."
>
> [3. 257–59]

Moreover, Chaucer's Pandarus offsets the force of his confession by capping it with a digression of nearly forty lines on the importance of keeping secrets; by the time he returns "to purpos" he has recovered his spirits, and the final emphasis of his speech is positive:

> "And kepe the clos, and be now of good cheere;
> For at thi day thow shalt me trewe fynde.
> I shal thi proces sette in swych a kynde,
> And God toforn, that it shall the suffise. . . ."
>
> [3. 332–35]

At every turn Pandarus avoids making explicit the manner in which his pandering is to compromise Criseyde; everything is left subject to Troilus's own will. And it seems to me that Troilus, vague as he is about the "fyn" of his own love, is equally unclear about the objective envisioned by Pandarus. Given his idealization of Criseyde and his conviction of his own unworthiness, her acceptance of even the most innocent "servyce" from him is bound to appear to him as potentially compromising. Such a compromise would seem to him a sufficient explanation of Pandarus's use of words like "treachery," and together with the need to keep such a relationship secret, it might well seem to explain Pandarus's concern about his own role and his insistence on "keeping tongue." It is true that Pandarus insists with what seems extraordinary candor that his persuasion of Criseyde "to doon thi lust, and holly to ben thyn" would appear in the world's eyes as "the worste trecherie / . . . that evere was bigonne" (3. 278–79). But Troilus's "lust" is an uncertain quantity; and he is only too likely to discern in Pandarus's words the threat of those dark and malign shapes—rumor, envy, malicious gossip—with which "the world" menaces the courtly lover. Such preoccupations, as well as his own special sense of *Dangier*,[19] would keep him from reflecting on the moral implications of Pandarus's characterization of their joint role.

Certainly there is no hint of misgiving, no sense that unpleasant realities are being glossed over, in Troilus's reaction to Pan-

---

19. At *Fil.* 3. 14. 6–7, Troiolo trembles lest he be overheard telling Pandaro of his love; at *Troilus* 3. 370–71, Troilus, knowing that only Pandarus can hear him, "quakes" at having to speak of his love at all.

darus's speech. Though Chaucer follows Boccaccio closely, a number of minor alterations in his version cause Troilus's feelings to appear more profound, more ingenuous, and less affected by the promise of fulfillment than in the *Filostrato*. The elaborate "spring" simile, which describes his response to Pandarus's promise (351–57), is adjusted to convey his feelings rather than his appearance.[20] His expression of gratitude goes beyond Troiolo's hyperboles to show him awed and moved by Pandarus's act of friendship, an act he sees as different in its essential nature from common pandering.[21] The purity of motive here imputed to Pandarus is, of course, Troilus's own, a projection of his assurance that there is nothing intrinsically wrong with the love Pandarus has negotiated. The same assurance, I think, must be seen as underlying his offer to arrange for Pandarus a similar relationship with one of his sisters.[22] It seems clear that he does not see even the married state of Helen as an obstacle to her entering into such an arrangement; hence he must see this arrangement in terms of a real "love of frendes" of the sort that Pandarus himself describes as common in Troy

20. In *Fil.* 3. 12 the face of Troiolo is compared to the glad aspect of the spring, while in *Troilus* 3. 351–57 the heart of Troilus is compared to the earth which the spring renews.

21. Cf. *Fil.* 3. 16. 4–5 (with the arbitrary hyperbole "hell and worse," "d'inferno e di peggio") with *Troilus* 3. 388–92, for which there is no precise counterpart in Boccaccio. At *Fil.* 3. 17. 7 Troiolo says that Pandaro has acted "as one should act for a friend"; cf. Troilus's wonder at Pandarus's "gentilesse, / Compassioun, and felawship, and trist" (3. 402–3).

Troilus's vindication of Pandarus by way of the logical distinction between similarity and identity (on the philosophical basis of which see Root's note on 3. 404–6) is highly dubious. His grasping at such an argument may reflect the anxiety Ida L. Gordon detects in this long speech (*The Double Sorrow of Troilus*, [Oxford, 1970], pp. 116–17). But it may also show his chronic inability to think of his own quest in sexual terms.

22. Thus I cannot agree with D. W. Robertson, Jr., "Chaucerian Tragedy," *ELH* 19 (1952): 26, that Troilus's offer in 409–13 is a sign that he has descended to Pandarus's moral level. On the other side it is hard to accept the view of Donald Howard, *The Three Temptations* (Princeton, N.J., 1966), p. 137, n. 86, that Pandarus and Troilus are avowing only "good intentions and loyalty." For both, says Howard, the offer to procure is "an exaggerated protestation of friendship which in each case carries the implication that the friend would forbear to ask so much." But Pandarus has in fact procured for Troilus if not his sister, at any rate his niece, to whom he is "he that I moost love and triste" (2. 247; cf. 3. 587). This can hardly be unclear to Troilus, and the only room for ambiguity seems to me to lie in Troilus's lack of understanding of what such a "servise" implies in concrete sexual terms.

(2. 369–79),[23] and that Helen appears to enjoy with his brother Deiphobus. All in all, the scene shows Troilus and Pandarus talking at cross purposes, Troilus unaware of Pandarus's true objective, Pandarus perhaps failing to recognize the extent of Troilus's innocence, and in any case, by his characteristic euphemism and indirection, helping to perpetuate it.

Pandarus's attempt to deal even this candidly with Troilus in this scene is unique in the first half of the poem. As a rule his purposes are better served by keeping Troilus in the dark and manipulating his innocence to ends of his own. A good example of his *modus operandi* is the speech that issues in the hatching of his first major ploy, the meeting at the house of Deiphobus. Pandarus begins by introducing more directly than ever before the idea of a face-to-face meeting between Troilus and Criseyde, but immediately offsets the possibly unnerving effect of this proposal on Troilus by presenting it not as a challenge to self-assertion, but as an opportunity for Troilus, in good courtly fashion, to display his suffering before Criseyde: "For in good herte it mot some routhe impresse, / To here and see the giltlees in distresse" (2. 1371–72). Pandarus then proceeds to anticipate Criseyde's resistance and interpret it in terms of courtly love psychology, imputing his line of thought to Troilus:

> "Paraunter thynkestow; though it be so,
> That kynde wolde hire don for to bygynne
> To han a manere routhe upon my woo,
> Seyth daunger: 'nay, thow shalt me nevere wynne';
> So reulith hire hir hertes gost withinne,
> That, though she bende, yit she stant on roote;
> What in effect is this unto my boote?"
>
> [2. 1373–79]

In creating this brief psychomachia, in which "kynde" is imagined as thwarted by "daunger" at the bidding of the "hertes

---

23. In proposing to Criseyde rather than to Troilus the strategy of using "love of frendes" as a "mantel," Pandarus diverges from the probable source of this notion in the *Roman de la Rose*. There the Friend advises the Lover to disguise his design on the Rose by pretending to a love that is lawful, pure, and sincere (7561–66), and the Lover is outraged by his cynicism (7765–75).

gost," Pandarus is dramatizing the basic, self-defeating tendency of Troilus's own imagination, which has established Criseyde and her feelings on a lofty and inaccessible plane from which he himself is excluded, leaving him as helpless as the lover outside the castle of Jealousy in the *Roman*. And having thus defined the situation in such a way as to impress upon Troilus a sense of his powerlessness to act, Pandarus goes on, as if shifting from the vantage point of Guillaume de Lorris to that of Jean de Meun, to define what is in effect his own role:

> Thenk here ayeins: whan that the sturdy ook,
> On which men hakketh ofte for the nones,
> Receyved hath the happy fallyng strook,
> The grete sweigh doth it come al at ones,
> As done thise rokkes or thise milnestones. . . .[24]
>
>   [2. 1380–84]

Despite the blatant innuendo in line 1382, the proverbial image developed here and in the stanza following conveys its meaning in a manner sufficiently general to keep Pandarus's objective from becoming too obvious, and his conclusion ("Men shal re-joyssen of a grete empryse / Acheved wel") is more general still. The implications Boccaccio's Criseida sums up in the terse characterization of her "broken honor" (*Fil.* 2. 138) could not be conveyed more smoothly. The point, I think, is to show Pandarus's effort not to create any uneasiness in Troilus regarding his ultimate intentions toward Criseyde. The effect becomes virtually that of an aside to the audience and is underscored by the quickness with which Pandarus reverts to idealistic terms in order to engage Troilus in his next stratagem:

> "Which is thi brother that thow lovest best,
> As in thi verray hertes privetee?"
> "Iwis, my brother Deiphobus," quod he. . . .
>
>   [2. 1396–98]

Troilus's reply here is his sole contribution to the scene: without

24. The tree-felling image may recall Ovid, *Met.* 10. 372–74, which describes the effect on Myrrha of her own thoughts; cf. *Roman* 3396–97, and below, ch. 3, n. 13.

in any way distracting him from his preoccupation with the inner experience of love, Pandarus has managed to involve him. Now Pandarus has the information he needs to prepare the dinner party which is the climax of Book 2, and the game is afoot.

In many ways the paradigmatic illustration of the relationship of Pandarus and Troilus, and of the contribution of the *Roman* to Chaucer's presentation of them, is a scene that we experience only through Pandarus's report of it to Criseyde and that may indeed be Pandarus's invention. In response to Criseyde's curiosity about Troilus's *courtoisie* ("Kan he wel speke of love?" [2. 503]), Pandarus describes how he "stalked" Troilus as he lay beside a well in the palace garden and heard him complain of his torments in love. One purpose of Pandarus's account is, of course, strategic: it provides Criseyde with a window on Troilus's emotional world, where love struggles to withstand "disesperaunce"; it shows her the completeness of his devotion and the keenness of his suffering on her account. But its obvious reference to the garden scene of the *Roman* also establishes Pandarus iconographically as god of love in relation to Troilus and shows Troilus as a virtual prisoner within the world of love allegory, his feelings and gestures utterly programmed by its conventions. Though we respond with Criseyde to the genuineness and depth of his feelings, we are aware at the same time that what gives these feelings rhetorical potency is the mediating presence of Pandarus, the artist and in a sense the god who oversees Troilus's innocently idolatrous pursuit of Criseyde.

Thus the association of Troilus and Pandarus involves much more than a superficial complementarity of innocence and worldly wisdom. There is a profound and finally irresolvable tension in the relationship between Troilus's essentially passive, contemplative attitude toward love and Pandarus's single-minded focus on the "fyn" of consummation. Pandarus becomes, in effect, that appetitive element lacking in Troilus's feelings toward Criseyde. As his desire begins to menace Troilus's radical innocence, his guidance becomes increasingly a matter of deception and seduction. In his role as artist he manipulates Troilus's idealism through the promise of a vaguely defined "blisse," and in general their collaboration depends on their placing very different interpretations on the nature and object of their common quest.

To illustrate further the radical difference between the responses of the two friends to their experience, I would like to expand this discussion beyond the frame provided by the *Roman de la Rose* and look briefly at a few passages in which Chaucer focuses on the very different ways in which imagination operates in them. For while Chaucer is, as I have suggested, rigorous in excluding from his poem any such comic resolution as that made possible in the *Roman* by the presence of the procreative Genius, he does develop the imaginative world of Troilus and contrast it with that of Pandarus in ways that open his own poem to a depth of meaning that is only dimly and confusedly adumbrated in the *Roman*.

In effect, Pandarus and Troilus embody two different aspects of the imaginative faculty itself as medieval psychology understood it. Pandarus represents the simplest level of imaginative behavior, that which isolates the desirable aspect of an object and draws our other conscious faculties into the service of our appetite to possess that object.[25] Thus governed by appetite, the imagination is reduced to a stimulus to ingenuity, machination in the interest of possession. Our experience of love thus becomes that pragmatic exercise whose rules are formulated half parodically in the *Ars amatoria* and its medieval equivalents, though the dominance and control that such rules imply serve only to disguise what is finally an enslaving compulsion.

As dramatized in the behavior of Troilus, the imagination is also responsive to aesthetic impulses, and tends, in its storing up of the images of sensory experience, to enhance that aspect of their attractiveness which approximates the ideal. To the extent that it remains free of the contaminating influence of physical desire, imagination dwells on this aspect of what it thus "loves" in an increasingly reflective way. Thus the imagination tends to cultivate the ideal that it senses is present in or symbolized by the

25. Pandarus is in many ways a textbook illustration of the appetitive function of the faculty known to medieval faculty psychology as *ingenium*. On the background of this and other aspects of imagination discussed in the following pages, see Wetherbee, "The Theme of Imagination in Medieval Poetry and the Allegorical Figure Genius," *Medievalia et Humanistica*, n.s. 7 (1976): 45–64.

loved object and moves toward a level of apprehension so intense as to suspend the activity of the will. At this level we intuit in what we love something that makes us yearn *beyond* possession, perhaps toward an ideal of which the beloved appears as a foreshadowing, or perhaps, nostalgically, toward a purity or a state of emotional integration we have lost and for which the ideal of union with the beloved serves us, consciously or not, as a substitute.

From the moment in Book 1 when we first see Pandarus and Troilus together we observe symptoms of the tension between their responses to love. Pandarus is as wholly given to action as Troilus to reflection; the mocking suggestion in his first speech that Troilus, miserable in the throes of his passion, has been seized by a fit of "hoolynesse" typifies his subversive attitude toward all things spiritual. Typical too is the indirection with which he operates, seeking to draw Troilus out of his languor by initiating a sort of chain reaction:

> Thise wordes seyde he for the nones alle,
> That with swich thing he myght him angry maken,
> And with an angre don his sorwe falle,
> As for the tyme, and his corage awaken. . . .
>
> [1. 561–64]

The awakening of Troilus's "corage" is the first step in the direction of the ultimately sexual goal that constitutes the *causa finalis* of Pandarus's activity in the poem, the "fyn of his entente." From the outset his imagination is devoted to devising a series of concrete, practical alternatives to the spiritual terms in which Troilus, left to his own devices, typically views his experience. While quickening Troilus's hope of "grace," Pandarus will gradually narrow and localize the definition of this grace until Troilus, for whom Criseyde is now a "goddess," is drawn to seek it in the physical consummation of his love for her.

The same relationship between the idealistic and the pragmatic is emphasized again when the friends separate at the end of Book 1. Having aroused Troilus's hope of realizing the "blisse" his impossibly idealized love seems to promise, Pandarus departs,

                         thenkyng on this matere,
          And how he best myghte hire biseche of grace,
          And fynde a tyme therto, and a place.
                                              [1. 1062–64]

The linking to a particular time and place of the "grace" Pandarus and Troilus pursue (and this is only the first of several
significant rhymings of "grace" and "place" in the poem) gives
us a sharp reminder of the finite nature of Pandarus's vision and
➤ how it will finally circumscribe the genuinely spiritual longings
of Troilus. The irony is sustained by the well-known simile that
follows, in which Pandarus's thoughts are compared to those of
an architect whose construct is a concrete embodiment of his
deliberate plan:

          For everi wight that hath an hous to founde
          Ne renneth naught the werk for to bygynne
          With rakel hond; but he wol bide a stounde,
          And sende his hertes line out fro withinne
          Aldirfirst his purpos for to wynne.
          Al this Pandare in his herte thoughte,
          And caste his werk ful wisly or he wroughte.
                                              [1. 1065–71]

The lines are imitated from the opening of the *Poetria nova* of
Geoffrey of Vinsauf, but Chaucer has significantly altered the
emphasis of his original. Geoffrey's equivalent to the "hertes
line" of 1068, "intrinseca linea cordis," is a wholly inner re-
source, a faculty of the "interior man," which traces in its archetypal form what is then, by a secondary process—the "hand of
the heart" giving place to that of the body—translated into its
outward imitation.[26] In Pandarus's case, by contrast, the "hertes

26. Geoffrey's emphasis on the interiority of the process he describes is very
clear in the lines in question, *Poetria nova* 43–48; ed. Edmond Faral, *Les Arts
poétiques du XIIe et du XIIIe siècle* (Paris, 1924), p. 198:

          Si quis habet fundare domum, non currit ad actum
          Impetuosa manus: intrinseca linea cordis
          Praemetitur opus, seriemque sub ordine certo
          Interior praescribit homo, totamque figurat
          Ante manus cordis quam corporis; et status eius
          Est prius archetypus quam sensilis.

line" is sent "*out* fro withinne" as the first stage of the creative
process, which thus becomes a process not of preconception, but
of reconnaissance. The point, I think, is that Pandarus has little
or no inner life in the sense that Geoffrey's example implies and
no archetypal preconception of what he seeks to realize. His
imagination is wholly oriented toward the material world and
operates pragmatically to give material expression not to his own
preconception, but to a materialist version of that of Troilus.
Throughout the poem we will see Troilus's idealism providing
the occasion, and at times the material, for the art of Pandarus,
which translates it into a form that, while paying lip service to
the ideal, is finally literal in the extreme. Geoffrey's architect is
an artist in a lofty traditional sense, a version of the *poeta pla-
tonicus;* but Pandarus is a mere craftsman, whose wholly practical
design will be realized within the four walls of an actual (and
already existing) house. The effect of Chaucer's allusion to
Geoffrey is thus to foreordain at the level of artistic principle the
subversion of Troilus's love and the foreshortening of the
poem's moral and spiritual vision, which will be the effects of
Pandarus's artistry.

But while Pandarus debases the artist's role, Geoffrey's original conception can help us appreciate the experience of Troilus.
His comparison of the poet to the architect, and by implication
to Plato's divine artist, reflects the influence of Bernardus Silvestris, Alain de Lille, and other poets and philosophers who,
working in the tradition of the *Timaeus* and late classical neo-
Platonism, had linked the activities of the imagination with the
most profound operations of the human mind.[27] In this tradition, and in company with the Genius of Jean de Meun, whose
sexual yearning for Paradise is in many respects a product of the

---

If a man has a house to build, his impetuous hand does not rush into
action. The measuring line of his mind first lays out the work, and he
mentally outlines the successive steps in a definite order. The mind's
hand shapes the entire house before the body's hand builds it. Its mode
of being is archetypal before it is actual.

27. See Kelly, *Medieval Imagination*, pp. 31–34. The implications of the underlying comparison with divine creation in Geoffrey's account and in Chaucer's use
of it are explored by Rowe, *O Love O Charite!*, pp. 100, 117–20. See also Fyler,
"The Fabrications of Pandarus," p. 116, and Bishop, *Chaucer's Troilus and
Criseyde*, p. 39.

same tradition, Troilus experiences his love of Criseyde on a
level of ideal perception which brings him to an intuition of the
pure source of imaginative vision, the divine goodness.

In the concluding stanzas of the *Troilus,* Chaucer hints at the
analogy, even the continuity, between the human and spiritual
dimensions of the love that "up-groweth" within us as we grow
toward maturity (5. 1835–40). Throughout the poem Troilus's
experience of this upgrowing, though finally abortive, is
charged with promise. When, contemplating Criseyde's beauty
in the mirror of his mind, he first resolves to devote his life to
her service in the hope of attaining grace (1. 365–71), we may
see no more than courtly hyperbole. But as the poem pro-
gresses, he lives out the implications of this language, responding in a way for which courtly poetry offers no precedent but
Dante, to that paradisal aspect of Criseyde's beauty which all
men may see, but which he alone perceives in his "brestes eye"
(1. 435). Even in the letter that is his final, futile appeal to her,
he can still declare her his agent of salvation, his Mary or his
Beatrice (5. 1419–20). Throughout the poem he associates her
with light and "blisse."[28]

In the process he rises to that awareness which Chaucer must
surely have felt to be the highest spiritual attainment of pagan
thought, the discernment in the harmony of the universe of the
operation of a love that manifests the beneficence of the Holy
Spirit:

> Than seyde he thus: "O Love, O Charite,
> Thi moder ek, Citherea the swete,
> After thi self next heried be she,
> Venus mene I, the wel-willy planete;
> And next yow, Imeneus, I the grete. . . ."
>
> [3. 1254–58]

The lines hark back to a rich medieval tradition of commentary
and philosophical poetry which had derived from Boethius and
the late classical neo-Platonist authors a philosophy of natural
love.[29] This "benigne love," the "holy bond of thynges," which

28. Rowe, *O Love O Charite!,* pp. 96–100.
29. On the background of these ideas see Tullio Gregory, *Platonismo medi-
evale: studi e ricerche* (Rome, 1958), pp. 100–154: Peter Dronke, "L'amor che
move il sole e l'altre stelle," *Studi medievali* 6 (1965): 389–422; and Wetherbee,
Platonism and Poetry in the Twelfth Century (Princeton, N.J., 1972), pp. 28–39.

Troilus then proceeds to invoke directly in the language of
Dante, manifests itself on all levels of human life, seeking always
to orient our physical, rational, and spiritual natures toward
fulfilling participation in the larger order.[30] Troilus's intuition
of the working of this power is prompted by a "genial" impulse
that is inseparable from sexual desire, but the participatory gesture is transformed by his "clene entente" into one of reverence:

> Whoso wol grace, and list the nought honouren,
> Lo, his desir wol fle withouten wynges.
> And noldestow of bounte hem socouren
> That serven best, and most alwey labouren,
> Yit were al lost, that dar I wel seyn, certes,
> But if thi grace passed oure desertes.
>
> [3. 1262–67]

These lines, imitated from Saint Bernard's prayer to the Virgin
in the final canto of the *Paradiso*, constitute Chaucer's most striking embellishment of the *tour de force* of Troilus's experience at
the center of the poem. That they expose in a uniquely vivid way
the confusion of earthly and divine in Troilus's view of love is
plain enough, but their more significant function is to set this
confusion in a larger perspective.[31] The previous stanza had
invoked a love whose natural expression would be participation
in the harmony of the universe. In the lines just quoted, Troilus
seems to have moved forward into the spiritual realm. He cannot consciously recognize the physical aspect of his state of feel-

---

30. There is no need to assume a single source for Troilus's prayer, but its
most striking details are also found in a gloss on the god Hymenaeus in a
commentary on Martianus Capella discussed and excerpted by Peter Dronke,
Fabula: Explorations into the Uses of Myth in Medieval Platonism (Leiden, 1974), pp.
100–118. Hymenaeus is first identified with the natural process of propagation,
which is glossed in turn by the quotation of Boethius, *De consolatione* 2, metr. 8,
13–18, on the love that rules the universe and binds together the order of things.
The commentator explains: "He is the holy spirit [*spiritus sanctus*] which infuses
into all things a certain ardent love [*quendam caritatis ardorem*]. He is called the
god of marriage, that is, the ordering power in the divinely ordained conjoining
of the elements [*sacre coniunctionis elementorum compositor*]" (p. 115).

31. Gordon, *Double Sorrow*, p. 37, emphasizes Troilus's confusion in 1254–74,
his inability "to distinguish between cupidinous love and charitable love," and
sees the invocation of Hymen as evidence that he is "blind enough to regard his
'acord' with Criseyde as equivalent to marriage." But this confusion seems less
important than the pure intuition that causes it, Troilus's vision of his own love
as participating in the cosmic marriage effected by divine love. See Rowe, *O Love
O Charite!*, pp. 106–8.

ing, and hence what is largely the stimulating effect of appetite
on imagination seems to him a manifestation of the divine bounty. Innocence, self-abasement, and awe collaborate with a genuine Boethian intuition of the integrative power of love, and for a
moment, in the stanza that marks the exact center of the poem,
his desire seems to have attained a spiritual fulfillment, a "place"
commensurate with his vision of grace:

> And for thow me, that koude leest deserve
> Of hem that noumbred ben unto thi grace,
> Hast holpen, ther I likly was to sterve,
> And me bistowed in so heigh a place,
> That thilke boundes may no blisse pace,
> I kan no more; but laude and reverence
> Be to thy bounte and thyn excellence!
>
> [3. 1268–74]

It is part of the peculiar poignancy of these lines that they
should define, in the very process of giving imaginative expression to Troilus's sense of grace, the "boundes" that render
his experience finite and transitory. The prayer that comes to a
climax here illustrates Troilus's love suspended in contemplation of an unattainable goal. The deep division between the
immediate inspiration of Troilus's desire and its ultimate object,
so elaborately dramatized in this portion of the poem, is the
condition of postlapsarian man, divorced by the flawed character of his will and reason from the simple fulfillment of his role
in the cosmic harmony and prevented by the same hard fact
from realizing in its full reality the grace he imagines to be
sustaining his love. Cut off both from full spiritual knowledge
and from a recognition of his concrete situation, he can only
"beat his wings," dwelling repeatedly on the wonder of his un-
deserved reward and his wish that he might somehow be of
service to Criseyde. But if the barrier that confines Troilus's
aspiration is impassible, it has seemed for a moment to be virtually translucent, and Troilus's experience takes us to the heart
of Chaucer's sense of the intrinsic capacity of the human spirit.

But Troilus is seduced and betrayed by the very beauty that
arouses him to ecstatic vision. He is utterly at the mercy of

Criseyde's contradictory appeals to his imagination and most intensely conscious of her paradisal aspect when most strongly subject to her physical attraction. There is nothing in literature that approximates the moment in which Troilus rises to the eloquence of Dante's Saint Bernard, only to "fall away" into the welcoming arms of Criseyde, but one further comparison may help to focus the irony of the situation and the deeply enigmatic character of the desire that creates it. In the strange and intricate lyric "Saturni sidus lividum," from the *Carmina Burana*,[32] a long description of the coming of spring, the dispelling of the clouds and gloom of winter by the warm sun, culminates in an elaborate analogy:

> Sic beati spes, halitus flagrans oris tenelli,
>> dum acclinat basium,
>> scindit nubem omnium
>> curarum; sed avelli
> nescit, ni congressio sit arcani medica duelli.

> Thus the hope of the blessed, the warm breath of a tender mouth offering a kiss, dispels the cloud of all cares. But it may not be wholly removed (? *or* "she does not wholly unveil herself"?) lest intercourse become the cure of the secret conflict.

The promise of the beauty of the beloved, idealized as *beati spes* (Dante's "speranza de' beati"), cannot be fully realized. Like Troilus's vision of the divine reality he senses in the beauty of Criseyde, the object of love is never fully disclosed. Union with the beloved offers no new vision and provides no resolution of the perennial conflict of imagination and desire, love and lust.

The betrayal of vision here is an inescapable danger, inseparable from the potential value of imaginative experience. Reason is light, says Hugh of St. Victor, but imagination, which can never wholly transcend its material origin as "bodily similitude," is to that extent shadow, an obstacle to illumination. Reason and imagination are united by the soul's "imaginary affection" and exist in a delicate balance. When their union takes place wholly

32. *Carmina Burana* 68, ed. Alfons Hilka and Otto Schumann (Heidelberg, 1930–41), vol. 1. 2, pp. 33–34.

in accord with nature reason is dominant, "circumscribing" by perfect understanding the nature whose image it perceives. But the bodily appeal of the image may subvert reason's power, and then, says Hugh in a striking image, imagination adheres to reason like a fleshly garment, contaminating perception with bodily desire.[33]

We can see these conflicting tendencies of the imagination coming to a head in a passage in which Troilus, for the first time, responds physically to the presence of Criseyde:

> This Troilus, with blisse of that supprised,
> Putte al in goddes hond, as he that mente
> No thyng but wel; and, sodeynly avysed,
> He hire in armes faste to hym hente.
>
> [3. 1184–87]

To be "surprised" is literally to be captured or seized.[34] To be "avysed" is to receive a prompting from within. In effect Troilus is "seized" and responds religiously, is "inspired" and responds physically. Though the wording of the passage carefully excludes conscious physical desire as a motive for Troilus's behavior here and he remains suspended in contemplation of his bliss for another hundred lines, his lower nature is evidently coming into play.[35] But he is incapable of isolating the components of this experience, which brings lust and exalted feeling into collaboration.

As in the "Saturni sidus lividum," what focuses Troilus's com-

33. *De unione spiritus et corporis*, ed. Ambrogio M. Piazzoni, *Studi medievali* 21 (1980): 887 (*Patrologia latina* 177. 288AB).

34. "Surprise" is used in a similarly complex way in *Purg.* 21. 63, in which Dante's Statius, describing the soul's release from penance, tells how the newly purified will "surprises" (*sorprende*) the soul with its new power to ascend to Paradise. On the possible significance of this moment for Chaucer, see below, ch. 8, pp. 228–31.

35. Is it in keeping with the interlocking of active and contemplative attitudes here to conjecture that Criseyde's comforting words in 1182–83 may have been accompanied by some intimate physical gesture? Such twofold encouragement might help to account for the complexity of Troilus's response and would lend an interesting ambiguity to his "putting al in goddes hond." But the temptation to overread is very strong in this part of the poem. Donald Howard, "Literature and Sexuality: Book III of Chaucer's *Troilus*," *Massachusetts Review* 8 (1967): 442–56, deals very well with Chaucer's skill in "avoiding intimate sexual detail to obtain an effect of erotic suggestiveness" (p. 446), but then offers a few suggestions of his own that go well beyond any hint in the text.

plex awareness is, of course, the beauty of Criseyde, which is at once "hevenyssh" and seductive in its appeal. Criseyde's "chere" becomes in effect a symbolic text, which Troilus is all too liable to read idolatrously, accepting its literal attractiveness as an end in itself, but which also seems to grant him an intimation of a higher reality, the divine source of all love and beauty. Troilus himself employs the vocabulary of reading when, in the aftermath of the consummation of their love, he is able for the first time to gaze steadily and without fear into Criseyde's eyes and finds himself disoriented in a way he does not understand:

> "Though ther be mercy writen in youre cheere,
> God woot the text ful hard is, soth, to fynde;
> How koude ye withouten bond me bynde?"
> [3. 1342–44]

Troilus never learns the answer to his question and never recognizes the fatal ambiguity of the relationship between the all-too-human Criseyde and the divine promise he had perceived intuitively in her countenance. And when, late in the poem, Chaucer offers his own "reading" of Criseyde, a description of her physical appearance which with masterly irony takes us to the heart of Troilus's dilemma, the ambiguity is shown to be finally beyond human resolution. Chaucer's portrait dwells on her flowing hair and the paradisal radiance of her eyes and ends with a deceptively simple couplet that states the fundamental enigma:

> And with hire riche beaute evere more
> Strof love in hire ay, which of hem was more.
> [5. 818–19]

What seems to be in question in these lines is the relation between the divine aspect of Criseyde's beauty, the "angelic" element the narrator had noted at her first appearance in the poem (1. 102), and that which arouses sexual desire. The linguistic device by which Chaucer analyzes this opposition is appropriate to its character, bypassing the conventions of rhetoric as the phenomenon itself eludes the categories of aesthetics and psychology. The narrator's words in the couplet just quoted are based on a corrupted text: in the poem of Joseph of Exeter from which Chaucer has borrowed his description of Criseyde's beauty, the word corresponding to "love" (*amorum*) had originally been "virtues" (*morum*).[36]

In Joseph's description the contest between beauty and morality is a cliché, a way of indicating that his heroine is as virtuous as she is fair. Chaucer cannot have failed to recognize this conventional descriptive formula and so must have adopted the obviously false reading deliberately, if he did not invent it himself.[37] Its effect is to transform what Joseph had presented as a perfect congruence of beauty and character, a notion fully appropriate to Troilus's idealizing vision, into an opposition between that same beauty and something called "love" which we may read in the terms of medieval psychology as an appeal to "animal" imagination, that earthly attractiveness with which the senses threaten to envelop our perceptions of the ideal.[38]

Criseyde's beauty, then, is itself finally a corrupted text. Its angelic perfection is contaminated by an erotic appeal that reflects both the corruptibility of her own malleable, "slydynge" character and the deeply flawed nature of the vision accessible to even so pure an imagination as that of Troilus in the absence of sure knowledge of the divine.

36. Chaucer's source is the portrait of Briseis in Joseph, *Frigii Daretis Ylias* 4. 156–62. Line 160, corresponding to *Troilus* 5. 818–19, reads "Diviciis forme certant insignia morum" ("The evidences of her moral character vie with the riches of her beauty"). Substituting *amorum* for *morum* would not affect the meter, and the change would be imperceptible when the line was read aloud. See Root, ad loc., who cites mss. of the *Troilus* in which the passage is glossed by the quotation of Joseph's lines with the *amorum* reading.

37. There can be no doubt that Chaucer's misreading is intentional. The formula being employed by Joseph becomes even clearer when he goes on in lines 161–62 to list examples of the *mores* of Briseis, beginning with *sobria simplicitas*, corresponding to the "sobre" and symple" of Troilus 5. 820.

38. See Wetherbee, "The Theme of Imagination," pp. 48–49.

[3]

History versus the Individual: Vergil and Ovid in the *Troilus*

Despite Chaucer's close and many-sided relationship with Boccaccio, Guillaume, and Jean de Meun, the *Troilus* is clearly a very different poem from the *Filostrato* or the *Roman*. Chaucer accepts their view of the social and psychological realities of human life and human love, and much in the *Troilus* is a variation on their treatment of the interplay of idealist and materialist attitudes and values; but the *Troilus* attains a grandeur and a final breadth of vision that are absent in these familiar sources. The aspirations of Troilus and the machinations of Pandarus are not only freed from the courtly world of the *Roman,* but set in a context of allusion to the mythic and historical themes of classical poetry which, even without the transforming perspective provided by Chaucer's use of Dante, would make the *Troilus* a poem of a different order.

The world of the poem's narrative is a much smaller place than the universe implied by its allusive framework, and one function of the framework is simply to accentuate the contrast between them. Chaucer's pagan characters live in a closed world. The attitudes they share—their preoccupation with love, their repudiation of history, their courtly code in all its aspects—and the private concerns that compartmentalize their lives are contrived, like the ingeniously medievalized Trojan setting, to point up their unawareness of the background against which they act out their story. The borrowings from Boccaccio and Jean de

Meun, the humor, the psychological realism, and all the resources of Chaucer the proto-novelist are finally means to the
same end. They fascinate us with the story's surface and thereby
make it an effective foil to the allusive conveyal of the realities of
the history and fate of Troy.

One obvious function of allusion to the classical poets is to
locate the action of the *Troilus* historically. In this respect, as I
have suggested, such allusion is Chaucer's deliberately chosen
alternative to the Troy-book tradition, and we must take seriously the care with which he makes his story correspond to the
histories of Troy and Thebes as presented in Vergil's *Aeneid* and
Statius's *Thebaid* and to the paradigm of world history in Ovid's
Metamorphoses. But allusion to these texts has a double function
in the *Troilus*. At the same time that it grounds the story in epic
history, it also constitutes a foil to the development of the hero
insofar as it isolates his experience, and endows it with a significance that is independent of his historical role and that finally
seems to transcend it. The purpose of this chapter and the next
is to show how Chaucer's perspective on Troilus is at once con-
gruent with that of Vergil and significantly at odds with it; how
allusion to figures from the *Metamorphoses* serves both to univer-
salize and to isolate Troilus's experience amid the flow of events
and to set off the private and spiritual nature of his love; and
finally how the opposition of individual and history emerges as a
major theme in the light of Chaucer's sustained and highly complex reference to the poetic history of Thebes.

Before attempting to justify my claim that the *poetae* are an
important source of meaning in the *Troilus* by examining the
sources of some of its classical allusions, I would like to establish
some ground rules. When is a classical reference sufficiently
pointed to justify our looking to a particular text for information? Probably the meaning of the *Troilus* will not be affected by
our failure to discover a source for Criseyde's two walk-on
nieces, Flexippe and Tarbe, or "oothre lasse folk, as Phebuseo";
but we may well want to know more about Myrrha or the daughter of Nisus than that one wept and the other sang. When, on
the other hand, is a correspondence too broad to justify a search
for specific linkages? To what extent do the *poetae* provide an

essential context for Chaucer's poem, and to what extent are they just a repository of poetic "lore," aids to amplification?

The question of the limits of allusion is, of course, a highly controversial one, even in regard to the work of modern poets whose meaning avowedly depends on the evocation of the themes and contexts of the poetry of the past. And no reader, however conditioned by and tolerant of the allusive freedom claimed by a T. S. Eliot, would approach the *Troilus* as he would "Prufrock" or "The Waste Land." But the comparison is not wholly far-fetched, for Chaucer's use of allusion in the *Troilus* does have certain affinities with Eliot's. Like Eliot, and perhaps with clearer justification, Chaucer creates a poetic world set in an irrevocable past, a world whose moral and spiritual values are fixed and circumscribed by constraints which no amount of imaginative sympathy can alter and which it becomes the function of allusion to define. And like Eliot's, Chaucer's treatment of his poetic world reflects a deep appreciation of the precedent of Dante, who provides a larger perspective on the classical *auctores* as they in turn define the spiritual horizons of Troy.

Certain basic assumptions underlie my treatment of Chaucer's allusions to classical poetry. First, I assume that Chaucer thought of the poems that are his privileged sources as structural wholes, that his use of the *Metamorphoses,* for example, implies a coherent reading of that work, both as a poem in its own right and in relation to the other works of his preferred authors. Second, I assume that his knowledge of the whole poem informs his use of it at a given moment, that he is deeply aware of broad affinities of theme and structure. Reference to a particular character, event, or image in another poem is often an invitation to the reader to set Chaucer's text side by side with its source for a time and consider the thematic, structural, and imagistic similarities between entire episodes.[1] Finally, I would suggest that Chaucer saw his canon of major *poetae* as forming a continuum, as presenting collectively a consistent and authoritative view of world history and human behavior. The precision and consistency with

1. See John M. Fyler, "The Fabrications of Pandarus," *Modern Language Quarterly* 41 (1980):118, n. 8, on the knowledge of classical texts that Chaucer seems to assume in his audience.

which the presentation of the ancient world in the *Troilus* complements and develops the world view of the *poetae*—a presentation that involves far more than the elaboration of Boccaccio's
narrative with "historiall" material—is one measure of the seriousness of Chaucer's response to their work.

This broad relationship to the *poetae* is at least as important as
any specific allusion, I think, and at the risk of seeming to have
patterned my argument on the model of *lucus a non lucendo*, I
would like to offer a tentative illustration of its importance by
considering the curiously oblique relationship between the
Troilus and Vergil's *Aeneid*, a relationship in which complementarity is the only obvious link. Though Chaucer unquestionably
knew the *Aeneid* very well, it is hard to see more than an occasional suggestive parallel in the *Troilus*: the heroes of both
poems, for example, are caught between their common servi-
tude to a large and irrevocable destiny on the one hand, and the
machinations of lesser powers—Venus, Juno, Pandarus—on the
other. In both poems the hero first appears only after an elaborate setting of the cosmic and historical stage. And more than
one critic has sensed a correspondence between the "smoky
reyn" that detains Criseyde at the house of Pandarus, making
possible the first introduction of Troilus into her bed, and the
storm that drives Dido and Aeneas to seek a common refuge in
their cave. Such correspondences could be multiplied, but it
would be hard to demonstrate the presence of deliberate
allusion.

Vergil's Troy is hardly recalled by Chaucer's, and such correspondences as can be detected are problematic. When Chaucer,
by a few deft strokes, hints at a possible affair between Helen
and Deiphobus, are we to think forward to the Vergilian conclusion of this affair, Aeneas's underworld encounter with a horri-
bly mutilated Deiphobus who tells of his betrayal by this same
Helen?[2] Certainly I cannot read the opening or the closing portion of the *Troilus* without recalling the panorama of the Trojan
war which Vergil's Aeneas, newly arrived at Carthage, discovers
inscribed on the portals of the temple of Juno. The panorama

2. See McKay Sundwall, "Deiphobus and Helen: A Tantalizing Hint,"
Modern Philology 73 (1975–76):151–56.

shows us, among other scenes, the Trojan people thronging the Palladion, where the story of Chaucer's Troilus begins, and it juxtaposes this scene with a picture of how that story ends:

> parte alia fugiens amissis Troilus armis,
> infelix puer atque impar congressus Achilli,
> fertur equis curruque haeret resupinus inani,
> lora tenens tamen; huic ceruixque comaeque trahuntur
> per terram, et uersa puluis inscribitur hasta.

> In another part Troilus, in flight, having lost his arms, a miserable boy and no match for Achilles, is drawn along on his back by his horses and empty chariot, still holding the reins. His neck and hair are dragged over the ground, and his inverted spear writes in the dust. [*Aen*. 1. 474–78]

This scene is hard to forget, but is it relevant to Chaucer's poem?

Chaucer, though he follows Boccaccio in making a brief reference to Troilus's death at the hands of Achilles, gives us no such view of his hero. In the lines just quoted we are already as far removed from the life of "joie" in Chaucer's Troy as we will be when Deiphobus in hell recalls for Aeneas the "false joys" of the city's last night (*Aen*. 6. 513–14). And yet the contrast between Vergil's perspective and Chaucer's can tell us a good deal about Chaucer's purpose in creating his own Troy as he did. Chaucer's Troy is a monument to the pursuit of false joys, a world that can exist only by excluding the realities of time and war. The pathetic fate of Vergil's Troilus, the boy warrior, is an appropriate extension of the role of Chaucer's "sely" Troilus, whose devotion to love is only the purest form of his city's fatal preoccupation with the pursuit of "joie." Though he cannot be shown to have had the passage in mind as he wrote, it is, I would argue, a legitimate test of the authenticity of Chaucer's vision of the world of ancient poetry that there is no essential inconsistency between his treatment of Troilus and Troy and that of Vergil. The story of Troilus leads into, and in a sense becomes, the story of Troy, and Chaucer has shown us part of the process of this identification.

I would suggest further that the Vergilian perspective on Troy and its fall is inevitably a portion of the burden of knowl-

edge which the narrator of Chaucer's poem must resist in order
to concentrate his energies on the affirmation of love. His own
perspective is comparable to that of Aeneas in the scene just
mentioned, in which the hero "feeds" on the *inanis pictura*, the
mere likeness of the fall of Troy, aware for the moment only of
the sadness of what he sees, yet strangely able to find grounds
for hope and a kind of redemption in the spectacle (*Aen.* 1.
450–65). The perils of this emotional vulnerability and the obliv-
iousness to destiny that it implies are suggested by Vergil's jux-
taposing of the image of his hero's fixation on the panorama of
Troy with an elaborate, quasi-mystical description of Dido, who
makes her first appearance at this point (1. 494–504). Chaucer's
narrator, too, invests a vain and desperate hope in his lovers,
and like Aeneas's it is a hope "at once founded on and nullified
by *picturae inanes*."[3] Like Aeneas acknowledging his destiny, the
narrator will finally be forced to withdraw from the world of
Troy with its short-lived loves and joys, after granting his
wretched youth a brief and futile (and unclassical) interval of
heroic wrath. But here the difference between Chaucer's perspective and Vergil's becomes critically important. For Aeneas,
recollection of the fall of Troy is a find of self-therapy; though
he allows himself to be entranced by this initial panorama, he
will go on to tell Dido the whole story, and in the process define
the larger purpose of his own exile and mission.[4] But Chaucer,
while he distances himself radically from the plane of his poem's
action, never diverts his gaze from the figure of Troilus. His
poem preserves an essential congruence with the *Aeneid*, and in
this sense is truly "subject" to the authority of the classical tradition. But at the same time the *Troilus* deals with precisely what
Vergil leaves unspoken, the story of the *infelix puer* that his
spear, as it writes in the dust of the battlefield, cannot tell, but
that gives his life a significance distinct from its historical meaning as an emblem of the vanity of Troy.

Very different from the significant but shadowy presence of
Vergil is the role of Ovid in Chaucer's poem. Ovidian allusion

---

3. W. R. Johnson, *Darkness Visible: A Study of Vergil's Aeneid* (Berkeley, 1976),
p. 106.

4. See Lee W. Patterson, "'Rapt with Pleasaunce': Vision and Narration in
the Epic," *ELH* 48 (1981):455–57.

informs the *Troilus* in several ways. The stance and attitude of both Pandarus and the narrator owe a great deal to the persona of the teacher-poet, the *magister amoris* of Ovid's amatory poems. The action is punctuated by allusions to individual stories, drawn not only from the *Metamorphoses* but from the *Heroides* and other of Ovid's works. The allusions to the love poetry, though they point up certain complexities of attitude in both Chaucer's poem and Ovid's love books which have not always been fully recognized,[5] are relatively straightforward, and largely a matter of tone and erotic doctrine. But the references to the *Metamorphoses* require us to come to terms with a range of the problems of interpretation posed by allusion. Though a few of these allusions function as little more than emblems, most extend well beyond the immediate contexts that allusion brings together, and at their most complex they enable us to discover correspondences between Chaucer's poem and fine details of Ovid's language and imagery which only an attentive reading of both texts together can bring to light.

To the extent that Ovidian allusion opens a window onto the world of the *Metamorphoses,* we may see Chaucer as an Ovidian artist, using allusion as Ovid himself used the theme of transformation, to arrest the movement of his poem and allow us to reflect on the interplay of forces at work within it. It is clear, too, that Chaucer's characters live their conscious lives in a largely Ovidian world in which the power of love, "that alle thing may bynde," is pitted against the efforts of human beings to withstand, control, or at least define the influence it exerts over their earthly destinies. There is change in Chaucer's Ovidian world, but no true metamorphosis. Troilus can identify himself with Daphne, whose transformation into a tree enabled her to escape the tyranny of love, or yearn, like Dante, for a metamorphosis of desire itself, but he cannot free himself from the reality of his situation. But here too the irony is Ovidian: for the metamorphosis that Ovid allows his characters and Chaucer withholds from his is recognized by both poets as all too often a symbol of vain hope, an expression of the human spirit's refusal to accept the human condition.

5. See ch. 5, pp. 152–53.

Though Troilus is consistently and almost exclusively the focal point of the most complex of these references, allusion to the *Metamorphoses* and other Ovidiana sheds light on Pandarus and Criseyde as well, beginning on the level of allusions made by the characters themselves. It is possible, indeed, to establish a hierarchy of complexity among the Ovidian references of the three principals in the story, a hierarchy that corresponds to their spiritual capacities and the complexity of involvement they feel with the gods and powers to whom they allude. Troilus truly believes in the gods and in the legends of their dealings with humankind. Criseyde and Pandarus, though, are almost totally engaged with practical realities, and the allusions that they make or that involve them reflect this practicality. When Pandarus compares Troilus's love pains to the sufferings of Niobe or Tityus, it is mere hyperbole; when he prays to be struck with lightning or afflicted with the torments of Tantalus if his intention toward Criseyde prove dishonorable (2. 1146, 3. 591–93), such punishments have no reality for him. Even the very obscure references to "corounes tweyne" and "Natal Joves feste" (2. 1725, 3. 150), which strike a vaguely religious note, seem finally to reflect only his abiding concern with the processes of generation.[6] Classical allusion is real for Pandarus only as it enters the world of the here and now: you can visit and see for yourself the marble tears of Niobe, and the Ovidian letter written to Paris by the abandoned nymph Oenone has evidently been circulating lately among the Trojan nobility (1. 699–700, 652–56).

Criseyde uses allusions to myth and the gods mainly to affirm

---

6. In 3. 150, word order suggests that "natal" denotes the function of the god rather than his "natal feste" or birthday. Here at least Pandarus may suggest the old gentlemen joking about christenings at Victorian weddings to whom C. S. Lewis compares him (*The Allegory of Love* [Oxford, 1936], p. 193). Far more obscure is Pandarus's appeal to Criseyde to exercise "the vertue of corounes tweyne" for the supposedly ailing Troilus (2. 1735). I can only add one more possible interpretation to the pile. In *Metamorphoses* 13, the wandering Aeneas receives from the priest-king Anius a bowl inscribed with the story of how Thebes was saved from a plague by the suicide of the daughters of Orion. When their bodies burned, twin boys emerged from the fire "lest the race should perish"; they became known as the *Coronae*, or Crowns (*Met.* 13. 692–99). Bernardus Silvestris alludes to Ovid's story in describing the twin *genii* whom he associates with the testicles, and who, like the *Coronae*, perpetuate the existence of the race (*Cosmographia* 2. 14. 157–62). Pandarus may be asking Criseyde to exercise a similarly revivifying function, though of course the sacrifice of her honor, which he eventually engineers, preserves neither Troilus nor Troy.

her good character and sincerity, most notably in a cluster of oaths to Troilus late in Book 4. Even these are disconcertingly juxtaposed with a glib account of how she will confound her priestly father's prophecies and undermine his devotion to Apollo with skeptical arguments and the promise of wealth (4. 1397–1400, 1408–14). When we hear a more genuine note, it is because her sense of security has been threatened: while Troilus can face an eternity of endless lamentation for the loss of Criseyde (4. 472–76), Criseyde needs to believe that they will somehow be reunited like Orpheus and Eurydice in a realm without pain, the "feld of pite," Ovid's "arva piorum" (4. 789–91).[7]

More poignant is a passage that provides a sort of coda to one of her strongest oaths. After invoking Juno's wrath should she prove false to Troilus, she ratifies her oath by invoking every god and goddess, from the celestial powers down to the "halve goddes" of the woods and fields, concluding, as if in triumph, "*Now* trowe me, if yow leste!" (4. 1534–47). The force of the vow is somewhat offset by the fact that it echoes Ovid's Jupiter, enumerating the *semidei* and other innocent nature spirits whose earthly peace is threatened by the treachery of Lycaon, in Ovidian history the first mortal to break faith with the gods (*Met.* 1. 192–98). But then Criseyde goes on:

> And thow, Symois, that as an arwe clere
> Thorugh Troie rennest ay downward to the se,
> Ber witnesse of this word that seyd is here. . . .
>
> [4. 1548–50]

Criseyde's purpose in these beautiful lines is, of course, to dramatize her declaration of fidelity and purity of motive, but they serve as well to contrast the order of nature with the practical and moral confusion of her own life.[8] So Dante's Francesca had

7. The most likely source of Criseyde's notion is *Met.* 11. 62–66, perhaps with a sidelong glance at the common mythographical association of Eurydice with the weakness of the flesh. See John B. Friedman, *Orpheus in the Middle Ages* (Harvard, 1970), pp. 105–14; Ida L. Gordon, *The Double Sorrow of Troilus* (Oxford, 1970), pp. 105–6.

8. Criseyde's lines recall Ovid's epistle of Oenone to Paris (already recalled by Pandarus at 1. 652–65), in which the nymph recalls Paris carving the same declaration, naming Xanthos instead of Simois, in the bark of a tree (*Heroides* 5. 25–32). As Fyler notes ("The Fabrications of Pandarus," pp. 116–18), the epistle goes on to forecast the fall of Troy.

prefaced her account of a life made chaotic by desire with a reference to her homeland, "where the Po descends to be at peace" (*Inf.* 5. 98–99).[9] The shift of tone and the evocation of a familiar landscape express Criseyde's instinctive resistance to the working of forces she can only partly understand, which are already beginning to undermine her sense of purpose. In the event, for all her assurances to Troilus, she will pass out of Troy as inevitably and finally as the river itself.

Criseyde's involvement with the course of events is implied again at the one moment when the narrator himself uses an Ovidian reference to comment on her role, an unobtrusive but pointed allusion in the course of the brief description of sunrise on the tenth day of Criseyde's absence from Troy—the day she is to return to the city. The lines set the continuity of a large and impersonal nature in contrast to Troilus's terrible anxiety:

> The laurer-crowned Phebus, with his heete,
> Gan, in his cours ay upward as he wente,
> To warmen of the est see the wawes weete;
> And Nysus' doughter song with fressh entente. . . .
>
> [5. 1107–10]

Outwardly cheerful and even optimistic, these lines veil a number of ironies. That Phoebus is "laurel-crowned" perhaps reflects the hopes of those who, like Troilus in earlier moments of need, appeal to his benevolence; but here that benevolence is shown diffusing itself with no respect to individuals. The very time scheme of Book 5 is a source of irony at this point, for we have already been shown the end of this same tenth day, when, after Criseyde's fatal interview with Diomede, Phoebus will be ushered out of the world by Venus without having in any way altered the course of events leading to Troilus's betrayal (1016–29).[10]

The allusion to Nisus's daughter emphasizes the irony of the situation. It recalls Ovid's tale of Scylla, daughter of Nisus, king

9. On the implications of these lines see Roger Dragonetti, "L'épisode de Francesca dans le cadre de la convention courtoise," in his *Aux frontières du langage poétique*, Romanica Gandensia, no. 9 (Ghent, 1961) pp. 100–101.

10. As Root points out in his note on 5. 842, Chaucer alters Boccaccio to achieve the ironic synchronization of events.

of Megara, who betrayed her father and his city by cutting off as he slept the lock of purple hair on which the safety of the city depended and presenting it to the city's enemy, Minos, king of Crete, as a token of love (*Met.* 8. 1–151). The theme of betrayal and the importance of the love offering are enough to suggest a parallel with the behavior of Criseyde, who is about to give over to Diomede the substance and tokens of a love that is as important as life itself to Troilus. Like Scylla, she is responding to the powerful physical presence of the enemy at a time when the fall of her city seems certain (60), and both women recognize that in thus yielding to the inevitable, they are performing what amount to acts of treason.

There are obvious differences between the two situations: where Scylla had betrayed her father for love, Criseyde is in effect betraying her lover to her father and his new allies. And Minos, whose knightly grace and beauty are described at length as they appear to Scylla and who recoils in horror at Scylla's offer to place in his hands the fate of her city and her father, seems far closer to Troilus than to the cynical Diomede.[11] Troilus, the virtuous lover, is cast in the role played in Ovid's story by the aged father, and this shift has the double effect of underlining the moral significance of Criseyde's infidelity to him and pointing up the utter impotence of Troilus himself at this stage in the poem. In Ovid's story Nisus is a wholly passive figure, whose only contribution to the plot is the lock of hair he surrenders while fast asleep.[12] In the final lines of the episode, after his city has finally fallen, he appears transformed into a hawk and seeks to avenge himself on Scylla, who flees in the form of a seabird, but the story proper is wholly concerned with the behavior of Scylla and her fatal attraction to Minos. In Chaucer's poem, then, the allusion to the story points up the situation of a Troilus who is the helpless victim of Criseyde's betrayal,

11. Chaucer may have recalled Scylla's fascination with Minos in describing Criseyde's first view of Troilus. With *Tr.* 2. 624–51 cf. *Met.* 8. 32–36.

12. Ovid does not even make clear how directly Nisus himself is affected by the loss of his lock of hair. It is introduced only as embodying "the security of the realm" (*Met.* 8. 10), and when Scylla tells Minos that in offering it to him she is in effect offering her father's head (93–94), she may mean either than Nisus is dead or just that Minos now has him at his mercy. In pre-Ovidian versions of the story the loss of the lock was fatal in itself.

whose relation to the events that adumbrate his city's fate is negative and unwitting. Much later, when Criseyde's betrayal of him has been made clear by unmistakable evidence, the confirmation of his worst fears will have a catalytic, almost a transforming influence on him, but for the moment, as Phoebus and the fortunes of Troy pursue their course, he is incapable of any initiative.

While the Nisus-Scylla allusion points up Troilus's utter insignificance on the level of history, the more typical function of the allusions that center on him is to draw us into the more private world within the poem where his experience is the sole concern and to call attention to the intrinsic quality of this experience. Victimization is a recurrent theme, and Chaucer, unlike Ovid, allows his lover-hero no release into the wish-world of metamorphosis. But the allusions to metamorphosis stories have the important effect of isolating Troilus's love and suggesting its inherent value, which external circumstance cannot affect and which gradually assumes a transcendent significance.

In Book 4, after the lovers have learned that Criseyde is to be sent away, they weep in one another's arms, and the narrator devotes a stanza to their tears, bitter as gall:

> So bittre teeris weep nat, as I fynde,
> The woful Mirra thorugh the bark and rynde;
> That in this world ther nys so hard an herte
> That nolde han rewed on hire peynes smerte.
> [4. 1138–41]

The sudden reference to Myrrha is bound to come as something of a shock. Though the narrator presumably intends us to recall her metamorphosis rather than her crime, it is hard to avoid reflecting on the possible implication for Chaucer of her disastrous love.

In one aspect Myrrha may be seen as an emblem of the victimization of the lovers: she came to grief through a passion for her father Cinyras which was brought to fulfillment by the contrivance of her nurse, and there are clear correspondences between the two situations. Troilus, longing for death and calling on the absent Criseyde, is discovered by Pandarus (1. 540–43), as Myrrha, saying her words of farewell to Cinyras, is overheard by her nurse, who rushes in to prevent her suicide (*Met.* 10. 378–88). In each case a long interrogation ensues, followed by the confession of love, the confidant's promise to arrange the affair, and finally the moment when the virgin lover is unwillingly led to the darkened chamber where the love is consummated. Myrrha's ingenuous sense of shame and horror is comparable to the mor-al-chivalric scruples and the powerful sense of *dangier*, dread, and vague guilt that encroach on Troilus's feelings as he approaches the moment of union with Criseyde.

Thus far the parallels are clear enough, and the allusion seems clearly designed to invite an extended comparison. But it seems equally clear that any such comparison must allow for the most striking feature of Myrrha's story, the incestuous character of her love. To the extent that we see Myrrha as the victim of a desire she resists until the connivance of the nurse more or less forces her to give in to it, her situation may be compared with that of Troilus, whose love in its sexual aspect is virtually the creation of Pandarus, an exploitation more than an indulgence of his feelings.[13] Myrrha's story, moreover, is one of several in this portion of the *Metamorphoses* which deal with youthful victims beset by passions that seem to contradict the purity of their natures. She is unique among these figures in that she is allowed, and finally forced, to put her desire into act, and its realization is not redeemed by any miracle like the transformation of Iphys or the animation of Pygmalion's statue. It is the manipulation of her feelings as much as the feelings themselves that accounts for her tragedy. In this respect the "unnatural" element in her love is comparable to the exploitation of the adolescent emotions of Troilus, whose dimly felt desires are realized chiefly because they coincide with the vicarious needs of Pandarus, and who in his own right would hardly have been capable of the course of action Pandarus pursues on his behalf.

Criseyde, of course, is also a victim in this situation: it is the

13. The nurse's office, like that of Pandarus, extends almost to the point of physically uniting the lovers (she is indeed said to "join their bodies," *Met.* 10. 464), though Pandarus's machinations are broader in scope. With the image of the falling tree which describes Myrrha's inner feelings, *Met.* 10. 372–74, cf. Pandarus's pragmatic use of the same image at 2. 1380–83.

lovers together who are compared to Myrrha as they share their
sense of betrayal by a design that has left them at the mercy of
circumstances. Criseyde too has been exploited by Pandarus,
and the continual emphasis on the natural bond of uncle and
niece, like Ovid's various reminders of the parental link between
Cinyras and Myrrha, emphasizes the ambiguous element in
their relations which is implied so strongly by the scene between
them on the morning following the lovers' first night together.[14]

But it is Troilus whose experience the comparison touches
most closely, for he is finally, like Myrrha, the least able of all
those involved to control the bent of his confused desires. The
horror of Myrrha's situation is in the ease with which her father,
who has already heard and unwittingly sanctioned her desire to
give herself to "a man like you," is drawn into active collaboration with the scheming of the nurse.[15] Though Troilus's desire
is more simply virtuous, the betrayal of his innocence involves a
similar collaboration between the other persons involved. In this
respect the Myrrha allusion is Chaucer's means of pointing to
that disturbing element in Troilus's experience which makes his
defloration at the hands of experienced adults so strikingly like
the gratification of a child's sexual fantasy by incredibly permis-
sive parents.[16]

As Chaucer's reference to Myrrha's perpetual weeping should
remind us, both she and Troilus, in their very different ways,
survive their betrayal. In one sense what both preserve is a sort
of negative existence: Myrrha transformed into a myrrh-tree
becomes a monument to her own remorse,[17] and Troilus lives
on in inviolate fidelity to a love that even he finally recognizes as
empty. But their very constancy in the face of betrayal argues
the integrity of feeling they have in common. Chaucer makes
this point indirectly by comparing the bitterness of the tears of
Troilus and Criseyde to that of gall or lignaloes (1137). Both of

14. See *Met.* 10. 421–22, 439–70; cf. *Tr.* 3. 1555–82 and below, ch. 5, pp.
163–64.

15. See *Met.* 10. 361–67.

16. See Helen S. Corsa, "Is this a Mannes Herte?" *Literature and Psychology* 16
(1966):184–91, who offers some tactful and plausible suggestions toward an
Oedipal reading of Troilus's swoon in Criseyde's presence at 3. 1092.

17. Her metamorphosis is a response to her prayer for a neutral condition in
which her sin may pollute neither the realm of the living nor that of the dead
Met. 10. 485–87).

these are purgatives, and the effect of the lovers' weeping, too, is to purge their painful feelings and "unswell" their hearts "by lengthe of pleynte" (1144–46). The effect is finally to draw them back into the world of their ongoing misfortune. But the working of time and physical process on the lovers' transient emotions has the further effect of setting off by contrast the constant element in Troilus's love which nature, time and circumstance, so decisive in the life of Criseyde, leave wholly unaltered.

But the most significant Ovidian moments for Troilus are the ones he himself recalls in the early stages of Book 3. These give us a particularly vivid insight into the instinctively religious element in his feelings, the special quality of belief that sets him apart. Their characteristic emphasis is anticipated in a remarkable passage that, though not clearly referable to any context in Ovid, prepares us for the cluster of Ovidian figures who fill Troilus's imagination as he approaches his first secret meeting with Criseyde. This passage details the strange and elaborate alibi that is his sole contribution to Pandarus's preparations for this night:

> That if that he was missed, nyght or day,
> Ther while he was abouten this servyse,
> That he was gon to don his sacrifise,
>
> And moste at swich a temple allone wake,
> Answered of Apollo for to be;
> And first to sen the holy laurer quake,
> Or that Apollo spake out of the tree,
> To telle hym whan the Grekes sholden flee,
> And forthy lette hym no man, god forbede,
> But preye Apollo that he wolde hym spede.
>
> [3. 537–46]

The detail necessary to the alibi is contained in the first three lines of the passage, and the loosely appended stanza following is a seemingly gratuitous embellishment. Though we may take it as Troilus's rehearsal of a prepared speech, the awkward ordering of its details suggests spontaneity, and the final couplet sounds a note of urgency. Once his thoughts have touched on prayer, the spiritual tendency of Troilus's feelings takes over:

the god is suddenly present to his mind, and he projects real awe and anxiety into the imagined setting.

When we see Troilus again, he has become wholly involved in the world of Ovidian mythology, a world in which his imagining of the quaking laurel becomes an identification with it, and his acute awareness of the imminent visitation of a divine and terrifying experience is ratified by a host of Ovidian archetypes. Troilus's evocation of these figures involves a strange mixture of religious submission and unwitting prophecy. Far off at the end of the poem, when his love idyll has been broken off by the departure of Criseyde and finally destroyed by the boar figure Diomede, Troilus's plight will be close to that of Adonis, killed by a boar at the moment of his emergence from the idyllic world in which Venus had sought to preserve his youthful beauty for herself. And it is to Adonis that Troilus, with unconscious irony but unerring instinct, compares himself in the first of a series of Ovidian prayers to the planetary deities:

> "And if ich hadde, O Venus ful of myrthe,
> Aspectes badde of Mars or of Saturne,
> Or thow combust or let were in my birthe,
> Thy fader prey al thilke harm disturne
> Of grace, and that I glad ayein may turne,
> For love of hym thow lovedest in the shawe,
> I meene Adon, that with the boor was slawe.

> "O Jove ek, for the love of faire Europe,
> The which in forme of bole awey thow fette,
> Now help; O Mars, thow with thi blody cope,
> For love of Cipres, thow me nought ne lette;
> O Phebus, thynk whan Dane hire selven shette
> Under the bark, and laurer wax for drede,
> Yit for hire love, O help now at this nede.

> "Mercurie, for the love of Hierse eke,
> For which Pallas was with Aglauros wroth,
> Now help; and ek Diane, I the biseke,
> That this viage be nat to the looth.
> O fatal sustren, which or any cloth
> Me shapen was, my destine me sponne,
> So helpeth to this werk that is bygonne."

> [3. 715–35]

As happens invariably when Troilus is allowed to reflect on his situation, this prayer shows him suspended, powerless, and afraid, at the center of a universe pervaded by love, but at the same time menacing, a projection of his own doubts. Beginning with an appeal to the power of love itself, the bounty and "mirth" of Venus, he descends in imagination through the spheres, calling on each planetary divinity in the name of love, yet dwelling irresistibly on the legends of more or less hapless mortals subjected to the consequences of more or less violent divine passion. The tales recalled form a perceptible sequence: after the harsh fate of Adonis, the emphasis on necessity, as reflected in the plight of the human victim of divine love, is steadily reduced. Europa's fate is left uncertain in Ovid's account; the story of Venus and Mars ends with a momentary suspension of the force of violent desire; Daphne's transformation may be seen as a successful evasion of the force of Apollo's passion; and Herse is apparently unaffected by the love of Mercury, who ends by exercising his divine power only on her sister Aglauros. Thus, while the references bear on Troilus's situation with growing immediacy, revealing his deep sense of dread in the face of love's power, they show him also insulating himself against the reality of his plight by fantasies of escape. The sequence concludes on what seems to be a note of capitulation: the reluctance to offend Diana may express a vague wish that his innocence and purity not be violated in the course of a "viage" which, as the concluding invocation of the Fates acknowledges, he accepts as inevitable.

While there are various ways in which the individual Ovidian stories may be seen as bearing on Troilus's situation, their collective function as a means of externalizing the basic tension between his inner fears and his sense of being at the mercy of higher forces is clear enough. But the presence of Ovid's little-known story of Mercury, Herse, and Aglauros is puzzling in several respects, and I would like to explore its possible relevance at somewhat greater length. As Chaucer's brief reference makes plain, the story begins as the story of Mercury's love for the Athenian princess Herse, but comes to center on the fate of Herse's sister Aglauros at the hands of Pallas-Minerva. Having refused to grant Mercury access to Herse except in return for a great sum of gold, Aglauros is punished by Minerva, who afflicts

her with a consuming envy of her sister. Aglauros is finally
turned to stone by Mercury himself when she tries again to deny
him entrance to the palace.

The relation of this story to Troilus's situation is problematic.
Is Troilus to be identified with the mortal object of the god's
desire or with the god himself? In the Ovidian context, moreover, Mercury's love functions almost wholly as the occasion for
the story of Aglauros, whose transformation is really the central
event of the tale. For this reason, although a number of suggestive correspondences seem to invite us to compare Ovid's
story with Chaucer's,[18] it is difficult to find a focal point for such
a comparison. Both stories deal with the would-be lovers' difficulties in gaining access to their ladies, but Mercury in his divine
assurance is a very different lover from the passive and timorous
Troilus, and he seems, moreover, to incorporate into his own
role much of the function of Chaucer's Pandarus. Moreover,
there is in the *Troilus* no obvious equivalent to the role played by
Aglauros. Though the story can finally be seen to bear precisely
and searchingly on the moment in Troilus's experience at which
Chaucer's allusion occurs, the reading for which I will argue
requires a detailed review of Ovid's narrative and a broad leeway
in considering the possible scope of Chaucer's reference to it.

As in so many episodes of the *Metamorphoses,* there is a mini-
mum of communication among the principals of the story.
Herse is wholly absent after Mercury's initial glimpse of her, and
the only interaction is in the confrontation of Mercury and
Aglauros. The remoteness of the characters from one another is
suggested by the simile that describes Mercury's initial reaction
to the sight of Herse: he circles over Athens

> Vt uolucris uisis rapidissima miluus extis,
> Dum timet et densi circumstant sacra ministri,

18. Aside from the correspondences noted below, we are given in each story a
careful blueprint of the house where the beloved sleeps. Herse's chamber is in
the *pars secreta* of Cecrops's palace, with the chambers of her sisters Pandrosos
(who plays no part in the story) and the watchful Aglauros on either side (*Met.* 2.
737–39). Criseyde, too, is placed in the innermost chamber of Pandarus's house,
which opens onto the hall where her ladies sleep, and to which Pandarus admits
Troilus through a secret "trappe." See also Michael Olmert, "Troilus and a
Classical Pandar: TC 3. 729–30," *Chaucer Newsletter* 1.1 (Winter 1979):18–19.

Flectitur in gyrum nec longius audet abire
Spemque suam motis auidus circumuolat alis. . . .

as the kite, swiftest of birds, when it has spied the remains [of a
sacrificed animal], but is fearful of the priests clustered around
the altar, flies in circles, not daring to withdraw, and hovers
about the object of its hope on beating wings. . . . [*Met.* 2.
716–19]

The attendant priests, whose concern with the rite of sacrifice
makes them an unwitting obstacle to the bird's predatory design,
anticipate in a neutral way the role to be played by Aglauros. She
does not at first oppose Mercury's desire to possess Herse, and it
is a peculiarity of her attitude that her opposition to the union
becomes more intense in proportion to her sense of its "divine"
meaning. She is at first willing to assist Mercury for a price, but is
later goaded to her fatal obstinacy by the very vividness with
which she imagines the splendor of the divine marriage her
sister is to enjoy:

Germanam ante oculos fortunatumque sororis
Coniugium pulchraque deum sub imagine ponit
Cunctaque magna facit. . . .

(Envy) sets her sister before her eyes, and her sister's fortunate
marriage, and the beautiful form of the god; and all these
things she magnifies. . . . [*Met.* 2. 803–5]

In the end it is a direct manifestation of divine power, Mercury's
opening of the doors of the palace (or of Herse's chamber?) with
his divine wand, that arouses Aglauros to the final effort of
resistance that ends in her petrification.

What underlies this paradoxical effect, the corrosion of
Aglauros's emotions by the mere imagining of her sister's divine
marriage, is her essentially materialistic conception of Mercury's
divinity, perhaps inspired in part by his golden-hemmed robe
and his promise to ennoble her with divine nephews and nieces
(734, 745–46). Hence her demand for a material share in the
divine bounty, "a great weight of gold": when she sees the god,
she sees gold, and it is in return for gold that she is prepared to

procure her sister. Her attitude is not only a human but also a spiritual failure. In an earlier episode she had disobeyed the command of Pallas and opened the chest that concealed the earth-born child Erichthonius (*Met.* 2. 552–61). Here again she shows herself incapable of appreciating either the divine power of Mercury or the implications of mystery in a god's love for a mortal. Her attempt to exploit the situation both repels the god and alienates Aglauros from human sympathy. Her final state is one of sheer hostility, but a hostility whose effect is turned inward, powerless against anyone but herself.

Aglauros's impiety and its grim effects help bring into focus certain complexities in the attitude of the narrator of the *Troilus*, whose mistaken identification of sexual fulfillment with the attainment of heavenly bliss reflects a similar materialism. The narrator differs from Aglauros insofar as he wants to see the lovers attain fulfillment rather than to thwart them, but he is obsessed by the same idolatrous conception of what their love represents, and his attitude toward them, though it falls short of Aglauros's hostility, shows its own symptoms of alienation. Thus he attacks with desperate energy those materialists and cynics who cannot recognize the ineffable wonder of love as Troilus and Criseyde experience it (3. 1359–79). Beneath the surface the narrator is vaguely aware that his intense commitment to love is only an attempt to evade his private frustration, his idealism a way of disguising a covetous design on the lovers which he cannot help, but which makes him deeply uneasy. Though he begins as a would-be "priest," seeking to use the story as a means of invoking the god of love on behalf of all lovers, he has in fact made the bliss the lovers are to attain through love into the vicarious object of his own deepest longing, an investment of feeling which, like Aglauros's, inevitably comes to express itself as a desire to share the wealth. Hence his initial reaction in considering the lovers' first night together is to ask

> Why ne hadde I swich oon with my soule ybought,
> Ye, or the leeste joie that was there?
>
> [3. 1319–20]

Reflecting on the meaning of their experience he is haunted by thoughts of "daunger" and fear, the voices of a host of imagined detractors, and the images of Midas and Crassus, archetypes of self-betraying greed.[19]

The conclusion of the Aglauros episode provides a final oblique comment on the narrator's situation. Mercury reappears, is ordered away by Aglauros, and responds by causing the doors to open with a touch of his wand. Aglauros, seeking to resist his entrance, finds herself powerless to move and is transformed to a stone. Nothing further is said of Herse or the result of Mercury's love for her; having punished Aglauros's impiety, the god simply returns to heaven (*Met.* 2. 814–35). The story thus shows what can result from self-abandonment to vicarious desire. Chaucer's narrator, as he contemplates the fulfillment of that desire, is wholly cut off from any authentic and fulfilling relation with the lovers. As the final confrontation in Ovid's story ends in silence, with Mercury returning to heaven and Aglauros reduced to a monument of materialized desire, so there remains an emptiness at the heart of the *Troilus*. Nothing is altered by the consummation of love: Troilus is left immersed in the delusive glow of his own unrewarded idealism, and the narrator reacts to the physical realization of his desire in baffled vehemence.

Like Aglauros's experience of the "divine" love of Herse, then, the narrator's experience of the love of Troilus for Criseyde has a life of its own. And as in the story of Aglauros, his private drama of vicarious desire and its disappointment threatens to draw all of the poem's meaning into itself by reducing the love story to a secondary function as the backdrop to this drama. But of course the *Troilus* and its narrator do not proceed to this profoundly Ovidian final term. What redeems them both is something invincible in the love of Troilus himself, a virtue that seeks to break out of the Ovidian world within which his love of Criseyde is realized and transcend the closure this world imposes on his experience.

This divergence would seem to be good reason for dropping the comparison with the story of Aglauros at this point, particularly as I am aware that I may be stretching to its limit my

19. See chapter 6 for a fuller account of the narrator's role in this scene.

readers' tolerance for allusions. But I would like to suggest that even the transcendent impulse of Troilus's love is implied by the allusive interplay between Chaucer and Ovid. My argument here depends on a passage that Chaucer does not explicitly recall in alluding to the Herse-Aglauros story, and my only justifications for singling it out are its strikingly emblematic role as an introduction to the Ovidian episode and its congruence with the theme and imagery of Book 3 of the *Troilus*. The passage I have in mind is the simile, already quoted, that describes Mercury's response to what is perhaps his only sight of Herse:

> . . . nec longius audet abire
> Spemque suam motis auidus circumuolat alis. . .
> [*Met.* 2. 718–19]

The image of the hovering bird, waiting suspended until the priests shall have completed their ritual task, links the roles of Troilus and Mercury and at the same time points to the vast difference between them. In its Ovidian context the simile dramatizes the passion that leads to the god's descent and also undercuts its magnificence. The reduction of Mercury to a bird of prey and Herse to a piece of sacrificial flesh prepares us for the cynicism with which Mercury will exploit his own divinity in announcing himself to Aglauros. If Aglauros's materialism is a fatal error, it is also true that the god himself, preparing to prey on the leavings of a religious rite, collaborates with her greed to create a travesty of divine descent.

As to the bearing of this passage on Troilus's situation, we may begin by considering the implications of the priests whose presence, in Ovid's simile, keeps the circling bird hovering at a distance. Unlike the free-ranging Mercury, whose love of Herse is a thing of the moment, Troilus's love involves his deepest feelings, and his devotion must be mediated by Pandarus and the poem's narrator, priests whose rites involve the appropriation of his love and its object to the service of their own needs and longings. They bring this love to fulfillment in a sacrament that is the realization not of Troilus's ideal, but of their own idolatry. Despite the religious awe of Troilus himself and his deep fear of profaning the mystery of love, he is being drawn steadily forward into the depths of the house of Pandarus.

In himself, however, Troilus is suspended like the hovering bird. On the one hand, he is drawn toward physical union with Criseyde; on the other, he yearns instinctively to transcend carnal involvement and realize his love in religious terms. Both tendencies are expressed through bird imagery. As Book 3 builds toward its climax and Troilus's sexual desire begins to surface, his first possessive gestures toward Criseyde suggest to the narrator the action of a bird of prey:

> What myghte or may the sely larke seye,
> Whan that the sperhauk hath it in his foot?
>> [3. 1191–92]

But despite the seeming decisiveness of the sparrowhawk's action, the rhetorical question "hovers" in relation to the action it seems to describe. It expresses the narrator's sense of awe and tension, but does not clearly reflect the attitude of Troilus himself, whose next act is to pray to "the bryghte goddes sevene" (3. 1204). Troilus, too, is hovering, fascinated but hesitant, and able to move forward only in response to clear encouragement from Criseyde.

A few stanzas later this picture of tentative aggression is balanced by the Dantean imagery of flight with which Troilus, suspended in contemplation of the beauty of Criseyde, expresses his sense of the working in him of divine love, the "holy bond of thynges":

> Whoso wol grace, and list the nought honouren,
> Lo, his desir wol fle withouten wynges.
>> [3. 1262–63]

Drawn from St. Bernard's prayer to the Virgin in the final canto of the *Paradiso* (33. 14–15), the lines develop an image of spiritual desire which Bernard had used in admonishing the Pilgrim a few lines earlier:

Veramente, ne forse tu t'arretri
  movendo l'ali tue, credendo oltrarti,
  orando grazia conven che s'impetri
grazia da quella che puote aiutarti. . . .

But lest perchance you fall back, moving your wings and thinking to advance, grace must be obtained by prayer, grace from
her who has power to aid you. . . . [*Par.* 32. 145–48]

Dante himself feels the impulse to fly on realizing, at the summit
of Purgatory, that the day has come when he is to be reunited
with Beatrice ("I felt my feathers growing for the flight," *Purg.*
27. 123). That Troilus experiences such a sense of elevation is
one of the most extraordinary features of the *Troilus,* and Chaucer's appropriation of the language of the *Paradiso* seems
intended to authenticate it as decisively as possible. But Troilus,
in the end, can only "beat his wings": he must inevitably descend
from the intensity of his preconception of Criseyde's "grace,"
and the ecstasy to which he has aspired serves only to make the
actual consummation of his love, by contrast, something of an
anticlimax. To the extent that allusion to Ovid's story identifies
Troilus with Mercury, it shows him to have followed a false god
who betrays his divinity to the pursuit of physical love and whose
descent into the world effects no divine event. Ovidian imagery
can take us to the center of Troilus's imaginative and spiritual
world, but the true meaning of his experience remains inaccessible to him and to the reader whose only guide is Ovid. It is only
when the same experience is reviewed from the transforming
perspective of Dante that Troilus's abortive spiritual flight assumes its full significance.

[4]

Thebes and Troy:
Statius and Dante's Statius

A t first sight there would seem to be no question about the importance of Statius for the *Troilus*. References to Thebes and its ill-fated rulers are strewn through the poem, culminating in the summary of the *Thebaid* itself, which is the centerpiece of Cassandre's speech to Troilus in Book 5. From the outset, as we have seen, the challenge facing Chaucer's narrator is defined in terms that recall Statius's narrative stance in the *Thebaid:* in the face of a full awareness of history—Criseyde's infidelity, Troilus's death at the hands of Achilles, the certainty of Troy's impending doom—the narrator must somehow withstand the pressure to despair symbolized by Tisiphone and let the full story of Troilus's love and loss unfold itself.

But it is also in connection with Thebes and its history that Chaucer makes his fullest use of what I have called the tradition of Lollius, referring directly and indirectly to several postclassical Latin and vernacular versions of the story of Thebes, and in the process raising the question of how this story can be made to constitute meaningful history. Pandarus, Troilus, and Criseyde recall the Theban past with frequency and familiarity, and the point of Cassandre's long response to Troilus's dream seems to be to stress the bearing of this past on the Trojan present. But the connection remains obscure. The cumulative effect of Chaucer's Theban allusions is to make clear that if there is a true and meaningful correspondence between

the histories of the two cities, it is inaccessible to the inhabitants
of the world of the *Troilus*. But for Chaucer the possibility of
making such connections is finally less important than the continuity of feeling that links him to Statius, the human sympathy
that helps both poets carry through their poetic tasks. Statius, as
I will try to show, is of all the *poetae* the one whose poetry deals in
the most radical way with the opposition between the claim of
individual experience to an intrinsic value and the view that
individual achievement is insignificant apart from its subservience to the larger inevitabilities of history. In the end, by effectively withdrawing Troilus from the world of history and affirming the unique significance of his love, Chaucer reveals himself
as a profoundly Statian poet. But through most of the poem we
can sense the possibility of this larger perspective only to the
extent that we see Chaucer's Theban allusions simultaneously in
relation to their Statian context and as they are perceived by the
characters in the poem, for whom this context is obscured by
their limited, pseudo-classical perspective.

Since the *Thebaid* is so little known, and since some of its most
suggestive qualities have been neglected even by Statius's few
commentators, I will devote the first part of this chapter to reviewing those aspects of the poem I see as bearing most closely
on the *Troilus*. C. S. Lewis remains the one critic who has sought
to explain Statius's potential importance for the Christian poet
on the basis of a careful reading of the *Thebaid*, and his brief
essay, while extremely useful, is basically an inventory of selected passages.[1] We must still begin by asking in broader terms
what this peculiarly violent poem had to offer the medieval poet
and why Statius's often despairing view of life should have lent
itself to revision from a Christian perspective.

At first glance the world of the *Thebaid* seems wholly dominated and obsessed by its own grim history. The poet presents
himself in the opening lines as disconcerted by the many inci-
dents of violence, impiety, and divine hostility which would have
to be considered if he were to trace the conflict of the sons of
Oedipus to its origins, and again and again in the poem the
course of Theban history is reviewed by those who have come to

1. "Dante's Statius," *Medium Aevum* 25 (1956):133–39.

see in it the predetermining pattern of their own misfortunes. Repeatedly the story of the campaign against Thebes is interrupted by extended historical digressions that show the present powerless to free itself from the clutches of the past. Nothing in the course of events runs counter to the emphasis established at the outset by the curse that Oedipus invokes on his two sons. Elaborate rituals in which the dead are invoked to guide the living, and laments and ceremonies for the newly fallen occupy a large portion of the poem, and the sense of loss pervades the final lines.

But Statius incorporates a remarkable number of assertions of the meaning and value of virtue and piety, which in their cumulative effect provide a counterforce to the prevailing emphasis of the history he is bound to relate. He seems to derive a kind of solace from identifying himself with youth, innocence, and purity and from bearing witness to the importance of their loss. It is chiefly through the deaths of the young that the curse of Thebes expresses itself: Adrastus, old and infirm, is the sole surviving Argive leader, and Creon and Oedipus outlive their sons. Youth, for Statius, is the chief repository of virtue, and in his response to these losses, his need to proclaim that "justice rewards the deserving," a sense of the value of human life is pitted against a frustrating awareness of the burden of fate and the moral indifference of the gods. The same concern with purity and innocence appears in his treatment of the sexual timidity of Argia, Deipyle, and Ismene, for whom there appears something inherently shameful in the necessary sacrifice of virgin purity demanded by sexual union.[2] Their capacity for such scruples seems to be associated in his mind with what amounts to a prelapsarian state, superior to strife and passion, but obviously incapable of survival in the world of the *Thebaid*. In the same spirit he presents an image of Juno in her maidenhood, timid in the presence of Jove, "not yet made angry by his adulteries" (10. 61–64). Though our view of this state of innocence is inevitably conditioned by our knowledge of intervening history, the impulse to recall it is very strong in Statius's poetry. A similar desire to make contact with a purer, more nearly primordial nature

---

2. See Lewis, "Dante's Statius," p. 139; Dante, *Convivio* 4. 25. 6–10.

informs the beautiful passage in which the pious seer Amphiaraus speculates on the meaning of augury:

> mirum unde, sed olim
> hic honor alitibus, superae seu conditor aulae
> sic dedit effusum chaos in nova semina texens,
> seu quia mutatae nostraque ab origine versis
> corporibus subiere notos, seu purior axis
> amotumque nefas et rarum insistere terris
> vera docent. . . .

> Though the cause is mysterious, this dignity has long been
> granted to birds, whether the creator of heaven so decreed
> while working vast chaos into the seeds of new life; or because
> they have come to soar upon the wind through a transforma-
> tion, their bodies altered from an original condition like our
> own; or because the purer air of heaven, and the remoteness
> of evil, and the rarity of their descents to the earth enable them
> to know truth. . . . [3. 482–88]

Such attempts to attain at least an intuitive or imaginative
liberation from the entrapment of the history-ridden world of
the poem take their most striking form in Statius's hints that a
happier afterlife rewards the virtue of at least some of his heroes.[3] The augur Maeon challenges Eteocles, condemning his
impious motives for pursuing war. He then commits suicide,
forestalling the king's wrath, and Statius envisions him enjoying
a new life in Elysian regions from which the guilt of Thebes is
excluded (3. 108–11). Amphiaraus, who is drawn down bodily
to the underworld without having undergone death in the usual
sense, is apparently conceded an exemption from the pains of
the underworld as a reward for his piety, and his companions
look forward to a day when he will be worshipped as a god (8.
206–7).[4] We are told explicitly that the spirit of the Theban hero

3. On this aspect of the poem see P. M. Kean, *Chaucer and the Making of
English Poetry* (London, 1972), 1:172–74. Kean, however, misinterprets the fate
of Capaneus, who can hardly be said to die "for the commonweal" (p. 173) and
who certainly is not "received in Elysium with universal praise" (p. 172).

4. This exemption is implied in the simile that compares Pluto to a lion who
is fierce while his opponent is strong, but who, once he has gained a decisive
advantage, is content to let his victim live (8. 124–26).

Menoeceus, whose expiatory suicide is held to have saved Thebes from defeat, ascends to the seat of Jove (10. 780–82).

There is probably no way to strike a precise balance between the optimism implied by Statius's spiritual intuitions and the prevailing gloom of the Theban world, and Statius seems not to have sought one. At a number of points we see him weighing alternate interpretations of religious institutions, and the conclusion of the *Thebaid* seems deliberately to withhold any judgment on the action of the poem. Throughout he makes an effort to affirm the value of the lives of his virtuous characters, but shows a deep desire to retreat from the grim realities of war and suffering into a celebration of the beauties of youth and innocence and nostalgia for a simpler, less history-ridden world.

From the outset Chaucer's allusions to Thebes show him concerned with the precarious situations of individuals in the grip of events. The first clear invitation to the reader to compare the stories of Thebes and Troy occurs at the beginning of Book 2, when Pandarus comes upon Criseyde and her ladies listening to the story of Thebes, and she summarizes for him the portion already told:

> "And we han herd how that king Layus deyde,
> Thorugh Edippus his sone, and al that dede;
> And here we stynten at thise lettres rede,
> How the bisshop, as the book kan telle,
> Amphiorax, fil thorugh the ground to helle."
> [2. 100–105]

The reading begins with the unwitting action of Oedipus and breaks off at the point of dealing with the fate of Amphiaraus, the noble priest of Apollo who had joined the campaign against Thebes despite his clear foreknowledge that he and his companions were doomed.[5] The chain of events and circumstances which links the two men at the crossroads to the disastrous war in which Amphiaraus meets his fate is as complex as the working of the love of Troilus and Criseyde into the pattern of the fate of

5. On the thematic implications of this interruption, which occurs in the *Thebaid* at the end of the sixth book, the mid-point of that work, see John Norton-Smith, *Geoffrey Chaucer* (London, 1974), pp. 90–91.

Troy.[6] It involves the same long history of confused dealings among humans and between humans and gods, conscious and unconscious breaches of trust and piety, and blindness or willful ignorance in the face of prophecy. Though capable of moments of vision, Troilus is, for the purposes of this comparison, the Oedipus of the Trojan version of the story, moving blindly along the preordained path of his double sorrow in pursuit of a personal goal that is a symptom and a symbol of the fatal blindness of the doomed city of Troy. Pandarus, who sets Troilus on the path that leads to his betrayal, is the very agent of blindness. When we see him at the beginning of Book 2, he is already at work on a master plan that will collaborate with the fortunes of war to visit pain and loss on Troilus and Troy. And it is utterly in keeping with Pandarus's plan that he should immediately distract Criseyde and her women from a story likely to give rise to disturbing reflections with a brisk "do wey youre book" (2. 111). Criseyde is already acutely conscious of living in a precarious situation within a city under siege, and it would not suit Pandarus's purposes to allow her to draw the obvious comparison between Thebes and Troy or to brood on the contrast between Amphiaraus's futile act of heroic loyalty and the more opportunistic conduct of her own father Calchas, who has lately abandoned Troy in response to the warning of "Apollo Delphicus."

More broadly, Pandarus's dispelling of such larger concerns as the fall of cities and the will of the gods prepares the way for a major extension of his own grand design. His interruption of the story of Amphiaraus becomes a symbol for his role as the subverter of all spiritual tendencies in the lives of those with whom he deals. Troilus, like Statius's priest, is a pious votary of Apollo. His piety gains him a momentary glimpse of the divine source of the forces that govern the life of the universe, and he is

6. This scene is the first of several tantalizing but inconclusive hints that there is a Theban link in Criseyde's own past. See David Anderson, "Theban History in Chaucer's *Troilus*," *Studies in the Age of Chaucer* 4 (1982):125–28, who suggests that Criseyde's mother "Argyve" (4. 762) was Argia, wife of Polynices. But the evidence would seem to be limited to the coincidence of names (Cassandre refers to Argia as "Argyve" at 5. 1509), and there is certainly no basis here for his further suggestion that the brooch Criseyde presents to Troilus (3. 1370–71) is the famous and fatal necklace of Vulcan worn successively by Cadmus's wife Harmonia, Semele, Jocasta, and Argia, who in the *Thebaid* presents it to Eriphyle, the wife of Amphiaraus (*Theb.* 2. 265–305, 4.187–213).

intuitively aware of the ominous bearing of these forces on his own life. The betrayal of his idealism will come about as a direct consequence of his submission to Pandarus, who goads him into abandoning contemplation in favor of an active pursuit of love. And at a broader level still, the fate of the virtuous seer suggests the plight of the poet narrator, at once privileged and burdened by his ability to see beyond the end of the love story; his vision is capable of encompassing "drede and sikernesse," tragedy and the possibility of spiritual redemption, yet he shrinks from the responsibility of his role and threatens to render his vision and *pietas* inoperative by his obsessive involvement with the tide of events.

Despite Pandarus's reference to a work on the siege of Thebes which contains "bookes twelve," and so is presumably that of Statius (2. 108), Criseyde calls her book a "romaunce," and her description suggests that she and her ladies have been listening to the story in a medieval version.[7] It is important that a romance version would omit the Statian aftermath of Amphiaraus's disappearance from the battlefield and the powerful eloquence with which he prevails against the anger of Pluto, vindicating his innocence and piety and avoiding the torments of Dis.[8] Such a version would set off the spiritual shortsightedness of Chaucer's characters, who seem powerless either to read a meaning into the literal history of events or to follow out the potential significance of individual embodiments of virtue or piety. It is also highly appropriate that the story of Thebes should be conveyed by the elaborate device of a romance within a romance. Whereas Statius's Thebans are burdened by an almost paralyzing awareness of the bearing of past events on their own lives, the historical perceptions of Chaucer's characters are mediated by courtly poetry, a form of civilized entertainment. They are effectively insulated by their own high culture from

7. The story of Oedipus and Laius is told in the *Roman de Thebes* but not in Statius, and the medieval poem refers to Amphiaraus as a "bishop." See Root, ad loc., and Anderson, "Theban History in Chaucer's *Troilus*," p. 120, n. 22.

8. *Thebaid* 8. 1–126. In the *Roman de Thebes*, which wholly omits Amphiaraus's posthumous fortunes, his death is called "orrible et fiere" (Guy Raynaud de Lage, ed. [Paris, 1969], line 5070). An alternate version describes him as slain by Pluto himself; see Root, ad loc. In his *Siege of Thebes* (ed. Axel Erdmann [London, 1911], lines 4039–58), Lydgate treats Amphiaraus as a sorcerer, justly punished with an eternity of "sorowe and meschaunce."

any functional awareness of the potential significance of the Theban archetypes to whom they compare themselves and their situation. Thus when Pandarus later in Book 2 expresses the wish that he may be struck by a thunderbolt if he intends any harm toward Criseyde in taking the role of Troilus's messenger (2. 1145–48), neither he nor we are likely to think at once of the most obvious precedent for such a fate, Jove's destruction of Capaneus upon the walls of Thebes.[9] And yet there is a curious similarity between the role of the blaspheming giant, who shouts down Amphiaraus's dire prophecies about the outcome of the Theban war (*Theb.* 3. 598–669), and Pandarus's coercive and occasionally bullying treatment of the reverence and misgivings of Troilus. Pandarus's *modus operandi* is, of course, less deliberately sacrilegious than Capaneus's reckless defiance of the gods, but the singlemindedness with which he pursues his campaign against Criseyde's honor in the face of all doubts and portents is a Trojan counterpart to Capaneus's insane bravery. An excessive preoccupation with love is the folly at the heart of the *Troilus* as the mad desire for royal power is the core of the action of the *Thebaid,* and the ultimate downfall of Troy is foreshadowed by the intensity of this preoccupation, the importance assumed by the "siege of Criseyde" in the midst of the larger war. Like the Argive champions, the besiegers of Criseyde fall prey to their own willful blindness, and this failure of perspective, Pandarus's relentless and shortsighted pragmatism and the blind idealism and fidelity of Troilus, become part of the larger process by which Troy betrays itself to the Greeks.

Amid this prevailing atmosphere, Chaucer's treatment of Antigone, the niece of Criseyde, is quietly telling. Chaucer certainly borrowed this figure from the *Thebaid,* and he preserves the vitality and idealism of the classical heroine in his Trojan maiden. Statius's Antigone, like all the young women of the *Thebaid,* is distinguished by her sexual purity as well as by the nobility of character which appears in her *pietas* toward the body of Polynices. We see her first just before the initial joining of battle, looking out from a tower at the gathering of the Theban

9. Pandarus seems to hint at the similarity when he declares that he would not deceive Criseyde "for the citee which that stondeth yondre" (2. 1146), presumably indicating the ramparts of Troy.

armies, and we view her through the eyes of the aged retainer
Phorbas, for whom she represents the hope of the future, the
one thing still worth living for in the guilty world of Thebes:

> "o mihi sollicitum decus ac suprema voluptas,
> Antigone! seras tibi demoror improbus umbras,
> fors eadem scelera et caedes visurus avitas,
> donec te thalamis habilem integramque resignem:
> hoc satis. . . ."

> "O my care, glory, and greatest pleasure, Antigone! For you I
> shamelessly postpone my descent to the shades, even though I
> will perhaps behold again the crimes and slaughter of your
> ancestors. So long as I may give you over inviolate and pre-
> pared for marriage, this is enough. . . ." [7. 363–67]

Chaucer's Antigone preserves the purity to which Phorbas responds so strongly. She is Antigone "the shene," "the white,"
and it is this quality that makes it fitting that she should appear
at a crucial stage in Chaucer's poem to speak for love at its most
idealistic and provide a complement to the idealism of Troilus.

But Chaucer has taken pains to distinguish the outlook of his
Trojan Antigone from that of her Theban original. Like every-
one around her she is preoccupied with love and takes a naive
delight in reassuring her aunt about its pleasures (2. 887–96).
Though we assume she knows no more of sexual love than what
she has learned from the "goodly maid" who composed the song
she sings (880), she is not only "white" but "fresshe" (887), a
term that, while it implies health and purity, hints also at eagerness, readiness, incipient desire.[10] As Troilus's emotional educa-
tion has been overseen by Pandarus, so Antigone has spent her
adolescent years in the house of Criseyde, and the idealism of
both has been influenced by their environment. Like the virtue
of Troilus, the innocence of an Antigone is compromised and
liable to manipulation in the Trojan milieu. In the central scene
of Book 2, where she makes her one significant appearance, her
passionately idealistic love song helps to fix the image of Troilus
in Criseyde's mind. Thus by a paradox wholly characteristic of

10. Cf. Pandarus's reference to his own "fresshe" heart at 2. 1096–99.

the *Troilus* the noblest qualities of this courtly embodiment of female purity are made to collaborate, with no prompting from Pandarus, in bringing the lovers together.

Chaucer's appropriation of Antigone epitomizes his use of Theban material throughout most of the *Troilus*, a mode of allusion that is ironic, always on the edge of parody, and highly conscious of incongruity. There is something inescapably comic about the preoccupation of Chaucer's Trojans with love; it is hard at times to remember that this folly and the code that legitimizes it are Chaucer's equivalent for the Theban madness, and they are all the more insidious for being so central to Trojan life. The same ironic awareness of love's power which enlists the virtues of Troilus and Antigone in the seduction of Criseyde is lurking just behind the coziness of Chaucer's treatment of the Trojan aristocracy, who are solicitous and busy about one another's lives and only too willing to take up the cause of a beautiful widow, each convinced that he is acting only "of his owen curtesie."[11] The combination of innocence and pride, true and false idealism in their chivalry is as different from the madness of the house of Oedipus as Pandarus from Capaneus, but we must finally take its contradictions and its potentially subversive influence equally seriously.

The fullest perspective on this aspect of Chaucer's use of the story of Thebes is provided by two related passages late in the poem which show Criseyde and Troilus viewing their situation against the backdrop of Theban history. Though brief in themselves and separated by several hundred lines, they are both dense in allusive content and intricately bound together by the events and literary contexts they evoke. In both, as so often in the poem, an allusion to Statian Thebes is set within an allusion to Dante, but both refer also to Ovid and less directly to Vergil. Together they constitute a summarial illustration of the problems of interpretation posed by the Theban references in the *Troilus*, and the broader problem of discerning historical continuity in the poem's world view.

11. On Trojan society in the *Troilus* see Mark Lambert, "*Troilus*, Books I–III: A Criseydan Reading," in *Essays on Troilus and Criseyde*, ed. Mary Salu (Woodbridge, Suffolk, 1979), pp. 114–18.

The first passage is part of an elaborate oath of fidelity in which Criseyde declares that if ever she prove false to Troilus,

> Saturnes doughter, Juno, thorugh hire myght,
> As wood as Athamante do me dwelle
> Eternalich in Stix, the put of helle.
>
> [4. 1538–40]

In the second passage Troilus, already fearing that Criseyde has abandoned him, prays to Cupid, and compares the loss he fears with the punishment inflicted by Juno upon Thebes:

> Now blisful lord, so cruel thow ne be
> Unto the blood of Troie, I preye the,
> As Juno was unto the blood Thebane,
> For which the folk of Thebes caughte hire bane.
>
> [5. 599–602]

Though the madness of Athamas was only one striking manifestation of Juno's wrath against Thebes, it is directly related to the origins of that wrath, and we may take these two passages as referring to the same story. The story begins with Jupiter's love for Semele, daughter of Cadmus and mother of Bacchus. Though Juno avenged Jupiter's infidelity by destroying Semele, her continuing anger against the pride and prosperity of Thebes led her to afflict Athamas, husband of Semele's sister Ino, with a madness that led him to seek the destruction of his wife and sons.

Chaucer's references to the two stories are further connected by their common source. Both may ultimately derive from the opening lines of the *Thebaid*, in which Athamas's madness and Juno's scheming are evoked together, but they also recall more immediately the opening of Canto 30 of the *Inferno*, the canto of the falsifiers, which begins

> Nel tempo che Iunone era crucciata
>   per Semelè contra 'l sangue tebano,
>   come mostrò una e altra fiata,
> Atamante divenne tanto insano. . . .

In the time when Juno was wroth for Semele against the
Theban blood, as she showed more than once, Athamas be-
came insane. . . .
[*Inf.* 30. 1–4]

Dante proceeds to recall Ovid's vivid account of Athamas's savage pursuit of his wife and children and then, as if anticipating
Troilus's forebodings, juxtaposes with this scene a reminiscence
of Ovid's depiction of the mad grief of Hecuba at the deaths of
Polyxena and Polydorus, the last act in the destruction of Troy:

E quando la fortuna volse in basso
    l'altezza de' Troian che tutto ardiva,
    sì che 'nsieme col regno il re fu casso,
Ecuba trista, misera e cattiva, . . .
    forsennata latrò sì come cane;
    tanto il dolor le fé la mente torta.

And when Fortune brought low the all-daring pride of the
Trojans, so that the king together with the kingdom was blotted out, Hecuba, sad, wretched and captive, . . . driven mad,
barked like a dog, so had the sorrow wrung her soul. [*Inf.* 30.
13–16, 20–21]

In both Dante's summaries and the Ovidian narratives on
which they are based, these two emblems of the fate of nations
bear quite different relations to the disasters visited on their
cities. Athamas is essentially a vehicle through which Juno's
wrath against Thebes expresses itself, and he disappears from
the story of the city after killing his son Learchus.[12] But Hecuba,
left alone to lament the obliteration of Troy and its royal house,
is the very image of the city's former glory and its fate. Once
"the image of flourishing Asia," she is now of all humankind the
one "for whom alone there remains a Troy."[13]
    The significance of these two figures to their stories is enough
to suggest a complementarity between their roles and those of

12. The story of Athamas and Ino is told in *Metamorphoses* 4. 416–542. Mid-
way in line 519, with the destruction of Learchus, the story abruptly stops being
that of Athamas and becomes wholly that of Ino and Palaemon.
13. See *Metamorphoses* 13. 484, 507–8.

Troilus and Criseyde. Viewed strictly in historical terms, in relation to the larger story of Troy, Criseyde, like Athamas, is
largely a vehicle. Her infidelity to Troilus is important chiefly as
a symptom and symbol of the fortunes of Troy, and it is appropriate that she disappear from the story of Troilus and his city
once she has abandoned them to their fate. Troilus, though, is
the very embodiment of Troy, the child of Hecuba, hailed as
"Ector the secounde," an image of the city and its nobility as they
see themselves—loyal, brave, deeply chivalrous, and high-prin-
cipled. When he is betrayed by Criseyde, Troy is betrayed in his
person.

But while Hecuba is a monument to the past greatness of
Troy, Troilus is inescapably identified with a Troy that is in the
process of betraying itself, and the noble qualities embodied in
him are fundamentally compromised. For this Troy harbors
Paris, Helen, and Pandarus as well as Troilus, Antigone, and
Hector, and all are involved in spite of themselves in a common
cause. Hector can argue nobly against the proposal to exchange
Criseyde for Antenor, declaring that "we usen here no wommen
for to selle" (4. 182) even while engaged in a war to defend the
honor of Helen. In the background, Pandarus and Criseyde
play for high stakes against the faction of "False Poliphete" (2.
1467–78), Pandarus procures his niece for a prince of the realm,
and Helen is or is not up to something with Deiphobus.

The ability of the Trojans to believe in their chivalrous integrity
in the midst of all this, which is evident in Hector's lofty tone in
the Trojan parliament and Deiphobus's eagerness to be
Criseyde's champion "with spore and yerde" (2. 1427), is Chaucer's version of what Dante in the passage quoted above calls the
"loftiness" (altezza) of the Trojans. In the Troilus this haughtiness
or idealized pride is represented as a blindness of the courtly
chivalric ethic to its own limitations. It is this same blindness that
enables Troilus to think of Pandarus's services on his behalf as an
act of "compassioun, and felawship and trist" rather than
"bauderye" (3. 395–403) and to defend Criseyde's good name to
the last in the face of overwhelming evidence. Chaucer seems to
have taken the flaws of chivalry and courtoisie very seriously, and it
is the gravity of this concern that has led many critics to sense that
the Troilus was in some measure conceived as a tract for the times

of Richard II. It is clear that the fall of Chaucer's Troy consists in the negation of this flawed idealism and that Criseyde's betrayal of Troilus is a central image for this process. When her false light is finally "queynt" in his mind, his fate merges with that of the city: he becomes the "unhappy boy" whose death Aeneas will see inscribed on the doors of Dido's temple. As in Dante's panorama, where "insieme col regno il re fu casso," where kingdom and king are "blotted out" together, Troilus and Chaucer's Troy are obliterated with the extinction of the ideal that had in a sense constituted the essential identity of both.

As so often when Thebes is conjured up in the *Troilus,* the incongruity between the actions and sufferings of Troilus and Criseyde and those of Athamas and Hecuba is as much to the point as the common identification of all four with national disasters. Just as Chaucer's Troy is not the tragic ruin that Ovid and Dante evoke through the figure of Hecuba, so Troilus and Criseyde fall short of tragic stature both in the role they play in the downfall of Troy and in their own fate as lovers. This disparity takes on added meaning when viewed in relation to *Inferno* 30, for there is a very similar incongruity in Dante's presentation. Having set up his Theban and Trojan scenes as a standard, Dante proceeds to complete the comparison as follows:

> Ma né di Tebe furie né troiane
>   si vider mai in alcun tanto crude,
>   non punger bestie, nonché membra umane,
> quant' io vidi in due ombre smorte e nude,
>   che mordendo correvan di quel modo
>   che 'l porco quando del porcil si schiude.

> But no fury of Thebes or of Troy was ever seen so cruel against any, in rending beasts, much less human limbs, as were two pallid shades that I saw biting and running like the pig when it is let out of the sty. [*Inf.* 30. 22–27]

As Dante well knew, the poems of Statius and Ovid on which he based his accounts of the "furies of Thebes and Troy" offer horrors far worse than those he associates with his two naked shades, and this knowledge, together with the comparison to runaway pigs, makes the movement of the introductory passage as a whole unmistakably anticlimactic. It is further puzzling to learn that the bestial shades are those of Myrrha and Gianni Schicchi, one the largely innocent victim of a passion she tried hard to deny, the other a Florentine remembered for a single rather comic act of mimicry and petty fraud. The standard of judgment implied by Dante's choice of examples is one by which Troilus, Criseyde, and Pandarus would stand equally condemned, but it is hard to understand why any of these figures should be relegated to this, the very "put of helle."

The answer to this question lies in the fact that Canto 30 deals with the tenth and lowest *bolgia* of the circle of the fraudulent and completes an analysis of fraud which had begun with the panders and seducers of Canto 18. Myrrha and Gianni Schicchi introduce this final stage, not because of the heinousness of their "crimes," but because these crimes provide vivid summarial images for the betrayal of self and of truth which all fraud involves.[14] Chaucer's allusions to *Inferno* 30 ask us to recognize that a version of this same sin is at work in the world of the *Troilus*. As the Dantean context makes plain, it is a sin born of a deep confusion about goals and motives, and insofar as allusion to Dante provides a setting for Chaucer's Trojan lovers, it points up their haplessness as much as their guilt. If they are falsifiers, it is because they themselves have first been deceived.

Further parallels might be drawn, but it is not clear how far we should press the comparison. We have already seen Chaucer making use of the figure of Myrrha to explore the lovers' situation, but it is impossible to know how well informed he would have been about a relatively obscure figure like Gianni Schicchi. Gianni's great achievement was to impersonate the newly dead Buoso Donati at the request of the dead man's nephew, dictating from the deathbed a will in Buoso's name, and contriving to gain for himself Buoso's prize possession, "the lady of the herd," a particularly fine mule (*Inf.* 30. 42–45). For Dante he represents worldly ingenuity, distracted by its own fictive power from a recognition that truth is at stake in human relations. To Chaucer

14. On the larger theological implications of this treatment of fraud see Roger Dragonetti, "Dante et Narcisse, ou les faux-monnayeurs de l'image," *Revue des études italiennes* 11 (1965):85–146; R. Allen Shoaf, "Dante's *Commedia* and Chaucer's Theory of Mediation: A Preliminary Sketch," in *New Perspectives in Chaucer Criticism*, ed. Donald M. Rose (Norman, Okla., 1981), pp. 83–103.

he might well seem a kind of Pandarus, acting in another's behalf to create and pursue false images and achieving ends from
which he himself derives an obscure gratification. Certainly
there is an obvious complementarity between the role played by
Gianni, the Pandarus-like enabler, and that of the innocent Myrrha, whose plight, as we saw in the preceding chapter, has much
in common with that of Troilus. Though Myrrha lets herself be
drawn by the ingenuity of her nurse to collaborate in a chain of
deceptions that violate *pietas* at the deepest level, falsifying and
so betraying the truth of her own nature and that of the nature
of love, she is hardly more an arch sinner than Troilus. The
horror of the guilt of both derives from its coexistence with
innocence.

Precise moral discriminations are beside the point here in any
case, for what we see illustrated in Myrrha and Gianni, as in the
lives of Chaucer's lovers, is the *process* of fraud, rather than the
moral gravity of the *crime* of fraud. From this point of view the
youthful vulnerability of the one and the overreaching ingenuity
of the other are as much to the point as their sinfulness. We are
invited to view them as involved in a process of which they are
unaware, at once collaborators and victims; it is necessary both
that we see them as individuals in their not very menacing frailty
and that we reflect on the nature of the process that has shaped
their lives.

It is a version of this same process, at work in love *paramours*
and in the subversion of nations and their institutions, that both
implicates and victimizes Troilus and Criseyde. The catalyst for
this process, we should recall, is that Boethian love whose role in
the *Troilus* is treated so ambiguously,[15] which "binds" the elements of cosmic life and submits human beings to the bondage
of unhappy passion. The power and menace of this love are
implied by the terms in which Chaucer invokes it in the Proem to
Book 3:

> Ye Joves first to thilke effectes glade,
> Thorugh which that thynges lyven alle and be,
> Comeveden, and amoreux hem made
> On mortal thyng. . . .
>
> [3. 15–18]

15. See chapter 1, pp. 49–52.

Such "effectes glade" include Jove's love of Semele, which Dante
points to as having first kindled the wrath of Juno against
Thebes (*Inf.* 30. 2). Like Semele, tricked by Juno and totally
destroyed as a result of her love affair with Jove, Chaucer's
lovers and Dante's symbolic sinners have trafficked with a power
they can neither withstand nor comprehend. It is a power all the
more treacherous for being a part of their daily lives:

> Ye knowe al thilke covered qualitee
> Of thynges, which that folk on wondren so,
> Whan they kan nought construe how it may jo,
> She loveth hym, or whi he loveth here,—
> As whi this fissh, and naught that, cometh to were.
>
> [3. 31–35]

The "covered qualitee" of love is a mystery in Boccaccio's version of these lines, a source of "marvel" (*Fil.* 3. 78. 5–8). Chaucer
is more analytical and traces the process of love's diffusion into
the world, gradually narrowing his focus from its cosmic to its
social aspect and so holding the small world of Trojan joy in the
same purview as the larger "glad effects" of love. As "wonder"
diminishes to mere curiosity, we descend into the world of Pandarus, who commends "love of frendes" as a "mantle" behind
which Criseyde may conceal her relations with Troilus. It is this
climate of intrigue that enables Troilus and Troy to persist in
their idealization of their life by concealing the flaws in their
chivalric practice beneath a veil of *courtoisie*. The force that origi-
nates as a manifestation of God's love for his creation has descended into the world and become a stimulus to secrecy, deception, and self-deception.

The message of these Theban-Trojan exempla, then, is
largely about the complexity of history and the importance of
keeping individual character and circumstance in mind as one
attempts to trace historical patterns. But we should note that in
the complexity of perspective which Chaucer's allusions to *Inferno* 30 provide there also lurks the danger of another kind of
"fraud," one that threatens the reader of the *Troilus* who goes
too far in identifying with the lovers and accepts the love story
too simply on its own terms. We too collaborate in the working
of fraud to the extent that we let ourselves be distracted from an

awareness of what is fundamentally at stake in human relations by the comic ingenuity of a confidence man or the pathos of love betrayed. To that extent we too become "Trojans," beguiled like Hector and Deiphobus by the plight of Criseyde and cajoled by Pandarus's stratagems on her behalf to the point at which we fail to see the implications of their behavior. At the center of Canto 30 Dante places a symbol of this danger, the figure of Sinon, the false Greek whose tears induced the Trojans to admit the wooden horse within the walls of their city. In doing so he is recalling the moral of Aeneas's account of how Sinon's "perjured art" had prevailed on the Trojans' compassion and magnanimity, allowing history to take them unawares. This moral can be applied to the impending downfall of Chaucer's Troy as well:

> credita res, captique dolis lacrimisque coactis
> quos neque Tydides nec Larisaeus Achilles,
> non anni domuere decem, non mille carinae.

> The story was believed, and we were taken by guile and by forced tears, we whom not the son of Tydeus, nor Larissean Achilles, nor ten years had overcome, nor a thousand ships. [*Aen.* 2. 196–98]

History, as the Theban references considered thus far present it, is compounded out of the weakness and short-sightedness of individuals. The allusions to Thebes by Chaucer's characters amount to a running gloss on their own enactment of a Trojan version of the downfall of the older city. A more controlled perspective seems to emerge in Cassandre's review of the events that have issued in Troilus's betrayal at the hands of Diomede. Her survey, which includes a summary of the narrative of Statius's version of the story of Thebes, gives the effect of an ordered composition, attentive to causation and recurrent patterns, and may well seem to provide the appropriate historical frame, the long view that has been so plainly absent in the other characters' tentative reflections on their historical situation.[16]

16. Norton-Smith, *Geoffrey Chaucer*, pp. 90–91, points to the importance of the recapitulation of Statius in "gathering together the destructive pagan past and its literary record, synchronizing its inevitability and its epical status with the declining Trojan present." But as I will suggest below, this seems to me to imply more continuity than Chaucer actually shows us: what ought to happen in Cassandre's speech rather than what does.

She first tells Troilus the story of the Calydonian boar and its slaying by Meleager. Next she passes to the role of Meleager's descendant Tydeus in the siege of Thebes, which leads her to the summary of Statius. Finally she "descends" to Diomede, the boar of the dream, bringing her discourse to bear, suddenly and unambiguously, on Troilus:

> "And thy lady, wher she be, ywis,
> This Diomede hire herte hath, and she his.
> Wepe if thow wolt, or lef; for, out of doute,
> This Diomede is inne, and thow art oute."
>
> [5. 1516–19]

Before considering Chaucer's purpose in making Statius's narrative the centerpiece of this dismal prophecy, it is important to note certain features of the speech as a whole. Cassandre's "historical" reading of Troilus's dream leads to an accurate gloss on the figure of the boar, but it is not therefore a valid *interpretation* of his situation. If Troilus is blind to any connection between his love and the larger world of events, Cassandre tends toward the opposite extreme, treating a mere sequence of events as if it constituted history.[17] Her world view is Ovidian in its delineation of a sequence of events with hints of recurring historical patterns and the working out of an underlying purpose. But it is an imbalanced Ovidian world she presents, dominated by the bare facts of historical change and utterly devoid of the irony and pathos with which Ovid himself, intervening at will, gives a human significance to the action of the *Metamorphoses*. Cassandre is wholly absent from the story she tells, and this seeming indifference is reinforced by the weaknesses in her narrative itself, which is marked by disjunction and the omission of traditional lore that might offset the effect of her fatalistic view of history. Meleager was the half-brother, rather than the ancestor, of Tydeus, a fact that robs Cassandre's genealogical emphasis of much of its force.[18] Moreover, the continuity implied by the

17. See Monica E. McAlpine, *The Genre of Troilus and Criseyde* (Ithaca, N.Y., 1978), pp. 170–72. Her discussion of Cassandre's role is the most thoughtful I have seen, though it is misleading as to the accuracy of Cassandre's interpretation of Troilus's dream and exaggerates the ambiguity of the dream itself.
18. Cassandre's assertion that Tydeus was descended "by ligne" from Meleager (1480–81) is probably due to *Filostrato* 7. 27. 2, in which Diomede's

emphasis on kinship is not developed. Diomede is associated with the boar because of his putative descent from Meleager "that made the boar to blede" (1515), but Cassandre offers nothing to suggest a meaning for this association and makes no attempt to link Thebes with Troy. Indeed one of the most striking things about her discourse is the discontinuity between its three sections. Having sketched the events surrounding the original boar slaying, she shifts abruptly, and with only the bare fact of kinship as an excuse, to talk about Tydeus and Thebes. Then her discourse takes another sudden leap, wholly omitting any reference to Troy or the background of the war and instead moving directly to Diomede and Troilus.

The sweep of Cassandre's historical survey, and its disjointedness, recall the headlong sequence of images at the opening of *Inferno* 30. The treatment of the "figure" of the boar, which is so powerful and enigmatic an image for Troilus, is an anticlimax very close to that effected by Dante's introduction of Myrrha and Gianni as wild pigs. But the difference between the two passages is far more important than these similarities; for Dante's use of mythic exempla raises intricate and searching questions about the involvement of the individual with his society and with history, while Cassandre's reduces the individuals she names to pawns, less important than the sequence of events in which they appear.

This contrast is particularly striking in Cassandre's summary of the *Thebaid*, which seems designed to produce the most starkly depressing effect. Not only does she obscure the origins of the war, making it seem a mere extension of the career of Tydeus, but the skeletal version she gives of the story reduces the bulk of the action to a mere listing of the deaths of the Argive heroes, and at times the narrative disappears altogether. For the princi-

---

grandfather is said to have slain the boar. Root, ad loc., notes that Chaucer could have found the proper genealogy in Boccaccio's *Genealogiae deorum gentilium* 9. 21. But the testimony of the mythographers is confusing. Meleager is said to be the ancestor of Tydeus in Lactantius Placidus's commentary on Statius, *Thebaid* 1. 463 (ed. Richard Jahnke, [Teubner, Leipzig, 1898], p. 52); cf. Lactantius's comments on 2. 727, 8. 706 (Jahnke, pp. 135, 404). In the compendium of the first Vatican Mythographer, c. 198 (G. H. Bode, ed., *Scriptores rerum mythicarum* [Celle, 1834], 1:60), Meleager is said to have been killed by his brother Tydeus, perhaps on the basis of *Thebaid* 1. 402–3.

pal source of Cassandre's summary is not the poem itself but the
twelve-line Latin *Argumentum* commonly found in manuscripts
of the *Thebaid*,[19] a plot summary that devotes a terse hexameter
to the main episodes of each of the twelve books of Statius's
poem. Nearly all the manuscripts of the *Troilus* contain the *Argumentum* as well, inserted after line 1498, the midpoint of Cassandre's summary of the *Thebaid*, and it is reasonable to assume
that the addition is Chaucer's own.

The *Argumentum* is a difficult text, dense with information and
cluttered with cumbersome proper names, and all the versions
found in the *Troilus* manuscripts contain obvious corruptions.
Moreover, even a text from which these flaws have been conjec-
turally removed gives a misleading impression of the action of
the *Thebaid* at a number of points, and these find their way into
Cassandre's version as well. Thus Cassandre's summary of
Thebaid 5,

> And of the holy serpent and the welle,
> And of the Furies, al she gan hym telle,
>   [5. 1497–98]

is based on the following line in the *Argumentum:*

> Mox furie Lenne quinto narratur et anguis.

The "furies" in question are the collective rage of the women of
Lemnos whose slaughter of their husbands is recounted to the
Argive host by the Lemnian exile Hypsipyle in the course of an
episode that is itself an interlude in the story of the siege of
Thebes. The "holy serpent and the welle" also figure briefly in
this episode in connection with the death of the infant Arch-
emorus. But in the *Argumentum,* and still more in Cassandre's
speech, these large images have outgrown their original context,
and they provide a backdrop for her account of the war which,
though portentous, is dehumanized and effectively meaningless,
its symbolic potential vast but finally incalculable.

More important than its specific inaccuracies is the bleak and

19. See F. P. Magoun, Jr., "Chaucer's Summary of Statius' *Thebaid* II–XII,"
Traditio 11 (1955):409–20.

impersonal character that Cassandre's reliance on the *Argumentum* gives to her version of Statius's narrative, particularly in her
account of the later books:

> Of Archymoris burying and the pleyes,
> And how Amphiorax fil thorugh the grounde;
> How Tideus was slayn, lord of Argeyes,
> And how Ypomedon in litel stounde
> Was dreynt, and ded Parthenope of wownde;
> And also how Cappaneus, the proude,
> With thonder dynt was slayn, that cride loude.
>
> She gan ek telle hym how that eyther brother,
> Ethiocles and Polymyte also,
> At a scarmuche ech of hem slough oother,
> And of Argyves wepynge and hire wo;
> And how the town was brent, she tolde ek tho. . . .
>   [5. 1499–1510]

In this account of the action of the *Thebaid,* the sense of inevitable doom has become dominant to the point of eliminating
any hint of an alternative perspective. Impassively, Cassandre
shows a succession of heroes who are destroyed, one after another, and that destruction is the end of it all. The burning of
Thebes is her own gloomily prophetic embellishment of the story, once again on the basis of a misleading detail in the *Argumentum,*[20] and she has nothing to say about the intervention of
Theseus, with its hint of redemption. Offering her version of
the *Thebaid* as evidence of Troilus's betrayal by Diomede, Cassandre bids her brother "weep if thou wilt, or laugh" (1518), but
she herself does neither: her view of the events with which she
deals is neither comic nor tragic, and the effect of her detachment is to enhance the impression of inevitability which her
summary conveys. Her prophecy is in effect dead poetry—a

---

20. Magoun, "Chaucer's Summary," p. 420, states that the burning of the city
is mentioned in the twelfth line of the *Argumentum.* But in fact *ignem* or *ignes*
refers to the funeral pyres of the Argives (the *busta* of *Theb.* 12. 798). Chaucer
would certainly have known this, and indeed was clearly fascinated by the ending
of Statius's poem; see *Knight's Tale* 994–97, which recall *Theb.* 12. 797ff., and esp.
2919–66, the long *occupatio* in which Chaucer lingers over Arcite's funeral as
Statius does over that of Parthenopaeus.

prophecy of doom like the inhuman *scritta morta* over the gateway of Dante's Inferno, a seeming confirmation of that fear to which the narrator of the *Thebaid* himself threatens to succumb at certain moments: that humanity is at the mercy of alien gods, that there is no higher controlling purpose, that all life ends in pointless destruction. By setting Statius's bleak narrative in an Ovidian frame and exploiting the suggestions of continuity and purpose which this framing device lends to the panorama of events, Chaucer achieves the chilling final effect of a complex and potentially heroic action which seems to come to nothing, effects no significant historical change, and issues in no metamorphosis or distinctive human gesture that might redeem the story in some small degree. History has been robbed of all meaning.

The point is not that Cassandre is wrong or that she is guilty of any malign intention in offering Troilus this grim perspective on his betrayal.[21] Cut off from authentic poetic sources, she is cut off as well from the humanity of the *poetae* and from their ability to locate the essential quality, what Statius calls the *virtus* of noble human actions. Thus she seems to suppress the most striking portions of the Ovidian story of Meleager, noting only that his presentation of the slain boar's head to Atalanta led to "a contek and a gret envye" (1479) before moving abruptly, and by way of a false genealogy, to Statius's story of Tydeus at Thebes. Yet the story of the boar is only a portion of the larger story of Meleager himself, a story whose potential significance as an image of Troilus's situation is far richer than the meanings Cassandre draws from her wealth of incident. A hero driven more by passionate love of Atalanta than by duty in his slaying of the boar, Meleager is goaded to a fundamental violation of *pietas* by a need to vindicate his love, slaying the brothers of his mother Althea when they question his right to present the boar's head to Atalanta. Althea casts into the fire the log to which Meleager's life has been linked by the Fates, and as it burns, he too is wholly consumed by a fire within himself. His death is both the punishment of his own folly and part of a larger scheme of divine

---

21. But see Henry H. Payton III, "The Roles of Calkas, Helen, and Cassandra in Chaucer's *Troilus*," *Interpretations* 7 (1975):11–12.

vengeance. Like Troilus, and Troy in the person of Troilus, he pays a terrible price for his love, and his death is in effect the climax of the national tragedy of Calydon.[22] It leaves a lingering sense of unfulfillment, offset only by Ovid's treatment of the similar death of Hercules in the following book of the *Metamorphoses*, an episode that ends not with utter loss, but with a powerful account of the hero's apotheosis (*Met.* 9. 239–71).

The neglect and near denial of individual heroism which are the most notable results of Cassandre's suppression of the human and potentially spiritual implications of her material appear even more sharply when her summary of the *Thebaid* is set against the original poem. Statius is deeply concerned with the quality of heroic action, and the most memorable moments in the *Thebaid* are those at which he focuses on individual heroes at moments of crisis. No reader of the poem can forget the last cannibalistic rage of Tydeus, the spectacular electrocution of Capaneus on the walls of Thebes, or the raw hatred in the final encounter of Polynices and Eteocles. But more distinctively Statian, and much more significant for our purposes in assessing Chaucer's debt to Statius, are his presentations of two young heroes, Parthenopaeus and Menoeceus, who exist to a great extent apart from the main action of the poem, and whose special qualities anticipate in many ways Chaucer's treatment of Troilus.

Of all the seven Argive heroes, the young Arcadian warrior Parthenopaeus contributes least to the action of the *Thebaid*, but his origins, his physical appearance, and his few heroic deeds are given special prominence. He is a uniquely privileged figure: from his primitive Arcadian background he derives an innocence that serves as a sort of insulation against the horrors of war. For him alone battle is a sport; Diana protects him and guides his arrows. His youthful beauty, reminding the Theban

22. When Meleager dies (*Met.* 8. 522–25), Ovid declares, "lofty Calydon is laid low [*iacet*]" (526); and while "iacet" is probably in large part metaphorical, Meleager's death leads directly to the dissolution of the royal house (526–45). Atalanta quietly disappears from Ovid's poem after the initial "contek" (425–36), but resurfaces, safe and sound, two books later. In an episode that Chaucer probably recalled in developing the role of Cassandre, Venus tells Adonis the story of Atalanta and Hippomenes in a vain attempt to dissuade him from hunting all beasts that meet the hunter head on (*Met.* 10. 560–707).

warriors of their own sons, makes them reluctant to attack him, and when he finally falls, both armies lament his death.

It would be hard to say with any precision what we are to see as embodied in Parthenopaeus or why his presence and fate should be so strongly emphasized. Very tentatively I would suggest that his embryonic heroism, and the elaborate means by which Statius dramatizes his beauty and innocence, are an adumbration of the fulfillment of something intrinsically noble, the ritual assumption of a kind of ideal natural manhood uncontaminated by any debasing passion and untroubled by a mature, worldly awareness of fate and responsibility. This ideal can hardly be elaborated, for it exists only as a promise, and the promise is inevitably aborted by circumstance.[23] The summons to war, though it finds Parthenopaeus already restless in Arcadia and eager for battle, is untimely, and in his final speech he acknowledges that recklessness has brought about his premature death. His role inevitably recalls the figures of Pallas and Camilla in the *Aeneid,* and we are probably to see in his brief intrusion into the world, as in Vergil's depiction of the obliteration of Saturnian Italy at the hands of the Trojans, a suggestion of the inevitably destructive effect of history on nature.

Whatever Statius's reasons for celebrating Parthenopaeus as he does, his motives may well seem to reduce themselves to mere nostalgia when this pastoral figure is set against the austere heroism of Menoeceus, the son of Creon, whose ritual suicide, undertaken in response to the prophecy of Tiresias that this alone can avert a Theban defeat, marks the spiritual high point of the poem. It is essential to Parthenopaeus's role that he exist as nearly as possible outside of history, while Menoceus, as the last of the Theban royal house, is deeply involved in the world of events. The opposition of the two heroes and the contrast in Statius's treatment of them is thus a particularly effective illustration of Statius's deeply ambivalent attitude toward the action of his poem.

But while Menoeceus is at least believed to have affected the course of history through his expiatory death, Statius gives less

23. As Parthenopaeus appears at the marshalling of the Argive host, the narrator expresses the hope that he may live until his strength becomes equal to his courage (4.253).

attention to the consequences of the act on this level than to the
transcendent character of the *virtus* that inspires his action. The
most significant contrast between the two young heroes is that
whereas Parthenopaeus functions chiefly as an unconscious reflection of the nostalgia and idealism of others, Menoeceus undergoes an inner, spiritual experience that is inaccessible to others. Before Menoeceus is introduced, we are shown the goddess
Virtus joyfully descending from the seat of Jove to make one of
her rare incursions into human life. Whereas the other heroes in
the poem are impelled in their final moments of valor by a *furor*
that intensifies their valor as death approaches, Virtus finds
Menoeceus already fighting at the height of his powers. Her
function is not to goad him to a heroic madness but to imbue
him with a sense of his spiritual mission. Assuming the form of
the priestess Manto, she compels him to forsake "mean battles"
and raise his mind to the contemplation of a higher destiny:

> . . . non haec tibi debita virtus:
> Astra vocant, caeloque animam, plus concipe, mittes.

> . . . This sort of virtue is not meant for you: the stars summon
> you; only set your mind on higher things and you will send
> your soul to heaven. [10. 664–65]

His death, despite its importance for Thebes, releases a soul that
has long been disdainful of bodily existence (774–75) and has
already entered into the presence of Jove even as *pietas* and *virtus*
bear his body to the ground (780–82).

Statius makes plain that Menoeceus's act has little or no effect,
either on the spiritual climate of the poem or on the course of
events. For a time it suspends the action of the war, as the Argives withdraw in reverence to allow the rejoicing Thebans to
stage an elaborate funeral and establish Menoeceus as a patron
of the city. But the interlude is brief, and the poet himself seems
to hint that its importance is overshadowed by that of the final
madness and destruction of Capaneus, as the war quickly resumes its bloody course. Creon's speech before Menoeceus's funeral pyre reaffirms his son's divine destiny, but it is also out of
grief for his loss that Creon is driven to prohibit the burial of the
Argive dead, a perversion of the meaning of Menoeceus's sacri-

fice which, together with the fact that Statius offers no final comment on his heroism, leaves his importance for the meaning of the poem as a whole uncertain.

The *Thebaid* ends on a similar note of uncertainty, all the more striking in that it represents a retreat from all that Menoeceus and his sacrifice seemed to represent. The Argive widows summon Theseus to the final campaign, which frees the city from domination by the house of Oedipus. Theseus's intervention has been seen as transforming the entire poem, making it finally "an epic not of sin but of redemption, a chronicle not of evil but of triumphant good."[24] But the poet himself offers no clear final assessment. With the release of tension following the death of Creon, all are drawn toward the dead—"vidui ducunt ad corpora luctus" (12. 796)—and the final lines of the narrative proper take the suspended form of a paralipsis, in which the poet, while denying his will or power to do justice to them, alludes briefly to the mourning over the Argive heroes and ends by hesitating for one final moment over the figure of Parthenopaeus:

> Arcada, quo planctu genetrix Erymanthia clamet,
> Arcada, consumpto servantem sanguine vultus,
> Arcada, quem geminae pariter flevere cohortes.

> The Arcadian, and how his mother cried out in her mourning; the Arcadian, his face still beautiful despite his loss of blood; the Arcadian, for whom the two armies felt equal grief. [12. 805–7]

In this lingering note of pity there is a hint of deep pessimism: it is as though *pietas* toward the dead were the one surely meaningful form of religious expression. Certainly there is no Statian equivalent to the remorseless *pietas* of the *Aeneid*, which assumes that the great achievement of the founding of Rome is worth its price in loss and slaughter.[25] Perhaps we are to see Statius's curious attachment to Parthenopaeus as symbolic of a purely

24. David Vessey, *Statius and the Thebaid* (Cambridge, 1973), p. 316. For opposed views see Giuseppe Aricò, "Adrasto e la Guerra Tebana," in his *Ricerche Staziane* (Palermo, 1972), pp. 109–31; John F. Burgess, "Statius' Altar of Mercy," *Classical Quarterly* 22 (1972):339–49.

25. See Burgess, "Pietas in Virgil and Statius," *Proceedings of the Virgil Society* 11 (1971–72):48–61.

personal attitude, a dissent from the harsh world of epic values for which no explicit justification could be given.

In the end, I think, we must see the *Thebaid* as dramatizing a conflict of values that Statius cannot resolve and of which the contrast in his treatment of Parthenopaeus and Menoeceus may be seen as symptomatic. Without attempting to suggest historical causes for his dilemma, we may see his poetry as suspended between what I will call traditional religion on the one hand, and, on the other, a dim perception of something very different, something genuinely transformative, which he can express only tentatively. The former, as manifested in the *Thebaid*, is largely the religion of cult and practice, devoted to the propitiation of the traditional gods and to the search for guidance through augury, necromancy, and the imputation of a symbolic value to good and bad fortune. In many ways it is a religion of culture, and its most strongly affirmative gestures involve a collaboration of *pietas* with artistic imagination: Amphiaraus's intuitive prob-ing of the meaning of augury is the act of a poet of meta-morphosis, seeking a symbolic pattern in the movement of the changing world. But this culture-religion is inevitably bound to the past and seems at times, as in the purely imaginative idealiza-tion of Parthenopaeus, to be reducible to mere nostalgia.

Against this half-poetic piety we may set those moments when Statius seems concerned with vindicating human life in the face of the hostility of the traditional gods and with affirming the meaning of virtue and suffering with no regard to their efficacy on the level of history. Menoeceus's experience of divine virtue and the immortality he gains through his suicide are clearly far more important in themselves than the temporary reprieve he earns for the city of Thebes. At such a moment, or again when he shows Coroebus and Amphiaraus gaining exemption from the cruelty of the gods by their eloquent affirmation of private virtue (1. 643–66, 8. 90–126), Statius suspends the power and authority of the traditional order, and by his increasing empha-sis on the divinity of Pietas and Virtus themselves, implicitly rejects it.

From the vantage point of the Christian poet, Statius's treat-ment of such a figure as Menoeceus is of crucial importance in illuminating his spiritual advancement relative to Vergil and

Ovid. As Lewis notes, Statius's affirmation of the heavenly provenance of the virtue that inspires Menoeceus answers directly a question left open by Vergil, who makes Nisus question whether his desire to do "something great" is divinely inspired or born of dangerous impulse.[26] Though Statius's conviction seems to waver somewhat when he is forced to descend from the theme of Menoeceus's transformation to deal with the "lofty virtue" of Capaneus, a virtue that "exceeds measure,"[27] the goddess who inspires Menoeceus is clearly of a different order, a sort of grace.

Certainly Dante saw in Menoeceus the potential resolution of the conflict of doubt, nostalgia, and religious intuition which the *Thebaid* leaves unresolved. The conversion of Statius as Dante presents it might be characterized as a full acceptance of the spiritual challenge represented by Menoeceus's fate, and it is appropriate the the confirmation of this conversion, Statius's major contribution to the spiritual theme of the *Commedia*, should be his discourse on the creation of the human soul (*Purg.* 25. 34–107). For the heart of this discourse, the account of the informing of the embryonic soul by divine *virtù* and of the soul's death and afterlife (68–87), is largely modeled on Menoeceus's experience of the inspiration of the goddess *Virtus* in *Thebaid* 10. In both cases the infusion is a glad bestowal of the divine on a creature that has attained a state of natural perfection sufficient to make it a worthy receptacle, and the effect in both cases is the absorption and reordering of the natural powers by the divine. This total transformation is conveyed in the *Purgatorio* by the wonderful analogy of the sun's heat, which unites with the juice of the grape to create wine (25. 76–78), and in the *Thebaid* by the more violent image of a tree struck by lightning, which "drinks" the fire and becomes consumed by its power (10. 674–77).[28] As Menoeceus's soul, immediately smitten with the love of death,

26. "Dante's Statius," p. 138; cf. *Theb.* 10. 628–37, *Aen.* 9. 184–87.

27. *Thebaid* 10. 827–36, 845–47. Capaneus states explicitly that his attempt to destroy Thebes single-handedly is also an attempt to deny the meaning of Menoeceus's sacrifice (845–47).

28. The suggestive phrase "raised up his spirit" (*erexit sensus*) (*Theb.* 10. 677) may perhaps be seen as corresponding to the lines in which the "new spirit" reconstitutes the active power of the embryonic human nature it informs (*Purg.* 25. 71–75).

moves unfalteringly toward the destiny that will translate it to heaven, so in the *Purgatorio* the soul, once perfected, lives only to die, and then, "without resting," goes forward to learn its destination in the afterlife.[29]

The liberation of Statius from the hellish world of Thebes to the point at which he becomes our authority for the freedom of the purified soul is one of the most important symbolic events in Dante's *Commedia*. And as I have already suggested, Dante's elaborate fiction, which becomes the prototype for his own assimilation and transcendence of the literary past in the *Purgatorio*, is highly significant for Chaucer as well. Indeed the experience of Dante's Statius is in certain respects closer to that of Chaucer's narrator than to Dante's own, and in the final stanzas of the *Troilus* Chaucer, too, will show himself deeply aware of having entered that area of poetic experience which the Statius cantos define.

In the *Thebaid* itself we can see in Statius's wavering between identification with Menoeceus and with Parthenopaeus doubts very much like those of Chaucer's narrator as he contemplates the story of Troilus. And though we cannot point to precise correspondences between the *Troilus* and the *Thebaid* comparable to those that illuminate Dante's appropriation of Statius, it is possible to see Troilus's role and the evolution of his heroism in Statian terms. In a broad sense Troilus is at once the Parthenopaeus and the Menoeceus of Chaucer's poem. Like Parthenopaeus he is a privileged figure, whose experience must fulfill the yearnings and fantasies of others, whose innocence must be preserved at all costs, and who exists on his own plane of reality, unaffected by the long war and the worldly stratagems of Pandarus. His imaginative world, his equivalent to the idyllic

29. The abrupt shift from the moment at which human nature is consummated by *virtù* to the moment of death (*Purg.* 25. 79–81) corresponds to the abrupt separation of spiritual from earthly when Menoeceus dies, and

> Pietas virtusque ferebant
> leniter ad terras corpus; nam spiritus olim
> ante Iovem et summis apicem sibi poscit in astris.

> Piety and Virtue bear his body gently to the ground; for his spirit has long since come before Jove, to demand for itself a place of honor among the highest stars. [*Theb.* 10. 780–82]

Arcadian atmosphere in which Parthenopaeus moves, is the lyric world of the religion of love, and he can have no ongoing existence outside that world. But he is also, like Menoeceus, the vessel of an inchoate spirituality, a virtue that withstands and finally overcomes the prevailing emphasis of the poem's action. Though we may see him as blind and pathetic in his adherence to an empty faith in the fidelity of Criseyde, we must also recognize something admirable in his own unfaltering commitment to love in the face of powerful temptations to despair.

Troilus will eventually become, like Menoeceus for Dante's Statius, a catalyst to the narrator's discovery of spiritual meaning beneath the surface of his poetic conception, but he must first undergo what amounts to an evolution from the status of a Parthenopaeus to that of a Menoeceus. In this respect Cassandre's Theban prophecy and her potentially devastating account of his dream may be seen as a crucial test, the shattering of his Parthenopaean idyll. His response to her speech clearly exposes the inadequacy of her view of human life and gives us a new and significant insight into his own.

Troilus answers Cassandre's claim that Criseyde has given her heart to Diomede not with a direct denial, but with the charge that Cassandre has slandered women in general, reinforced by the counter-example of the heroic virtue of Alcestis, who gave her life for her husband:

> "For whan hire housbonde was in jupartye
> To dye hym self, but if she wolde dye,
> She ches for hym to dye and gon to helle,
> And starf anon, as us the bokes telle."
>   [5. 1530–33]

There is a special aptness in the citation of the example of Alcestis. Though it does nothing to vindicate Criseyde, it raises questions about the value of private virtue which point up Cassandre's indifference to the quality of human actions. The Alcestis reference also provides a valuable index to the combination of genuine virtues and severe limitations that Troilus will exhibit in the final stages of his story. It is significant that Alcestis's legend was unknown to the Middle Ages in any classical

literary version. It survived only in the compendia of the mythographers, so that its meaning was largely determined by the
moralizations conventionally associated with it in mythographic
tradition. To this extent Troilus's vision shares the limitations of
Cassandre's: he is as much at the mercy of the pseudo-classical
tradition as she is in his dependence on mythographical exempla
that lack the reinforcement of authentic poetry. But unlike Cassandre's fatalistic view, which diminishes the significance of the
individual, the example of Alcestis illustrates a triumph of *pietas,*
a submission to fate which is at the same time a willed, virtuous
act.

In the bare-bones version transmitted by Fulgentius and the
Vatican mythographers, the story of Alcestis is as follows: she
was the wife of the Greek king Admetus, who had won her, with
the aid of Apollo and Hercules, on terms proposed by her father, by successfully harnessing to his chariot a lion and a boar.
Alcestis's self-sacrifice was undertaken in response to the prophecy of Apollo that only thus could Admetus be saved from a fatal
illness. After her death Hercules brought her back from the
underworld and restored her to Admetus. For the mythographers, Admetus is the human mind or spirit, subject to
fear ("quasi quem *ad*-ire poterit *metus*"), and Alcestis is the spiritual courage (*animositas* or *praesumptio*) to which he aspires. In
pursuit of her he yokes the lion ("mental virtue") and the boar
("bodily virtue") and it is this integrated virtue, symbolized by
Hercules, which affirms the spiritual destiny of man by meeting
the challenge of death.[30]

The limitations of Troilus's view of Alcestis are clear: in recalling her story he makes no mention of its final and crowning
event, her liberation by Hercules and her restoration to Admetus; indeed he seems unaware of this event, declaring instead
that after descending into hell she "starf anon" (1533). Here we
may see the fatalism that strictly limits Troilus's sense of his own
destiny as a lover, reducing Alcestis to the role of a virtuous

30. See Fulgentius, *Mitologiae* 1. 22 (*Opera*, ed. Rudolph Helm [Leipzig 1898],
pp. 33–35); Mythographus 1. 92; 2. 154; 3. 13. 3 (Bode, ed., pp. 31, 128–29,
247–48). The story is given without the moralization by Hyginus, *Fabulae*, no.
51; Lactantius Placidus on *Thebaid* 6. 359 (Jahnke, ed., p. 318); Boccaccio,
Genealogiae 13.1. Cf. Chaucer, Prologue to the *Legend of Good Women* F 511–16, G
499–504.

suicide and causing him to ignore altogether the implications of
Hercules' act of redemption, just as Cassandre ignored the sacrifice of Menoeceus and the redemptive role of Theseus in the
Thebaid. Troilus, moreover, has utterly failed to harness the lion
and the boar in his own life; they are represented in the opposition between himself and Diomede, the boar-figure of his dream
whose intervention in his life he is for the moment psychologically incapable of recognizing.[31]

But there is nobility as well as futility in Troilus's position at
this point in the story, and there is much in the comparison of
Alcestis to remind us of his positive qualities. When he points to
her fidelity and her noble exercise of free choice, he is unwittingly pointing to the presence of similar qualities in himself, a
fidelity that values love more highly than his own life and survives uncompromised when his love is betrayed. Though he is
mistaken in his insistence on believing that Criseyde has re-
mained loyal, his refusal to abandon that conviction in the face
of Cassandre's revelations is admirable. The spark of virtue that
enables him to assert the claims of fidelity at the very moment
when his own faith in love is most strongly threatened by despair
is itself an example of the sort of spiritual capacity that her view
of human existence wholly ignores. If his love remains centered
on Criseyde and never attains the full dignity of the patriotic
and religious virtue of Menoeceus, it is nonetheless the essential
force that enables him to survive and transcend the potentially
overwhelming implications of his story.

In the end this latent spirituality will emerge more decisively.
After the emotional intensity of Troilus's love has been convert-
ed for an interval into heroic wrath, he will be granted a moment
of transcendent awareness. But Chaucer, like Statius, leaves certain aspects of his hero's role unresolved and assigns no final
value to his spiritual evolution. Troilus's virtue is left in suspension, in a spiritual void, and there is no category of genuine
religious experience to which we can refer the Boethian perspective on life and love which he attains immediately after his
death in battle. In the end, hero and narrator part company

31. Troilus is compared to a lion at 5. 830, in the course of a portrait that is
balanced against that of Diomede.

once and for all. Leaving Troilus to the care of Mercury, the narrator steps outside the poem's pagan world and his vision shifts, as in the *Thebaid,* from the affirmation of heroism to a sense of the pathos of human loss. In the final stanzas of the poem we look back at Troilus from another world, as Statius looks back at the funeral pyre of Parthenopaeus, or as Dante's Vergil recalls the lost, half-pastoral Italy where Turnus, Camilla, Nisus, and Euryalus met their deaths (*Inf.* 1. 106–8). But there are hints of future promise in this vision of the loss of innocence and the long history of the sacrifice of youthful heroism. As Dante and Statius discern new meanings in the ancient ideals of *virtus* and *pietas,* so Chaucer's narrator is finally compelled to respond to Troilus's spiritual yearnings by giving expression to intuitions of his own. In the end, as for Dante's Statius, these intuitions become the means to the narrator's full psychological and spiritual liberation from the world of his poem.

[5]

Dante and the *Troilus*

In comparison to the obliqueness and ambiguity of Chaucer's use of classical sources in the *Troilus*, the most striking characteristics of his allusions to Dante are their directness, boldness, and prominence. The *Troilus* begins and ends with allusions to the *Commedia;* a quotation from the climactic prayer of the *Paradiso* marks the high point of Troilus's ecstasy in Book 3, and many details invite us to compare his love for Criseyde with that of Dante for Beatrice. The solemnity of the context thus created is startling, and it is startling, too, to find even Pandarus playing a Dantean part and inviting us to compare him with Dante's Vergil at his most magisterial. At the very center of the *Commedia* Vergil states the great principle of the omnipresence of love:

> "Né creator né creatura mai,"
> cominciò el, "figliuol, fu sanza amore,
> o naturale o d'animo. . . ."

> "Neither Creator nor creature, my son, was ever without love, either natural or of the mind. . . ." [*Purg.* 17. 91–93]

We are surely intended to recall these lines as we listen to Pandarus's famous declaration that all men and women are suceptible to "loves hete/Celestial, or elles love of kynde" (1. 978–79).

Of course, much of the point of such passages lies in the parodic manner in which they reflect their originals. Dante's love of Beatrice grows over the course of his journey into a spiritual realization of her role as a vessel of truth. Troilus, by contrast, has been deeply deceived in his worship of Criseyde, and it is only by refusing to recognize this fact that he can preserve the faith that gives his life meaning. In a similar way the "celestial" love Pandarus substitutes for Vergil's elective "love of the mind" is a mere balloon, a vague nothing introduced only to be dismissed, enabling Pandarus to concentrate on the kind of physical desire he understands. Where Vergil goes on in the lines just quoted to remind the Pilgrim that the "good fruit" of his lofty discourse is largely common knowledge ("and this you know," 93), Pandarus shrouds his prosaic view of love in mystery, citing "wyse lered" as authority for his assertions (976). Vergil proceeds to distinguish the unfailing bent of natural love from the liability of elective love to perceptual, emotional, or rational error (*Purg.* 17. 94–105); Pandarus can succeed in his role as Troilus's guide only by concealing and exploiting this liability as it expresses itself in Troilus's desire for Criseyde.

But these ironies cannot be considered apart from more positive implications. Chaucer has appropriated the resources of the greatest Christian poet to show us through Troilus's experience what human love is in itself, as well as what, being merely human, it cannot be; what rich spiritual capacities are implied by its aspirations as well as how inevitable it is that any worldly attachment, valued too highly, will betray these aspirations. We must take seriously the meaning that Troilus perceives at the heart of his love for Criseyde, though we must also recognize that his sense of having realized that meaning is illusory and that he is in constant danger of "falling away" from the heights of his imaginative vision into despair.

Chaucer's use of Dante is not confined to isolated moments of high parody. Throughout the poem Troilus, Criseyde, and Pandarus appear and reappear in situations enhanced by allusions that invite us to compare them with Dante, Beatrice, and Vergil. A number of important structural elements of the *Troilus* are best understood in reference to the *Commedia*, and the central portion of the poem contains a sequence of significant allusions that amount to a sustained parody of the climactic events of the *Purgatorio*.

The best starting point for considering this aspect of the *Troilus* is the opening of Book 2, in which both the narrator and Pandarus are located in Dantean terms. The narrator's situation is focused in the opening stanza of the Proem:

> Owt of this blake wawes for to saylle,
> O wynde, O wynde, the weder gynneth clere;
> For in this see the boot hath swych travaylle
> Of my konnyng that unneth I it steere.
> This see clepe I the tempestous matere
> Of desespoir that Troilus was inne. . . .
>
> [2. 1–6]

Despite the tormented syntax and disjointed statement, the lines clearly recall the opening of the *Purgatorio:*

> Per correr miglior acque alza le vele
> omai la navicella del mio ingegno,
> che lascia dietro a sé mar sì crudele. . . .
>
> To course over better waters the little bark of my genius now
> hoists her sails, leaving behind her a sea so cruel. . . . [*Purg.* 1.
> 1–3]

Dante is here celebrating the release of his imagination from the deadly pressure of the *Inferno,* where poetry is generated by frustration and ends inevitably in a sense of loss, into a world in which spiritual and poetic fulfillment are possible. The raising of the sails of imagination represents a new freedom to respond to his inspiration in full confidence that it will not betray him. The narrator of the Troilus seeks to establish a similar orientation as he embarks on the story of Troilus's emergence from the inferno of his despair to the hope of a realization of his love for Criseyde. But it is clear that Chaucer's narrator is still at the mercy of something "tempestous" in his material: the violence of his first three lines dramatizes the lack of control made explicit in the fourth, and the uncertain emphasis of "O wynde O wynde," which seems to be nothing more than a purely phonic echo of the *omai* of Dante's second line, suggests an utter confusion as to the nature of the force that drives his poem forward. The recourse to an allegorical gloss in lines 5 and 6 is a clear acknowledgment of the lack of inner coherence in the stanza. The effect of the passage as a whole is to dramatize the problem with which the narrator plays in a gingerly fashion in the remainder of the Proem to Book 2, that is, his lingering anxiety as to the kind of influence being exerted on him by the story he is bound to tell.

The narrator's conscious misgivings extend only to a vague awareness of something in the story that is not wholly attuned to his own "sentement," and he is able, with characteristic misguided humility, to attribute the discord to his own insensitivity to the nuances of language. But underlying these symptoms are the same problems of motivation and control that surfaced in the poem's opening appeal to Tisiphone. In those lines also, Statius bears significantly on the narrator's dilemma. The opening lines of Book 2 recall not only Dante but a cluster of similes from the *Thebaid,* in which the image of the storm-driven sailor is used to illustrate the growing madness of the sons of Oedipus. Polynices, rushing through the night from Thebes to Argos, where he will raise an army to lead against his brother, is compared to a navigator caught by a winter storm, who has lost his bearings and so "stands, bereft of purpose [*rationis inops*], amid the violence of sky and sea" (1. 372–73). The simile seems inappropriate at first because the navigator is wholly suspended while Polynices is acting with outward decisiveness, making his way through dense forest and beating back the menacing undergrowth (376–79). But Polynices' faculties and motivation are not his own, for they have become wholly subject to Tisiphone and the wrath of Jove. The hapless sailor represents the thwarting of conscious purpose while Polynices' actions represent submission to an inescapable fate.

Statius presents Eteocles's situation in the same terms. The shade of Laius, sent by Jove to goad him into preparing for war, rebukes his inactivity by comparing him to a helmsman who idly neglects the rigging and rudder of his ship while a storm gathers around him (2. 105–8). And when disaster strikes in the form of Tydeus, who destroys the Theban cohort sent to ambush him,

Eteocles' response is illustrated by an image that is very close to Chaucer's—that of a sailor, tricked by the deceptive brightness of the stars into leaving a friendly port, only to be overwhelmed by a great storm:

> ipse quidem malit terras pugnatque reverti,
> fert ingens a puppe notus, tunc arte relicta
> ingemit et caecas sequitur iam nescius undas. . . .

> he would rather be on land, and struggles to turn back, but a
> strong south wind astern carries him along; at last, abandoning
> his own skill, he groans, and heedlessly lets the blind waves
> draw him on. . . . [*Theb.* 3. 28–30]

The lack of self-control implicit in the disjunction of the simile used earlier of Polynices has here become the focal point of the comparison. Where Polynices had appeared outwardly to be choosing his course, Eteocles recognizes that he is powerless in the face of events and cannot free himself from a role about which he fees a deep ambivalence: "now he feels ashamed of his undertaking, now he repents his shame" (3. 22).

Chaucer's narrator is unaware of the implications of what he experiences as a difficulty in directing the course of his narrative, but he too, like the helpless navigator, accepts the limitations of his art, disclaiming authority for the events taking shape in his poem and the atmosphere that surrounds them:

> O lady myn, that called art Cleo,
> Thow be my speed fro this forth, and my Muse,
> To ryme wel this book, til I have do;
> Me nedeth here noon othere art to use.
> Forwhi to every lovere I me excuse,
> That of no sentement I this endite,
> But out of Latyn in my tonge it write.
>
> [2. 8–14]

The "darkness," which represented the narrator's alienation from the joys of love in Book 1, has here become an inability to respond with assurance to the nuances of the language of love, an internalizing of his sense of alienation which leaves him by his own account powerless to do anything more than imitate his author's "Latin" as best he can.

The appeal to Clio, Muse of history, also points to Statius, again by way of Dante. Though none other of the *poetae* invokes her,[1] Clio appears twice in the *Thebaid,* first in the opening book, where she helps the poet recall the roster of heroes who fell in the cause of Polynices (1. 41–45) and again in Book 10, in which she is summoned to tell the story of Menoeceus's glorious suicide (10. 628–31). It is typical of Statius's uneasy relation to his epic task that he should subsume under a single, neutral authority events of such diverse character and significance, refusing to distinguish the inspiration that prompts him to tell of Amphiaraus or Menoeceus from that which elicits his nostalgia for Parthenopaeus or his awe at the violence of Capaneus. It is clearly a similar desire to avoid taking full responsibility for his story that leads Chaucer's narrator to ask Clio to help him cast it in rhyme.

Statius's appeals to Clio are also noted by Dante's Vergil, who points to the discrepancy between the impression created by Statius's poetry and the clear evidence of grace provided by his presence in Purgatory:

> "Or quando tu cantasti le crude armi
>   de la doppia trestizia di Giocasta,"
>   disse 'l cantor de' buccolici carmi,
> "per quello che Clïò teco lì tasta,
>   non par che ti facesse ancor fedele
>   la fede sanza qual ben far non basta.
> Se così è, qual sole o quai candele
>   ti stenebraron sì, che tu drizzasti
>   poscia di retro al pescator le vele?"

"Now when you sang of the cruel strife of Jocasta's twofold sorrow" said the singer of the Bucolic songs, "it does not appear, from that which Clio touches with you there, that the faith, without which good works suffice not, had yet made you faithful. If that is so, then what sun or what candles dispelled

1. The one near-exception is Ovid's noninvocation of "Clio and Clio's sisters" in *Ars amatoria* 1. 27 (quoted below, p. 153).

your darkness, so that thereafter you set your sails to follow
the Fisherman?" [*Purg.* 22. 55–63]

The image of the sailing boat recalls the opening lines of the
Purgatorio and so contrasts the uncertain character of Clio's inspiration with the sure sense of purpose that the Christian
Statius now shares with Dante. We are bound to share Vergil's
puzzlement at the contrast between Statius's early darkness and
his present state of purity and true belief. The problem is one we
will have to deal with in considering the conclusion of the
Troilus. For the moment, however, I would note only that the
passage just quoted, which brings together Jocasta's twin sons,
her "double sorrow," the image of the sailing boat with which
Statius illustrates the brothers' condition, and the uncertain inspiration of Clio, is a clear precedent for Chaucer's use of the
same imagery. The effect of Chaucer's allusions in the opening
stanzas of Book 2 is thus to identify his narrator with Statius in
his most "Theban," least Dantean aspect, and to set his story at
this stage of its unfolding in jarring contrast to the process of
spiritual release that Dante traces in the *Purgatorio*. At the same
time, by establishing a frame for the Proem with the clear allusion to *Purgatorio* 1 in the opening lines, he implies the ac-
cessibility of a Dantean perspective and the possibility that his
narrator, like Dante, will find a way out of the dilemma in which
we see him, caught amid the dark waters of his ancient source.

But having thus located his narrator vis-à-vis the larger thematic world of the *poetae*, Chaucer seems to shift his ground in
the remainder of the Proem, and deals with the narrator's predicament as an insensitivity to the poetic values associated with
medieval love poetry. He does so, moreover, in terms that
strongly recall Dante's discussions of poetic language:

> Wherfore I nyl have neither thank ne blame
> Of al this werk, but prey yow mekely,
> Disblameth me, if any word be lame;
> For as myn auctour seyde, so sey I.
> Ek though I speeke of love unfelyngly,
> No wonder is, for it no thyng of newe is;
> A blynd man kan nat juggen wel in hewis.

Ye knowe ek, that in forme of speche is chaunge
Withinne a thousand yeer, and wordes tho
That hadden pris, now wonder nyce and straunge
Us thinketh hem, and yit thei spake hem so,
And spedde as wel in love as men now do;
Ek for to wynnen love in sondry ages,
In sondry londes, sondry ben usages.

[2. 15–28]

The narrator's gloomy comparison of himself to a blind man
with no sense of color resembles Dante's rebuke to those "idiots"
who burst into song with no understanding of poetic construc-
tion so that "we feel scorn for them just as for a blind man
making distinctions among colors" (*De vulgari eloquentia* 2. 6. 3).
Chaucer goes on to discuss the mutability of language (22–25) in
terms that closely resemble those of *Convivio* 1. 5, in which the
nobility and permanence of Latin are contrasted with the unsta-
ble and corruptible vernacular. The attitude toward the vernacular which this last passage seems to imply is, of course, one
that Dante later strongly rejected, explicitly in the *De vulgari
eloquentia* and implicitly in his encounters with earlier Italian
poets in Purgatory. In setting this passage side by side with the
image of the blind man, Chaucer is suggesting contradictory
motives for the narrator's dislocation. On the one hand his language is "unfeeling" because he is himself insensitive to love; on
the other he is accurately rendering his author's meaning, but
historical developments have rendered this meaning remote and
strange.

In either case the narrator's attitude toward his own language
is one of extreme diffidence, and it is clear that in claiming to be
at the mercy of his auctour, and hence of the language and
behavior of a bygone time, he is evading problems that lie much
closer to home. In large part his difficulties reflect the peculiarly
hybrid character of the *Troilus*: it is very hard, as we have seen,
to adopt a consistent narrative stance toward a medieval romance that makes a radical assertion of its adherence to the
tradition of the *poetae*, a pagan love story told from the perspective of Dante and the *Roman de la Rose*. But at this point these
larger problems of authority are less apparent than in the Proem

to Book 1. The plot of the *Troilus* has been reduced for the moment to the unfolding of Pandarus's practice of the art of love, a "usage" which, if it is not simply universal, is as typical of medieval culture as of that of the ancient world.

Ovid had pointed to the problem the art of love poses for the "serious" poet when he disclaimed for his *Ars Amatoria* the traditional sources of poetic inspiration, insisting that his real Muse was experience:

> nec mihi sunt uisae Clio Cliusque sorores
> seruanti pecudes uallibus, Ascra, tuis;
> usus opus mouet hoc: uati parete perito;
> uera canam. . . .

> Clio and Clio's sisters did not appear to me as I tended my flocks in the vales of Ascra; practice inspires this work: defer to the experienced bard; I will sing about real things.... [1. 27–30]

Like Ovid, the narrator of the *Troilus* is preparing to sing of "real things." But he enters on his task with none of Ovid's bravado: he is not so bold as to repudiate Clio, history, and tradition, but his relation to them is anxious and confused. The *poetae* cannot provide a model for his undertaking, and he must finally take full responsibility for his account of love. But there is clearly something in the "practice" he is about to describe that disturbs him and makes him fear that his audience will reject it (29–35). The real practitioner of love's art in the *Troilus* is neither the narrator nor his hero, but Pandarus. Pandarus's motives and methods, while they do serve to bring love to fulfillment, reveal in the process the cynicism and emotional impoverishment that are inseparable from the Ovidian love doctor's philosophy: a distrust of spontaneous feeling, doubts about the possibility of intimacy, and a sense of deprivation far closer to real bitterness than the "unlikeliness" to which the narrator himself confesses.[2]

2. On this aspect of the *Ars amatoria* and its narrative persona, see H. M. Leicester, Jr., "Ovid Enclosed: The God of Love as *Magister Amoris* in the *Roman de la Rose* of Guillaume de Lorris," forthcoming in *Res Publica Litterarum*.

The action of Book 2 opens with a view of Pandarus and a second allusion to Dante, which confirm the narrator's misgivings and build on the allusion to the *Purgatorio* with which his Proem begins. Though it is May, the time of "bawme" and gladness, Pandarus is introduced by a description that points up his alienation from the season and gives substance to the narrator's uneasiness about his own language by twice stressing the contradiction between Pandarus's ability to "speke of love" and his distempered state of mind:

> That Pandarus, for al his wise speche,
> Felte ek his parte of loves shotes keene,
> That koude he nevere so wel of lovyng preche,
> It made his hewe a day ful ofte greene;
> So shope it, that hym fil that day a teene
> In love, for which in wo to bedde he wente. . . .
>
> [2. 57–62]

In the following stanza Pandarus lies "half in a slomberynge" while the swallow Procne sings of her tragic marriage and its violent end:

> The swalowe, Proigne, with a sorwful lay,
> Whan morwen com, gan make hire waymentynge,
> Whi she forshapen was, and evere lay
> Pandare a-bedde, half in a slomberynge. . . .
>
> [2. 64–67]

The singing of Procne closely echoes a similar account in the *Purgatorio* (9. 12–14), but whereas in Dante her function is largely emblematic, here her song is urged on Pandarus with a peculiar vehemence. Her role would seem to be completed by the first three lines of her stanza (64–66), which correspond closely to Dante's description. But after the narrator has shifted to Pandarus, and the narrative seems about to resume, Procne unexpectedly reappears, and now

> so neigh hym made hire cheterynge,
> How Tereux gan forth hire suster take,
> That with the noyse of hire he gan awake.
>
> [3. 68–70]

The association of Pandarus's arousal with the content, as well as the noisiness, of Procne's song points up not only the moral implications of Pandarus's role, but also the complexity of his motivation. It is another of the many instances in which private feelings seem to be interwoven with his office as "fictile power" and motive force.[3]

We can learn a good deal about Dante's relation to the *Troilus* by comparing the context of Chaucer's allusion with that of its source in the *Purgatorio*. There Procne's song signals that hour before dawn "when our mind, more a pilgrim from the flesh and less captive to thoughts, is in its visions almost divine" (*Purg.* 9. 13–18). The sleeping Dante dreams of being borne upward by an eagle to the fiery outer boundary of the sublunar world and wakes to learn from Vergil that while asleep he was carried by Saint Lucy to the threshold of Purgatory. There is an obvious contrast between the rich suggestiveness of the divine visitation in Dante's scene, in which the interplay of dream and visionary reality calls attention to the complexity of Dante's spiritual situation and the intricacy of his relation to Vergil, and the way in which Chaucer focuses our attention on Pandarus's thoughts and feelings. The original function of the image of Procne, as of the figure of Ganymede to whom Dante compares himself within the dream (22–24), is to dramatize the uncertainty of the Pilgrim's response to his initial experience of divine "ravishment." This response is comparable to Troilus's identification of himself with Adonis, Daphne, or Europa when love and Pandarus begin to encroach on his deepest feelings. Pandarus by contrast is concerned with a simpler kind of ravishment. The final image in Dante's account of the dream episode is of the beautiful eyes of Lucy, indicating to Vergil the entrance of Purgatory (61–63); Chaucer leaves us with the leering innuendo of the line in which the narrator sends Pandarus off on his mission to Criseyde: "Now Janus, god of entre, thow hym gyde!" (2. 77). The effect of the allusion is thus to contrast Pandarus's mission with Vergil's and to make still more plain what had been implied by the narrator's hapless evocation of the opening lines of the

---

3. See John Norton-Smith, *Geoffrey Chaucer* (London, 1974), p. 177; Marvin Mudrick, "Chaucer's Nightingales," *Hudson Review* 10 (1957–58):71–74 (repr. in *Chaucer's 'Troilus': Essays in Criticism*, ed. Stephen A. Barney [Hamden, Conn., 1980], pp. 93–95).

Purgatorio at the beginning of the Proem to Book 2: this is not
the world of the *Commedia,* and the quest on which we are em-
barked is not a spiritual one; Pandarus is not Vergil, and the
realm into which we are being led, with Criseyde at its center, is
not Purgatory.

For better or worse, however, Pandarus *is* the Vergil of the
Troilus: he mediates to Troilus the favor of the lady in whom
Troilus's hope of bliss resides, and he brings Troilus to the
threshold of that bliss, though he himself, like Vergil, is excluded from it. Chaucer echoes Dante in dramatizing Troilus's
gratitude for Pandarus's guidance.[4] But Troilus never feels the
unity of purpose that enables the Pilgrim to tell his Vergil that "a
single will is in us both" (*Inf.* 2. 139). The rush of feeling that
makes his heart "spread for joy" when Pandarus announces
Criseyde's willingness to receive his attentions (2. 979–80) is
followed not by a decisive setting forth, but by an expression of
utter helplessness (981–87).[5] Where Vergil's art and genius
have the function of sustaining and articulating Dante's experience of spiritual self-discovery, Pandarus's are applied to preparing Troilus to experience a false, worldly paradise. His eloquence, in contrast to Vergil's is not prompted by heavenly
powers but by the pressure of a preoccupation with erotic love
which is itself conditioned by frustration.

It is thus wholly appropriate that Troilus, the Pilgrim of
Chaucer's poem, should have no part to play in a scene that
corresponds to Dante's initiation into the experience of Purgatory. The stages in his progress toward sexual bliss are attained
through wholly external manipulation on Pandarus's part and
bear only an incidental relation to the Dantean aspect of his love.
Whereas the roles of Vergil and Dante are so closely interrelated
that Vergil is a necessary element of Dante's own consciousness,

4. *Troilus* 2. 967–69; cf. *Inferno* 2. 127–29. Boccaccio also follows Dante
closely at this point (*Fil.* 2. 80. 1–4, 6, which repeat *Inf.* 2. 127–30, 132), but
there are several correspondences between Chaucer and Dante which have no
equivalent in Boccaccio. Both the Pilgrim and Troilus make declarations of
submission to their guides (*Tr.* 2. 974–75, *Inf.* 2. 140), and Troilus, like the
Pilgrim and unlike Troiolo, feels the effect of his experience in his heart (*Tr.* 2.
979–80; cf. *Inf.* 2. 131, 136–37).
5. Lines 981–87 correspond to *Fil.* 2. 88, but Chaucer achieves an irony that
has no equivalent in Boccaccio by moving them forward so that they follow
immediately the stanza in which Troilus had declared "al brosten ben my bondes"
(976).

Troilus's progress toward fulfillment takes place in two spheres, the contemplative and the practical, which are almost completely separate, and requires only minimal communication between himself and Pandarus. His role as a lover is almost entirely invented for him by Pandarus, and he is brought to the physical consummation of love while preserving his consciousness unsullied by carnal thoughts. If Vergil is effectively reason for Dante, Pandarus can be said to perform the function of sexual desire and of that Ovidian ingenuity that desire stimulates. Like Vergil he is intimately involved in shaping his protégé's response to the promise of his experience, but the response he elicits remains almost entirely subliminal until the moment of consummation in Book 3.

Pandarus cannot, of course, resolve matters wholly on his own. His power to direct and exploit Troilus's activity as lover depends on Troilus's first being in love, and there is something in Troilus's love, an equivalent to what Dante feels as "good courage" (*Inf.* 2. 131), which the role imposed on him by Pandarus is inadequate to circumscribe. His spiritual idealism is never, as it were, fully incarnated in the lover of Criseyde, but continues to exist on a separate plane of contemplative vision to which he is capable of withdrawing even as he lies with Criseyde in his arms. It is this idealism—the virtue that exists in potential before his discovery of love and survives the betrayal of his love by Criseyde—that finally determines his awareness, and ours, of the meaning of his experience, at a level of which Pandarus is sublimely unaware.

The compartmentalizing of the experience of Troilus and Pandarus is only one instance of the fragmented perception of reality that typifies the pagan world of the *Troilus*. Like the disjointed prophecy of Cassandre and the self-deluded chivalric pride of the Trojan aristocracy, the inability of Troilus and Pandarus to appreciate one another's goals and motivations reflects the incoherence of a world view that is chronically worldly and shortsighted, incapable of placing personal and social values in a historical and spiritual perspective. One of the chief purposes of Chaucer's allusions to Dante is to provide us with just such a perspective, and this purpose appears particularly clearly in his use of Dante's dream scenes.

Troilus is Chaucer's equivalent to Dante's Pilgrim, and his

absence from the scene introduced by the song of Procne at the
beginning of Book 2 means the absence of any equivalent to
Dante's dream of the eagle. Pandarus, of course, has no dream
at all; it is a symptom of his lack of an inner dimension that, lying
half asleep, he should hear only the "cheterynge" of Procne
about Tereus's rape of her sister Philomela and be aroused by it
to set in motion the seduction of his own niece. But later
Criseyde has a dream, centered like Dante's on possession by an
eagle (2. 925–31). Its position in the second half of Book 2
precisely corresponds to that of Pandarus's nondream in the
first, and it is introduced by a reference to the song of the
nightingale which complements the reference to the swallow
Procne in the earlier scene.

Rather than auguring a spiritual experience, however,
Criseyde's dream is an anticipation of physical submission to
love, and its details express perfectly the limitations of her character and outlook:

> And as she slep, anon right tho hire mette,
> How that an egle, fethered whit as bon,
> Under hire brest his longe clawes sette,
> And out hire herte rente, and that anon,
> And dide his herte into hire brest to gon;
> Of which she nought agroos, ne no thyng smerte;
> And forth he fleigh, with herte left for herte.
>
> [2. 925–31]

Most obviously the dream illustrates Criseyde's anticipation of
accepting Troilus as her lover: that an exchange of hearts takes
place, rather than simply the ravishing of Criseyde's, hints at her
confidence in Troilus's "trouthe." The absence of fear ("she
nought agroos") suggests that her responsiveness has been informed by the confident idealism of the song of Antigone, which
she had heard shortly before falling asleep. But at the same time
there is a marked emphasis on the physical: the exchange of
hearts recalls the occurrence of the same motif in the final stanza
of Antigone's song (872–73) but Chaucer has transformed the
idealizing cliché in a way that emphasizes physical action. He has
done so, moreover, by adapting the imagery of violence from

Troiolo's dream of the boar in the *Filostrato* (8. 23–24), and the effect is to superimpose on the more immediate significance of the dream a prevision of Criseyde's still unforeseen surrender to the more aggressive love of Diomede.[6]

One effect of this double focus is surely to point up the limits of Criseyde's power to provide for herself in love by foreshadowing the dissolution of her love for Troilus. But the dream also hints very gently at a reason for this failure by suggesting that the love of Troilus does not wholly meet Criseyde's expectations. The love for which she prepares herself through the long build-up of Books 2 and 3 contains an element of force, of "ravyne," which is wholly lacking in Troilus's behavior toward her. Ostensibly—certainly to Criseyde's conscious awareness—this lack of aggression is part of the unique beauty and *gentilesse* of Troilus as lover, and in terms of the larger purposes of the *Troilus* it is a symptom of what makes his love most deeply meaningful. But to the finally worldly nature of Criseyde, in her hour of need, Troilus's love will come to appear as no more than a confection of abstract virtues, and she will turn for solid comfort to Diomede, perhaps without knowing why she does so.

Thus a dream announced by the portentous idealism of Antigone's song and centered on a powerful Dantean image of divine visitation not only fails to deliver the dreamer from her bodily state but also emphasizes the depth of her engagement with the here and now.[7] Rising for a while to an appreciation of Troilus's virtue, Criseyde will fall away again into the material world, without having realized in any way the visionary dimension that is so real a part of Troilus's experience of their love. The utter circumscription of Criseyde's dream world is a clear

6. See Joseph E. Gallagher, "Criseyde's Dream of the Eagle: Love and War in *Troilus and Criseyde*," *Modern Language Quarterly* 36 (1975):118. When an exchange of hearts is mentioned again, it is with reference to Diomede rather than Troilus (5. 1517).

7. A number of details precisely oppose Criseyde's dream experience to that of the Pilgrim. Where Dante's eagle is unbearably radiant ("terribil come folgor," *Purg.* 9. 29), Criseyde's is almost grotesquely vivid ("whit as bon," 926). Dante is borne upward to the sublunar sphere of fire (30), while Criseyde apparently remains in her bed. Dante and his eagle "burn" together until the intensity of the imagined fire "scorches" and awakens him (31–33); Criseyde's eagle performs his exchange of hearts painlessly, and the dream evidently ends without awakening her (932).

indication of how radically separate the world of the *Troilus* is
from that of the *Purgatorio*. A similar gravity governs the dream-
ing of Troilus himself. Though his waking experience of love is
charged with spiritual intuition, his dreams are centered on
worldly events: he is abandoned or taken captive (5. 249–52) or,
in the dream of the boar, confronted with the blunt fact of the
physical reality of his betrayal by Diomede, a message he cannot
read and from which he immediately recoils into his private love
world. The final effect of the dreams in the poem is much like
that of Cassandre's discourse: a bleak, secular prophecy that
expresses both the interconnection of the lives of the characters
and their essential separateness: the obsessive energy of Pandarus's scheming, the utter dislocation of Troilus's inner life,
and the practical and self-regarding terms on which Criseyde
responds to both.

The most striking and puzzling allusion to a dream scene
from the *Commedia*, though it is not connected to any dream in
the *Troilus*, occurs in Book 3 in the stanza that announces the
coming of day after the lovers' first night together:

> Whan that the cok, comune astrologer,
> Gan on his brest to bete, and after crowe,
> And Lucifer, the dayes messager,
> Gan for to rise, and oute hire stremes throwe,
> And estward roos, to hym that koude it knowe,
> Fortuna Major . . .
>
> [3. 1415–20]

The emphasis on signs and meanings in this passage calls attention to itself. The interpretative role of the cock and the message
conveyed by Lucifer are part of the common order of daily
events, but the trailing reference to Fortuna Major seems
intended to emphasize the obscurity of this figure. The same
emphasis is evident in the passage that is Chaucer's source for
this reference, *Purgatorio* 19, in which Dante describes the time
just before dawn

> quando i geomanti lor Maggior Fortuna
> veggiono in orïente, innanzi a l'alba,
> surger per via che poco le sta bruna . . .

when the geomancers see their Fortuna Major rise in the east
before dawn by a path which does not long stay dark for it . . .
[*Purg.* 19. 4–6]

The term *Fortuna Major* was employed in geomancy, a mode
of astrological calculation in which configurations of dots created by the geomancer without reference to the heavens were
correlated with patterns perceptible among the stars of the
zodiacal signs and referred to the authority of one or another of
the seven planets as a basis for interpretation.[8] For both Dante
and Chaucer such bastardized astrology is probably a symbol of
the random and often spurious means by which human understanding creates for itself a sense of coherence and purpose. In
the *Commedia* the figure introduces Dante's dream of the Siren, a
female figure who is grotesquely malformed and inarticulate
until endowed with beauty and eloquence by the effect of fleshly
desire on Dante's imaginative perception of her:

> Io la mirava; e come 'l sol conforta
> le fredde membra che la notte aggrava,
> così lo sguardo mio le facea scorta
> la lingua, e poscia tutta la drizzava
> in poco d'ora, e lo smarrito volto,
> com' amor vuol, così le colorava.

> I gazed upon her: and even as the sun revives cold limbs
> benumbed by night, so my look made ready her tongue, and
> then in but little time set her full straight, and colored her
> pallid face even as love requires. [*Purg.* 19. 10–15]

Thus endowed, the Siren sings seductively to the Pilgrim until
the sudden appearance of a *donna santa,* at whose admonition
Vergil seizes her and tears away her garments to expose the
foulness within. Dante awakes at the foul smell she gives off and
finds himself in broad daylight.

8. On the medieval practice of geomancy, which involved no scientific
knowledge and was classed with the more dubious forms of astrology and magic,
see Paul Tannery, *Le Rabolion: traités de géomancie arabes, grecs et latins,* in his
Mémoires scientifiques, vol. 4 (Paris, 1920), pp. 318–411; for a medieval discussion
of the properties associated with Fortuna Major (which, however, seems to have
no special bearing on either poet's reference to the figure), see Tannery, pp.
380–82. A book made for Richard II in 1391 (now MS Bodley 581) contains
geomantic material.

The scene that Fortuna Major introduces in the *Troilus*, in which Criseyde and Troilus exchange dawn-songs and vows of fidelity, has none of the ugliness of Dante's treatment of the Siren. But the relationship between dreamer and dream in the *Purgatorio* passage anticipates some of the most striking features of Chaucer's dawn-song sequence and its aftermath. Both Troilus and the Pilgrim are suspended in contemplation of a beauty that, like the patterns traced by the geomancers, derives its meaning from their own subjective needs. As Dante's eager gaze endowed the Siren with beauty, so it is the credulous desire of Troilus that sustains Criseyde's dominant role in the dialogue in which they respond to the coming of dawn and gives her words an absolute value for him. Her equivalent to the Siren's song is her initiation of the dawn-song sequence; she usurps the role normally taken by the male lover in the dawn song and elicits from Troilus an almost mechanically symmetrical response.[9] But it is Troilus whose total involvement with love is emphasized, who refuses to accept the need to separate, and who insists on prolonging the ritual of songs and vows in which the scene consists. His sense of reality is subject to Criseyde's influence to the point at which she comes to seem to him the center of "al the lyf ich have" (1477). As the Siren had arrested and turned aside her victims in mid-voyage (*Purg.* 19. 19–22), so Troilus is led to repudiate the affairs of the day and the cares of the city, asking only that Criseyde remain true to him. This request draws from her a protestation of fidelity so heavily freighted with appeals to God to witness her sincerity as to make us wonder whether anything but Troilus's invincible trust in her sustains her words.

The dawn scene ends with Troilus's departure, and we follow him home to his own chamber, where he communes, Dante-like, with the image of Criseyde in his mind, wholly oblivious to the physical desire that has now become an element in his devotion (1541–47). There is no shocking revelation like Vergil's unveil-

---

9. On the incongruities in Chaucer's use of the *alba* (dawn song) see Robert E. Kaske, "The Aube in Chaucer's *Troilus*," in *Chaucer Criticism*, ed. R. J. Schoeck and Jerome Taylor, 2 vols. (Notre Dame, 1960), 2:167–79. On the conventions Chaucer adjusts, see Jonathan Saville, *The Medieval Erotic Alba* (New York, 1972), pp. 153–55, 213–14.

ing of the Siren to waken him from his amorous delusion. But
the parallel with the Siren dream is sustained for us by the
strange and, for most readers, unsettling scene between Pandarus and Criseyde on the morning following the night of love.
Pandarus appears while Criseyde is still in bed, and his banter-
ing quickly reduces her from indignation at his having betrayed
her into Troilus's arms to a kind of coquettishness. He then
proceeds to thrust himself upon her with increasing urgency,
rummaging under the bedclothes, proffering his "sword," and
finally kissing her, before the narrator steps in to divert our
attention:

> I passe all that which nedeth nought to seye,
> What! god foryaf his deth, and she also
> Foryaf, and with hire uncle gan to pleye,
> For oother cause was ther non than so.
> But of this thing right to theffect to go,
> Whan tyme was, home to hire hous she wente,
> And Pandarus hath hoolly his entente.
>
> [3. 1576–82]

As always, we may take the narrator's tone of hearty reassurance
here as a sign that he has missed the point: phrases like "I passe
al that," and "right to theffect to go," which had earlier expressed his eagerness to hasten on the sexual climax, are now
used in an attempt to gloss over what is taking place between
Criseyde and her uncle. The high good humor of "What! god
foryaf his deth" fails to obscure the glaring ambiguity and potential blasphemy of the phrase in this context, and the con-
clusiveness of the final line obviously raises more questions than
it answers. But there is no sure way to determine the object of
Pandarus's "entente" here; we cannot tell just what takes place
between uncle and niece, and we do not need to know. The real
meaning of the scene, reinforced by the parody of Dante that
lies behind it, is in the utter betrayal of Troilus it represents, the
travesty of his pure devotion in its combination of blatant innuendo with suggestions of blasphemy. Once again, as with the
refractive use of the dream episode of *Purgatorio* 9, the meaningful event, the encounter of Pandarus and Criseyde which

corresponds to the moment of moral enlightenment in the Siren scene, takes place wholly outside the sphere of Troilus's consciousness, exposing his deluded sense of Criseyde's worth without in any way disabusing him of it.

A note of caution is necessary at this point. In casting Criseyde as the Siren in the scenes just discussed, I do not mean to compare her in her own person to the "ancient witch" whom Vergil unmasks. As many critics have pointed out, there is no reason to doubt Criseyde's good will toward Troilus at this point in the story; even her bedroom scene with Pandarus has been praised for its tact, and Pandarus's behavior has somehow been read as showing an avuncular sympathy with young love.[10] It is only when contrasted with the innocent idealism of Troilus, for whom she is "inly fair" (1606) and who describes the effect of sexual fulfillment in almost Pauline terms as instilling in him a "newe qualitee" (1653–55), that her acceptance of Pandarus's advances is compromising. The scene brings us down to earth, and its bald suggestiveness is unique in the poem, a departure from the prevailing courtly decorum fully as striking as Troilus's earlier appropriation of the climactic prayer of the *Paradiso* to express his ecstasy just before the consummation of his love.

Indeed the Dantean allusions that point up the contrast between Troilus's great moment of visionary ecstasy and Pandarus's achievement of his debased "entente" also define symbolically the terms on which Troilus's experience of love is to be evaluated. They show us that his remarkable capacity to experience love on spiritual terms has as its corollary a terrible vulnerability to corruption and betrayal on the earthly level. In addition they emphasize Troilus's radical innocence. Unlike Dante in the earthly Paradise, Troilus brings no history of involvement with "false images" to his confrontation with Criseyde. He is experiencing love for the first time, and Chaucer

10. See C. S. Lewis, *The Allegory of Love* (Oxford, 1936), pp. 193–94, and Arthur Mizener, "Character and Action in the Case of Criseyde," *PMLA* 54 (1939):65– 81 (repr. in *Chaucer's 'Troilus': Essays in Criticism*, ed. Barney, pp. 55–74). For Mizener the morning-after scene is "a beautiful presentation of two witty but tactful people" (p. 75; Barney, p. 64). Contrast Paull F. Baum, *Chaucer: A Critical Appreciation* (Durham, N.C., 1958), p. 147, who suggests that line 1582 ("And Pandarus hath hoolly his entente") is in a sense the climax of the poem: "After this," he observes, "there is no more laughter."

manages to convey the effect of his discovery of bliss in virtually prelapsarian terms.

We can better appreciate the significance of Troilus's experience if we consider its Dantean aspect in a broader and more sequential way, by comparing the central portion of Book 3 of Chaucer's poem to the final cantos of the *Purgatorio*. The tension between inner vision and external circumstance which comes to a head in Troilus's confrontation with Criseyde at the house of Pandarus can be seen as the antithesis of what Charles Singleton has called "the pattern at the center" of the *Commedia*, the elaborate ritual of Dante's reunion with Beatrice in the earthly Paradise at the summit of Purgatory.[11] In both cases the encounter effects a significant transformation. Under the stern tutelage of Beatrice, Dante emerges from a quest he had inevitably conceived in largely private and erotic terms and after a painful process of self-recognition comes to learn that his experience has prepared him for true participation in Christian history, as a citizen of "that Rome whereof Christ is a Roman" (*Purg.* 32. 102). Troilus on the other hand approaches his great encounter with confused and uneasy intimations of the divine mystery at the heart of his love, but the initiation he undergoes draws him away from such concerns into physical lovemaking. Dante's experience concludes for our purposes with the pageant of the history of the church which prepares for Beatrice's prophecy of deliverance. Troilus is irrevocably alienated by his experience from any such larger awareness as Dante attains. If Dante's experience is a recovery of purity and vision, a *restauratio*, Troilus's is a falling away, a descent into the world of false pleasure from which Dante has been liberated once and for all.

The introduction of Troilus and the Pilgrim into their respective paradises constitutes the crowning achievement of the artistry of their guides. Vergil throughout the *Commedia* has devoted his "art and genius" to the reorienting of Dante's reason and will. His final speech, in *Purgatorio* 27, signals the completion of his work and frees Dante to pursue his pleasure in response to the beauties of a Paradise that is the fulfillment of Vergil's own

11. *Commedia: Elements of Structure*, Dante Studies, no. 1, (Cambridge, Mass., 1957), pp. 45–60.

dream (*Purg.* 28. 139–41). Pandarus, too, is realizing a dream or fantasy of his own in the achievement of Troilus's quest, but his "engyn" has operated in a wholly external way, manipulating and constraining his pupil rather than informing and strengthening his will. Where Vergil releases Dante into the "sweet air" of a realm whose unchanging climate rewards the Pilgrim's own hard-won stability, Troilus is confined to a "litel stuwe" (3. 601) until drawn by Pandarus, under cover of a darkness made darker still by a "smoky reyn," into a windowless inner room. Vergil is in sure touch with Dante's feelings and can urge him forward by promising the advent of Beatrice, confident that the Pilgrim is morally and psychologically prepared for his encounter with her (27. 133–42). But when Pandarus comes to summon Troilus to the "hevene blisse" that awaits him in Criseyde's chamber, he finds his pupil uneasy, recalcitrant, and wholly incapable of self-determination. Troilus's response to Pandarus's promise of reward is near panic. Whereas Vergil concludes his enterprise once and for all by commending Dante's reconstituted will, "free, upright, and whole" (140), and his last words in the *Commedia* are a bestowal on Dante of the crown and mitre of self-command (142), Pandarus is compelled to rebuke the "wrecched mouses herte" of his disciple, throw a fur robe over his shirt, and literally drag him into the presence of Criseyde (736–42).

The same parodic contrast is evident in the psychological states of the two lovers, manifested at this crucial stage in the imaginative processes by which both translate their experience into mythic terms. Again the opposition is striking: in place of Dante's sense of undergoing a metamorphosis of desire (*Purg.* 27. 123), Chaucer gives us Troilus's catalogue of hapless mortals pursued in love by gods. The brief reminiscences of Europa, Adonis, Herse, and Daphne emphasize the dominance of the gods' passion, and the only human feeling clearly indicated is the "drede" that leads to the transformation of Daphne.

Dante is initiated into Paradise by Matelda, who, in addition to guiding him toward his reunion with Beatrice, provides a focus for the lingering sexual element in his adoration. As he gazes at her, he is reminded of Proserpina at the moment of her ravishment, and her eyes seem as full of love as those of Venus when, accidentally wounded by Cupid's arrow, she fell madly in love with Adonis (*Purg.* 28. 49–51, 63–66). This emphasis on the erotic has puzzled commentators,[12] but should remind us that Matelda, like the Siren, is the embodiment of an imaginative experience rather than a sacramental one. Though her beauty is not, like the Siren's, wholly of Dante's own making, and while it shows him capable of realizing Paradise in imaginative terms, it is inevitably conditioned by that long service as a poet of love which has been his preparation for Paradise. His desire here is a metaphor for the experience of grace that Beatrice will grant him, very much as Menoeceus's visitation of divine virtue is Dante's Statius's metaphor for the creation of the intellective soul.

Troilus's thoughts also tend naturally to dwell on myths of love, but his sexual feelings are at odds with his spiritual intimations. Under the pressure of a confused sense of being psychologically and physically "possessed" by love, his impulse is to avert the sort of engagement Dante imagines and longs for. Dante is yearning back from a world conditioned by the loss of primal innocence toward the state in which innocent desire was possible, and Matelda is largely the projection of this yearning. Troilus is faced with the loss of his own innocence, and his imaginative response is a series of mythic images of his helpless state. Where Dante compares Matelda's innocent rapture to the longings of Ovid's amorous Venus, Troilus invokes that same Venus in the name of Adonis, the object and in a real sense the victim of her love (3. 720–21).

The difference between the two lovers' relations with their guides is pointed up again when Troilus is brought face to face with his lady and finds he can no longer depend on his mentor for reassurance. Where Vergil had withdrawn his support only after rendering Dante psychologically capable of enduring the agony of self-recognition he must undergo as Beatrice chastises him, Pandarus has prepared for this confrontation by inventing

12. For Charles Singleton, *Journey to Beatrice*, Dante Studies, no. 2, (Cambridge, Mass., 1958), pp. 213–14, the unthinkability of Dante's entertaining sexual feelings toward Matelda is itself an argument that we must read the scene allegorically. The literal view is well defended by Emerson Brown, Jr., "Proserpina, Matelda, and the Pilgrim," *Dante Studies* 89 (1971):39–46.

the story that Troilus suspects Criseyde of having given her love
to "Horaste" (792–98). Faced with Criseyde's elaborate display
of grief at his suspicion, Troilus is utterly demoralized. In place
of Dante's powerful expression of sorrow and love in response
to Vergil's sudden disappearance (*Purg.* 30. 49–54) we see
Troilus forced to the inescapable recognition that through his
involvement with Pandarus he is guilty of complicity in a plot
both dishonest and, worse, unsuccessful:

> "O Pandarus," thoughte he, "allas, thi wile
> Serveth of nought, so weylaway the while."
> [3. 1077–78]

Dante finally comes to terms with the history of his pursuit of
false images and is made to confess a guilt that his whole previous experience in the *Commedia* has conditioned him to recognize. Guided by the song of the pitying angels, he weeps in
anguish (*Purg.* 30. 94–99) and is then drawn forward to a confession of his error. Troilus, whose moral awareness has been
systematically subverted, has no sustaining ritual to help him
express his true feelings and can only disclaim responsibility for
his role in the game Pandarus has played. He sheds no tears, and
though he is dominated by a keen sense of guilt, he cannot
acknowledge it. He feels himself damned by his complicity to a
moral and emotional limbo, so alienated from Criseyde by Pandarus's deceptions that his feeble protestation of innocence
("god woot that of this game, / Whan al is wist, than am I nat to
blame" [1084–85]) has the effect of a dying man's last words.
And the swoon that follows is described in terms that make it the
emotional equivalent of death, a suspension of the operation of
his bodily spirits and hence of all feeling:

> And every spirit his vigour in knette,
> So they astoned or oppressed were.
> The felyng of his sorwe, or of his fere,
> Or of aught elles, fled was out of towne;
> And down he fil al sodeynly a-swowne.
> [3. 1088–92]

The intensity of Troilus's experience here reflects the implo-
sion upon him of an unendurably powerful feeling of unworthi-

ness and the conviction that Criseyde's *dangier* has banished him from her favor once and for all. Though his sense of guilt is confused and inarticulate, a conflict of feelings only dimly realized, rather than the vivid "recognition" of Dante (*Purg.* 31. 88), his crisis attests to the depth of his commitment to love and the reality for him of the threat of annihilation which that commitment entails. Because he has believed so profoundly in the power of Criseyde's love to bestow a "grace" that is virtually the gift of life, the quasi-death he had experienced on first encountering her gaze in the temple of Pallas (1. 306–7) has now become associated in his mind with the loss of her favor. He is for the moment "despeired out of loves grace," and his whole nature acquiesces in the abandonment of life itself, which is his imaginative response to this loss.[13]

Of course, this death is only a prelude to the miracle of his reawakening to find himself restored to favor. The crisis has the practical effect of literally introducing him to the bed of love, but leaves him "wonder sore abayst," in a state of suspension between spiritual and physical experience. His moral and psychological dislocation are made worse by the fact that Criseyde is much less concerned with proving his character and submitting him to penance than with defending herself from suspicion, and when she miscalculates the effect of her tears, causing Troilus to swoon, she too becomes desperate. Thus, instead of the stern but all-confirming "ben son, ben son Beatrice," we are shown Criseyde bending over Troilus's inert body and promising him "in his ear"

> "Iwys, my dere herte, I am nat wroth,
> Have here my trouthe, and many another ooth;
> Now speke to me, for it am I Criseyde."
> But al for nought . . .
>
> [3. 1110–13]

Where Beatrice rebukes Dante's moral childishness and admonishes him to live up to the manhood seemingly implied by his beard (*Purg.* 31. 61–69), confident that the shame will ultimately

---

13. See the excellent analysis of this moment in Jill Mann, "Troilus' Swoon," *Chaucer Review* 14 (1979–80):327–28.

strengthen him, Criseyde's chiding of Troilus ("is this a mannes game?" 1126) merely exposes the hapless innocence in which he had been led to play the "childissh jalous" (1168).

But Troilus's swoon, like the loss of consciousness Dante undergoes under the pressure of intense contrition (*Purg.* 31. 88–90), is a rite of passage. Dante revives to see the face of Matelda moving above him as she bears him through the absolving stream (31. 91–96); Troilus finds himself in bed, with Criseyde doing "al hir peyne" to bring him around (1118–20). Dante's absolution from his old error is symbolized by his emergence from the stream into the dance of the Cardinal Virtues, who "cover him with their arms" as they dance about him (31. 103–5); Troilus's, more simply, by the gesture of Criseyde herself:[14]

> hire arm over hym she leyde,
> And al foryaf . . .
>   [3. 1128–29]

Though Troilus will require some further assurance of his forgiveness, his emergence from Purgatory to a state of readiness to receive the promised bliss is essentially complete at this point. We have already traced the arc of his *paradiso*, the intensity of feeling which rises to issue in his beautiful prayer to divine love before descending again into the material world. But it is possible to pursue the analogy of the *Purgatorio* a stage further and to recognize that the revelation that completes Dante's experience in the earthly Paradise also has its negative equivalent in the *Troilus*.

In *Purgatorio* 32, after a second loss of consciousness, Dante awakens to see again Matelda. She points out Beatrice, transformed from her earlier, almost unendurable splendor to reappear as the reflected glory of truth revealed, the guiding wisdom of the church in the world, seated on the bare ground and guarding the chariot that is the image of the church. Beatrice grants Dante a vision of the earthly history of the church, repre-

---

14. Criseyde is perhaps recalling Dante's description of the Virtues when she compares herself to Prudence with her three eyes at 5. 744–45; cf. *Purg.* 29. 131–32.

sented as a series of violations visited upon the chariot itself (*Purg.* 32. 109–60). A diving eagle strikes the chariot, causing it to roll like a ship in a storm; a ravenous fox tries to enter it but is repelled by Beatrice; the eagle reappears and enters, leaving the car adorned with his plumage; a dragon comes out of the earth and breaks open the bottom of the car. Then the chariot itself is transformed into a monster; a harlot appears seated on its back, attended by a giant who kisses her repeatedly until, when she looks lustfully at Dante, he beats her from head to foot and finally drags both monster and harlot away into the forest.

Such densely symbolic panoramas are a temptation for the medievalist, who tends to see in them what he most wants to see. And it would be an arbitrary exercise at best to seek any too precise relation between this vision and the events of *Troilus.* Nonetheless, I would suggest a broad parallel between Dante's imagery and that which the *Troilus,* by various means, concentrates around the person and bed of Criseyde. As the repeated violations of the church lead to its corruption and finally the Babylonian captivity of the Avignon papacy, so the equivalent images in the *Troilus* trace the effects of the encroachments of Pandarus, Troilus, Diomede, and history itself on the freedom and integrity of Criseyde.

Like the chariot of Dante's vision, Criseyde is first assailed by the eagle of her dream,[15] then with increasing importunity by Pandarus, and at last by Troilus. Her union with Troilus, I would suggest, corresponds to the second descent of Dante's eagle upon the chariot. Representative originally of the endowment of the church with temporal goods, it is equivalent in Chaucer's scheme to the materialization of love. Without in itself involving any base motive (Dante himself concedes that the "feathering" of the chariot had been done "perhaps with sincere and kind intent," 138), the union nonetheless marks a stage in a process of corruption by material things which leads to eventual harlotry.

Pandarus's role is easily enough related to that of the heretics and false counselors who corrupt the church from within by

15. Mario Praz, *The Flaming Heart* (New York, 1958), pp. 39–40, suggests a number of correspondences between the imagery of Criseyde's dream and that of the pageant of *Purgatorio* 32.

claiming to speak with true authority and whom Dante represents by the fox, "starved of all good food" (120), that seeks to
enter the chariot. I think Chaucer is also recalling this scene as
he describes Pandarus's dealing with Criseyde on the morning
after the consummation. Like Beatrice, Criseyde recognizes
Pandarus for what he is—"fox that ye ben" she calls him
(1565)—and recognizes the danger of his "wordes white"
(1567); but she has already acquiesced in his design on her, and
the scene in which he reveals the effects of his "starvation" by
seeking to act out that design in his own person, literally or
symbolically, merely confirms its corrupting effect.

The remaining events of Dante's vision, the dragon's damag-
ing of the chariot, its metamorphosis, and the final scene of
harlot and giant, may be loosely correlated with the disruptive
events of the war and Criseyde's later, far more compromising
submission to the blasphemously uncourtly Diomede. These
specific matters are less important than the broad Dantean pattern of which they form a part, which enables us to gauge the
dimensions of Troilus's experience of love and recognize the
seriousness with which Chaucer views both the love and its betrayal. The point of this elaborate borrowing from the *Commedia*—the casting of Pandarus as arch-heretic, Criseyde as Siren
and harlot and her bed as a mock church—is not simply to
condemn their moral and spiritual blindness, though we should
certainly be warned by it not to let sentimentality obscure our
awareness of these failings. Its primary function is to provide a
setting in which to consider the love of Troilus for itself, and the
identification of these lesser characters with evil archetypes becomes meaningful only to the extent that we see Troilus's vision
of love as comparable to Dante's. The scene between Pandarus
and Criseyde completes the parody of Dante which I have called
the "pattern at the center" of the *Troilus* by giving us a powerful
image of the violation of Troilus's devotion and by setting this
violation in an allusive context that makes it not simply a human
betrayal but the desecration of something at least potentially
divine. It exposes in the most forceful way the emptiness at the
heart of Troilus's love, the failure of that love to integrate the
spiritual and physical elements in his experience. There is no
meaningful connection between the Criseyde of Troilus's vision

and the Criseyde who incarnates that vision: she is now a Siren, now a Matelda, now prophetically a harlot, but never a *beatrix*. The pattern at the center of the *Troilus* has no true center, no sacred presence or transforming event to offset the steady descent of Troilus's love from vision into materiality. Allusion to Dante makes us aware of this absence, which Chaucer's hapless and self-deceived narrator could not have done by himself, and by forcing us to view Troilus's betrayal in a context that emphasizes its enormity, provides an intimation of what we and the narrator will finally come to realize as the true spiritual dimensions of the poem. But this final discovery will take place only after Troilus himself has lived through the consequences of his betrayal and come to his own posthumous realization that "felicite," whatever it may be, lies far beyond the love of Criseyde.

The next significant allusion to Dante occurs at the beginning of Book 4, where Chaucer introduces Troilus's grief over the threatened loss of Criseyde with a version of the tree simile from *Inferno* 3. As noted in Chapter 1, this simile in its original context helps us focus on the process of Dante's introduction to the world of the dead (see page 40). Troilus, too, is preparing to descend into a psychological inferno more hellish than any of his woes hitherto, a world in which he will commune in imagination with Proserpine, Oedipus, and other "ancient suffering spirits." It would be hard to imagine a more powerful comparison than Dante's simile.

But neither Troilus's situation nor Chaucer's treatment of it is simple. Troilus's desperate state is at least partly of his own making, and his hopelessness is shown at certain moments to be almost willful. The rhetoric in which he yearns for death, imagines an afterlife of perpetual mourning, and rationalizes his present inactivity as an imposed condition is a genuine reflection of his sense of loss and abandonment, but it has in it an element of self-indulgence and melodrama that suggests that it is an emotional substitute for something else. What it replaces, I think, is the passion of the early stage of Troilus's sexual involvement with Criseyde, a passion that had reached its physical and emotional peak in Book 3 and is now becoming a steadily weaker bond between them, so that both unconsciously acquiesce in the separation that threatens them. As Dante undergoes the

vicarious experience of death and damnation in his *Inferno*, so
Troilus's rhetorical and emotional energies collaborate in an
imaginative rehearsal of the experience of loss, an exercise that
leaves him psychologically diminished, powerless to alter the
destiny that Criseyde's scheming prepares for him.

Here as so often in the poem it is necessary to maintain a
double view of the experience of Troilus. In Book 3 we must
recognize the comic incongruity of the juxtaposition of his ecstasy with Pandarus's "bysynesse" and at the same time take his
spiritual experience seriously in itself. So in Book 4 we must
recognize the ironic breach between what is actually taking place
and what seems to Troilus to be taking place and at the same
time respect the deep emotion that so distorts his sense of reality
as to force him to live out the experience of loss on what seem to
him life-and-death terms. This complex focus is already implicit
in Chaucer's use of Dante's image of the tree deprived of its
leaves to describe Troilus's feelings as he lies alone in his chamber contemplating the Trojan parliament's decision to exchange
Criseyde for Antenor:

> And as in wynter leves ben biraft,
> Ech after other, til the tree be bare,
> So that ther nys but bark and braunche ilaft,
> Lith Troilus, byraft of eche welfare,
> Ibounden in the blake bark of care,
> Disposed wood out of his wit to breyde,
> So sore hym sat the chaungynge of Criseyde.
>   [4. 225–31]

The simile has a very different character from that of the allusions to *Purgatorio* and *Paradiso* in Book 3. There we were given
broad analogies of structure and iconography that enabled us to
isolate and assess the specially privileged qualities of Troilus's
experience without the necessity of analyzing his feelings closely.
Here, by contrast, we are taken to the very heart of Troilus's
emotional condition.

As I suggested in chapter 1, Dante's version of this simile
shows a marked shift in the direction of subjective and vicarious
emotion when compared with the passage in Vergil which is its
source. Chaucer carries Dante's alteration of Vergil's image a

step further. Where Dante, like Vergil, begins by comparing dead souls to falling leaves, Chaucer introduces the leaves only for the purpose of emphasizing strongly the bareness of the tree itself, which is reiterated by the interpolation of a wholly original line (227). But as he develops the image, though its initial effect remains coherent and powerful, its stark power gives way to an increasing irony and an emphasis on the implications of narcissistic self-consciousness in the Dantean version. Troilus as we behold him is lying on his bed, and when we are quietly reminded of this by "lith" in 228, it is as though the tree in the simile were lying down as well, prostrated by the shock of losing its foliage. The effect is to offset somewhat the force of "byraft of ech welfare," and a similar effect is conveyed in the next line, in which the vivid and somber image of Troilus bound by "the blake bark of care" is both enriched by the suggestion of metamorphosis and weakened by the distracting hint of a pun on "bark." In the next line the metamorphosis theme is undercut by an unmistakable pun on "wood," and the self-consciousness latent in the simile as a whole surfaces in its application to a Troilus who is "disposed," as if by a careful decision, to lose his wits.

The comic element in the stanza is not, of course, its whole point, and there is a danger that such an analysis of it will go too far in distracting attention from the force of Chaucer's image and the obligation to take it seriously imposed by its context in literary tradition. Chaucer's use of Dante in the *Troilus* is never merely facetious, and if it is clear by the end of the stanza that Troilus's feelings have not brought him as close as he imagines to "the woeful pass," it is clear as well that he has been rendered helpless by them, "bound" to undergo an experience that very strongly resembles despair.[16] But the comedy *is* unmistakably there, and its function is to distance us a little from his reactions. The tree simile shows Troilus's reactions being programmed by Dante's, which in turn are controlled by Vergil's. The governing

16. Norton-Smith, *Geoffrey Chaucer*, p. 202, aptly contrasts with these lines those earlier passages in which the emergence of hopeful thoughts in Troilus has been compared to the growth, and even the recovery after frost, of plants and leaves. One may also compare the conflict of strong feelings under whose pressure he had intuitively identified himself with the metamorphosed Daphne at 3. 726–27.

presence of convention is thus strongly emphasized, and in the long scene that follows we see the strength of Troilus's feelings affirmed and at the same time undermined by the conventional means through which they are expressed.[17]

In Book 5 the actual departure of Criseyde provokes a more authentic despair, but at the same time revives the idealizing and spiritual tendencies of Troilus's love. As he reviews the "proces" of his romance, he recapitulates its private, Dantean aspect in a way that confirms its inviolate status and provides him with the emotional strength to withstand the revelation of his betrayal. This retrospective process is climaxed by the long letter that represents Troilus's last direct address to Criseyde. This letter is very different from its counterpart in Boccaccio (*Fil.* 7. 52–75), which deals openly and somewhat melodramatically with Troiolo's sense of abandonment and his fear that Criseida has betrayed him. In Troilus's letter everything is muted. He mentions the bare facts—Criseyde has been gone two months and he has not heard from her—but they are interspersed with repeated apologies for his presumption in mentioning them, and his only hint at any misgivings about her conduct takes the form of an appeal for her forgiveness for having harbored such thoughts:

> "And by the cause ek of my cares colde,
> That sleth my wit, if aught amys masterte,
> Foryeve it me, myn owen swete herte."
>
> [5. 1342–44]

Later he goes so far as to remind her of the obligations of "trouthe" (1386), but he speaks with the same lack of conviction that crippled his attempts to dissuade her from leaving in Book 4[18] and immediately retreats again into the depths of his humility, asking only for leave to die if he has been guilty in any way or if Criseyde no longer wishes to see him (1387–93).

This life-or-death view of his condition assumes a new urgency here. It is Troilus's way of expressing not only his deepest

17. See chapter 7.
18. Lines 1395–96 clearly echo 4. 1490–91, in which Troilus fears that neither "routhe" nor "trouthe" will enable Criseyde to resist the attractions of life among the Greeks. Cf. also 5. 1585–89.

fears but also the depth of his feelings of love and need, and we
can hear an increasingly prayerful note in his request:

> "That hereupon ye wolden write me,
> For love of god, my righte lode-sterre. . . ."
>   [5. 1392–93]

Here, as at several points in the early books, Troilus seems almost to be invoking two gods at once, and in the final stanzas of
the letter his sense of radical dependency on Criseyde becomes
itself a religious state. It is to Criseyde that he prays, "With hope,
or deth, delivereth me fro peyne" (1400). In the lines that invoke
her beauty—lines in which Troilus expresses for the first time
since her departure a strong desire for something other than
death—it is almost as though he were looking forward to a vision
of that beauty in a realm beyond bodily existence:

> "Iwys, myn hertes day, my lady free,
> So thursteth ay myn herte to byholde
> Youre beaute, that my lif unnethe I holde."
>   [5. 1405–7]

So Dante, praying to Beatrice near the close of the *Paradiso*,
looks forward to the point at which his soul will be released from
his body in a state of exalted love worthy of her favor (*Par.* 31.
88–90). Like Dante's, the prayer of Troilus is his final direct
address to his "glorious lady," and like Dante's it claims for her
the status of a unique manifestation of divine grace. Dante
declares,

> "di tante cose quant' i'ho vedute,
>   dal tuo podere e da la tua bontate
>   riconosco la grazia e la virtute . . .
>
>   . . . . . .
>
> "La tua magnificenza in me custodi,
>   si che l'anima mia, che fatt' hai sana,
>   piacente a te dal corpo si disnodi."

> "Of all those things which I have seen I acknowledge the grace
> and the virtue to be from your power and your excellence. . . .
> Preserve in me your great munificence, so that my soul, which

you have made whole, may be loosed from the body, pleasing
unto you." [*Par.* 31. 82–84, 88–90]

Troilus in a kind of desperate earnest imputes virtually the same
powers to Criseyde:

"In yow lith, whan yow list that it so be,
The day on which me clothen shal my grave.
In yow my lif, in yow myght for to save
Me fro disese of alle peynes smerte!
And fare now wel, myn owen swete herte!"
[5. 1417–21]

These lines represent not only Troilus's farewell to Criseyde,
but the completion of the Dantean phase of his career. Like all
of Troilus's Dantean gestures, this final, consummate praise of
Criseyde is in one sense meaningless; even Troilus will soon
have to acknowledge that she has betrayed him. But from another point of view the prayer is a final confirmation of the
strength and integrity of Troilus's imaginative idealism. The
allusion to Dante is a kind of seal, attesting to the depth of
feeling that produces this final affirmation and reminding us
that Troilus's love of Criseyde has been and will remain the most
important thing in his life, a *vita nuova*. Together with the memory of the time when Criseyde's palace had been "enlumyned
with sonne of alle blisse," this wholly private perception of her
meaning for him will endure to the end, unaffected by the historical realities that are soon to be forced upon him by Cassandre's prophecy, the death of Hector, and the sight of
Criseyde's token on the captured armor of Diomede. Chaucer
has allowed his pagan hero to say of Criseyde "that which was
never said of any woman" save Beatrice, and it is the same conception of Troilus's love as a religious vocation that will allow
him at his death to ascend to the eighth sphere. In the meantime
the realization of his betrayal will convert Troilus's conscious
feelings from love to heroic wrath, but the Dantean element in
his experience continues to exist intact beneath the outward
violence of his last days, and it is as both a visionary lover and an
embodiment of heroic virtue that we must view him at the close
of the poem.

[6]

Character and Action:
Criseyde and the Narrator

I t is clear that the reading of the *Troilus* implied by the
patterns of allusion I have traced in the preceding chapters
places a radical emphasis on Troilus's experience as the
poem's central concern. It is he to whom love happens, he who
experiences it as the descent of a divine force and in whose
sensibility its effects are realized in their full complexity. It is as
his story that the action of the poem begins and ends, and it is
through identification with him that the narrator is led to his
discovery of the transforming power of love in the poem's final
stanzas. Equally clearly, the program of allusion that places
Troilus so centrally must cast the other characters in the poem as
in some measure unadmirable or false. To the extent that
Troilus is a potential Dante figure, Criseyde and Pandarus, in-
terposing themselves between his spirit and the objects of its
visionary imaginings, must constitute a pseudo-Beatrice and a
false Vergil.

It is obvious that this view imposes unrealistic restrictions on
our response to these characters and to the world they live in. If
Troy appears as an erotic prison when set in relation to Statian
Thebes and the Dantean Purgatory, it is also a world peopled by
sympathetic human beings, living their lives amiably and often
nobly. This is the world in which Pandarus and Criseyde are at
home and with which the narrator himself is most concerned

through the bulk of the poem. And if all of these characters are severely limited in their power to appreciate the special virtues of Troilus's private world, his ability to function in their world is equally limited. Troilus's reality consists precisely in the authenticity of his experience of love, and except at certain moments of brilliant psychological intuition, Chaucer conveys this experience by means of convention. In contrast to the minutely rendered and highly individualized postures of Criseyde, Troilus's behavior is almost mechanical in its ritual quality, as utterly programmed in accordance with the standard moralizing and courtly dogma of the narrator's comments on it as that of proud Bayard himself. Appealing in his trusting innocence, Troilus is also humorless and self-absorbed. In contrast to his tendency to express himself in prayer, song, and apostrophes to the absent Criseyde is a marked inability to engage in ordinary social intercourse. As Robert Henryson was to see clearly, Troilus is ultimately the prisoner of his own unique qualities, and that spark of virtue that will illumine his experience for the narrator and for us does not bring him fully to life.

Since sympathy is all we are finally allowed to feel for any of the pagan characters in the *Troilus,* it is important to recognize the fullness of Chaucer's human vision, his generosity to his too worldly characters, and his awareness of what is lacking in his unworldly hero. And yet when all is said, Troilus's virtue remains the poem's central concern, and every other major character must be seen as having been created largely to set off that virtue. The purpose of this chapter is to demonstrate that the roles played by Criseyde and the narrator in the story of Troilus are reinforced by a thorough and fully consistent characterization which shows them to be, for all their undeniable appeal as human creatures, incapable of anything like the integrity or aspiration of Troilus. These shortcomings are obvious enough in the case of Pandarus, whose office is essentially to complement Troilus's love with practical ingenuity and physical desire; but I will argue that Criseyde, too, though she possesses an inner dimension wholly lacking in Pandarus, is similarly cut off from participation in love as Troilus undergoes it. From the moment we first see her to the end of her final speech she is bound to the

world and worldly security by a besetting preoccupation that is
as much her *modus vivendi* as love-idealism is the condition of
Troilus.

The narrator, too, is a character in the story, and my larger
argument about the *Troilus* depends to a great extent on viewing
him as like the other characters both in his unreflecting involvement with the action and in his failure to recognize and respond
to the distinctive quality of Troilus's love. I have already suggested the nature of his involvement as it is dramatized in the
opening Proem, in which a potentially overwhelming fatalism
and an intuitive charity are held in suspense by his desperate
need to affirm the attainment of erotic "gladness" as an end in
itself. In my final chapter I will analyze the process by which the
narrator breaks away from this obsessive attachment to the love
story at the end of the poem and comes to terms with it in a new
way. Here I want to concentrate on his experience in the center
of the poem, and specifically in the aftermath of the consummation scene, in which he finds himself disoriented and alone, cut
off from Troilus's spiritual idealization of his love and from the
vision of a heaven of erotic delight which he himself had imagined, yet unable to focus on the lovers' actual situation and
willfully blind to his own. Even his expressions of joy are never
wholly free from an undertone of doubt, and his uncontrollable
anxiety prepares us for the abrupt shift from the lyric celebra-
tions of love and Venus that punctuate the later portions of
Book 3 to the somber Proem of Book 4, in which Fortune and
the Furies are conjured up and the narrator becomes suddenly
aware of the quick passage of earthly joys.

Up to this point, however, the bright world and its inhabitants
are well served. Like the Baker Street Irregulars who ransack
the Sherlock Holmes stories for evidence about the life and habits of their hero, all readers of the *Troilus* have their pet clues to
the history and situation of Criseyde. My own favorite passage is
that in which she responds to Pandarus's claim that she is about
to be sued—again—by "false Poliphete":

> Yit of hym selve nothing wolde I recche,
> Nere it for Antenor and Eneas,

That ben his frendes in swich manere cas.
But, for the love of god, myn uncle deere,
No fors of that, lat hym han al yfeere. . . .

[2. 1473–77]

"Poliphete" is presumably the Trojan priest of Ceres mentioned
by Vergil (*Aen.* 6. 484). His quarrel with Criseyde evidently involves money, perhaps revenues derived from the involvement
of both Poliphete and Criseyde's father Calchas in the activities
of the Trojan priesthood. Since Criseyde is evidently well-to-do,
they are presumably playing for high stakes.[1]

Criseyde's swift assessment of the pros and cons of what she
takes to be a real situation suggests an experienced, practical
politician. Her decision not to contest the claims of Poliphete
because, as she goes on to assure Pandarus, "withouten that, I
have ynough for us" (1478) suggests that Pandarus too is involved in these complex matters. This passage, moreover, is just
one of many that allude to the web of shared experience that
joins uncle and niece, suggesting that each has knowledge of
what Henry James might call the "abysses" in the other's life. It
is evidently understood among Criseyde's household that very
private matters are discussed between them (2. 215–17)—
though Chaucer artfully avoids telling us what they discuss—
and at times they seem to employ a sort of code (2. 1111–13).
We can never be sure how much shared sexual innuendo passes
between them (" 'Nay, therof spak I nought, a ha!' quod she"),
nor can we understand fully the import of the jokes and games
they play or interpret her sudden intense bursts of laughter.
Finally, of course, they do not wholly open themselves to one
another: Pandarus does not hesitate to sacrifice Criseyde's
honor in the pursuit of his own obscure desires, and he in turn is
eventually betrayed, as Troilus is, by that deep-seated instinct
for self-protection in Criseyde which he has previously exploited

---

1. Criseyde considers herself a woman of substantial means (2. 750–51), as is
further suggested by her house (or palace) with its paved parlor (2. 82), extensive
garden (2. 820–22), and rich furnishings (2. 1228–29 and by the size of her
household (she comes to dinner attended by a retinue of "nine or ten" women at
3. 598). E. T. Donaldson, "Chaucer and the Elusion of Clarity," *Essays and Studies*
25 (1972):29–31, shows how artfully Chaucer presents this and other information about Criseyde's situation.

so effectively. But like James's Gilbert Osmond and Madame Merle, they know one another as well as such people can be known.

No amount of detective work will ever yield sure answers about Criseyde, but it is clear that she is a woman whose circumstances must inevitably play a very important role in her life. She is evidently older than Boccaccio's Criseida, with adolescent nieces in her charge; her status in Troy is perhaps uncertain;[2] and she has substantial material interests to protect. She is not a person likely to be much given to idealism in her pursuit of love or to enter willingly into a love relationship on any but her own terms.

All of this is very evident in the scene of Book 2 in which, after Pandarus has confronted her with the prospect of loving Troilus, she sits down alone to think things over. During Chaucer's long examination of her state of mind, the effect of Pandarus's eloquence is reinforced—first by the appearance of Troilus himself, then by the insistent return to her mind of that sense of his "worthiness" that Pandarus had emphasized, and finally by the song of Antigone, with its affirmation of the noble lover's worthiness as a bulwark against all peril. But it must be emphasized that Criseyde *thinks* things over: the word "thought" occurs more than a dozen times in the 200-odd lines that describe her reaction to the prospect of reciprocating Troilus's love, and detail after detail points to the control and deliberation of her response. In the end, Pandarus, circumstance, and love itself have their way with her; we are left feeling that she could not have escaped her situation any more than Troilus could have escaped his.[3] But by the time she finds herself "at dulcar-

2. Though 5. 956–57 suggest that Criseyde was born at Troy, a chance remark by one of the women who visit her on learning of her imminent departure suggests that she may not always have lived there (4. 690). See also ch. 4, n. 6.

3. See the excellent discussion of Donald Howard, "Experience, Language, and Consciousness: *Troilus and Criseyde*, II, 596–931," in *Medieval Literature and Folklore Studies: Essays in Honor of Francis Lee Utley* (New Brunswick, N.J., 1970), pp. 189–91 (repr. in *Chaucer's 'Troilus': Essays in Criticism*, ed. Stephen A. Barney [Hamden, Conn., 1980], pp. 175–77). My reading of this scene diverges from Howard's fine analysis chiefly in its emphasis: where he examines interactions of thought and feeling to show the complexity of Criseyde's response to love, I seek to distinguish her response from that of Troilus by pointing out instances of her relative self-awareness.

non" (3. 931), no longer able to maneuver, she knows what is at stake on the practical level in a way that Troilus never does.

The stanzas that describe Criseyde's reaction to her first sight of Troilus are worth comparing with the single stanza of Book 1 in which Troilus responds to the sight of Criseyde:

> And of hire look in him ther gan to quyken
> So gret desir, and swiche affeccioun,
> That in his hertes botme gan to stiken
> Of hir the fixe and depe impressioun;
> And though he erst hadde poured up and down,
> He was tho glad his hornes in to shrinke;
> Unnethes wiste he how to loke or wynke.
>
> [1. 295–301]

As verbs like "quyken" and "stiken" indicate, Troilus's experience *happens to him,* and his only action is to instinctively "draw in his horns," a gesture of submission that anticipates the imagined death of his vital spirit in 306–7. The consuming nature of the experience is summed up by the narrator's comment, "blissed be love, that kan thus folk converte" (308).

Criseyde is prepared for her sight of Troilus by the shouts of the crowd and the excitement of her household and is able to observe from her private vantage point his becoming blush of embarrassment as he is greeted with cheers. Having "allowed" (the active verb is important) the sight of him to reach her heart, she asks with a faintly ironic self-awareness "who yaf me drynke?" (651).[4] Something has happened to her, too, and in a minute she too will blush, but nothing about her reaction is simply spontaneous; each stage is joined to the next by an interval of "thought." Criseyde blushes at "hire own thought" of who

4. Howard finds the "drink" image suggestive of "unguarded attraction" and "a feeling as yet undefined" ("Experience, Language, and Consciousness," pp. 176–77; Barney, pp. 162–63). I would point to the very fact that Criseyde has such ready recourse to a comparison as evidence of self-awareness, particularly in contrast to Troilus's wholly unreflecting reaction to his first sight of her. As David Grossvogel observes (*Limits of the Novel* [Ithaca, N.Y., 1968], p. 69), the image hints at an evasion, even an abdication of moral responsibility. Moreover, if the image of intoxication does not define her experience, it does circumscribe it: we are warned by it not to expect anything like Troilus's religious response to his first sight of Criseyde and perhaps reminded as well that Criseyde has had some prior experience of the potentially disorienting effect of love.

Troilus is and what she has been told of him; "with that thought"
she pulls her head inside the window (a deliberate action that
provides a literal counterpart to the shrinking in of Troilus's
horns in the stanza just quoted) and then in privacy, "within her
thought," reflects on what she has heard and seen.

The narrator's comment on the scene, by its utter inap-
propriateness, completes the contrast: some, he says, will feel
that Criseyde has fallen too readily in love with Troilus at first
sight, but they are wrong:

> For I sey nat that she so sodeynly
> Yaf hym hire love, but that she gan enclyne
> To like hym first, and I have told yow whi;
> And after that, his manhod and his pyne
> Made love withinne hire for to myne;
> For which, by proces and by good servyse,
> He gat hire love, and in no sodeyn wyse.
>
> [2. 673–79]

The narrator has his own reasons for insisting on the positive
effect of Troilus's "pyne" and "servyse," and we have already
been told that Criseyde is impressed by how much Troilus has
suffered for her (663–65). But it seems clear that these lines
imply a far more conventional experience of *fin amor* than we
have in fact been shown. We cannot describe precisely the process by which "he gat hire love," but clearly we must give much
credit to Pandarus's maneuvering and Criseyde's careful calculation of her own advantage, conditioned in some measure by her
previous experience of love. Troilus's own role is suggested
more accurately, though indirectly, by the narrator's further
reflection:

> And also blisful Venus, wel arrayed,
> Sat in hire seventhe hous of hevene tho,
> Disposed wel, and with aspectes payed,
> To helpen sely Troilus of his woo;
> And, soth to seyn, she nas not al a foo
> To Troilus in his nativitee;
> God woot that wel the sonner spedde he.
>
> [2. 680–86]

Far from urging his love on Criseyde with charm, guile, or
"maystrye," Troilus is emphatically "sely Troilus"—virtuous, innocent, hapless, simple, wretched, holy, to mention just a few of
the meanings the word can have in Chaucer. He is the passive
object of Pandarus's and Criseyde's concern, dominated by love
and powerless to resist in any way the constant pressure it exerts
on his life.[5]

It would not, of course, be fair to Criseyde to argue that Chaucer's point is simply to balance her worldly self-interest against
Troilus's spiritual self-abandonment. Criseyde is sensitive to the
appeal of love as well as to its possible practical advantages, and
as her inner debate is traced over the next hundred-odd lines we
recognize that a real obstacle to acquiescence is her knowledge
of what love can cost in emotional terms. It is clear, indeed, that
her emphasis on practical considerations is at least partly a way
of evading the harder questions that, as she knows from experience, must be faced. But her "cloudy thoughts" (768) are not
Troilus's forebodings about the effects of a divine power dimly
perceived. She is concerned with her freedom and reputation
and the harm that gossip and misunderstanding can do to both.
The urgency that such reflections create, though real, does not
last long. Suspended between the two sides of her inner debate,
Criseyde refuses to commit herself, and this section of Book 2
ends with unexpected abruptness:

> Now hoot, now cold; but thus bitwixen tweye,
> She rist hire up, and wente hire for to pleye.
> [2. 811–12]

Thus a crisis that has been building slowly over twenty stanzas is
dismissed in a single line. Clearly Criseyde is not vexed by contraries as powerful as those "windes two" that had rendered
Troilus utterly helpless (1. 417–18).

Of course, Troilus is not the only one for whom love is a
serious matter; Criseyde, on her own pragmatic level, is intri-

5. As Stephen Barney remarks, "When we see Criseyde alone, she is weighing alternatives; when we see Troilus alone, he is wishing" ("Troilus Bound,"
Speculum 47 [1972]:446).

cately involved in coming to terms with what love represents to
her. The difference between the two is illustrated in a way that
does justice to both by the song of Antigone and Criseyde's
response to it. Like a Broadway director unveiling the production number that will celebrate the heroine's discovery of love,
Chaucer creates a rich garden setting and introduces at a moment's notice a "grete route" of attendant ladies (818–22). Given
this build-up, we may well be surprised when the heroine herself
does not take center stage, though it is wholly in character for
her to avoid doing so. But the song, a veritable *summa* of the
quasi-religious conception of *fin amor* that has consumed
Troilus, is clearly aimed at Criseyde's heart. Antigone, in the
intensity of her virginal devotion to love, offers a celebration of
something like erotic fulfillment untroubled by any of the
doubts with which Criseyde has been engaged, a love "withouten
jalousie or strif," everlasting and secure:

> "But I with al myn herte, and al my myght,
> As I have seyd, wol love unto my laste
> My deere herte, and al myn owen knyght,
> In which myn herte growen is so faste,
> And his in me, that it shal evere laste.
> Al dredde I first to love hym to bigynne,
> Now woot I wel, there is no peril inne."
>   [2. 869–75]

Criseyde's reaction to the song in the four stanzas that follow
is carefully drawn. There is a poignancy in her response to the
chirpy enthusiasm of Antigone: her gentle irony and affectionate amusement do not quite conceal a note of genuine yearning,
and Chaucer ends the scene by pointing to the delicate balance
of her feelings:

> Criseyde unto that purpose nought answerde,
> But seyde: "ywys, it wol be nyght as faste."
> But every word which that she of hire herde,
> She gan to prenten in hire herte faste,
> And ay gan love hire lasse for tagaste

Than it did erst, and synken in hire herte,
That she wax somewhat able to converte.[6]

[2. 897–903]

Here Criseyde comes as close as at any point in the poem to making a direct response to love. But even here her response is controlled. It is veiled by her comment on the coming of night, which is half a dismissal of, half a reflection upon the subject of her conversation with Antigone; and it is described in terms of the deliberate act of printing. Only now does Criseyde approach that moment of "conversion" that Troilus had undergone in the first instant of beholding her, and even now she does not consciously cross the threshold of commitment to love. The effect of Antigone's song amounts to a renewal of "thought" (915). Criseyde is less on guard than at any previous moment: the final three lines of the stanza just quoted form a distinct syntactic unit that describes a separate, ongoing process taking place subliminally within her heart. But even this subliminal process inclines her to love only "somewhat." Even when it has been completed at the subconscious level of her eagle dream, it shows her acquiescing only in a carefully qualified act of physical possession.[7] Rather than opening a window onto the spiritual possibilities of love, Criseyde's dream is conditioned and circumscribed by her experience of love in this world.

Thus, though Criseyde's response to love is more complex than that of Pandarus, it is affected even at the deepest level by a chronic worldliness. Chaucer makes this point again at the one other moment in the poem when we see her unconscious, after she faints away in the course of her interview with Troilus in Book 4. There is a curious sense of deliberation in the narrator's description of this inner crisis—

Hire woful spirit from his propre place,
Right with the word, alwey o poynt to pace

[4. 1152–53]

6. It is appropriate to the state of Criseyde's feelings that the end of this stanza marks the exact midpoint of the narrative portion (excluding, that is, the forty-nine-line Proem) of Book 2.

7. See ch. 5, pp. 158–60.

as though Criseyde's spirit, on the point of suiting action to word, were waiting to see the effect of her outward appearance before finally forsaking her body. One gathers from 1221–22 that her "goost" does at last come forth, but that it lingers close at hand, with a circumspection worthy of its mistress, to keep an eye on the course of events.[8]

Essentially the same limitations appear in a different form at those moments when we see Criseyde responding directly to Troilus. From the beginning she is aware of his worthiness and *gentilesse* (2. 701–4) and pleased that he is no boaster (724), and as the relationship develops, she comes increasingly to value his self-discipline and deference (3. 475–78). His devotion seems to her to offer "a wall of steel" against any abuse of her honor (479–80), and her utter confidence in his "trouthe and clene entente" is emphasized even as they lie in one another's arms (3. 1226–29). But all of these qualities are valued chiefly insofar as they serve Criseyde's desire to avoid constraint, the chatter of "wicked tongues," or physical pain. From a different point of view they point up a lack of aggressiveness which, however well suited to "love of frendes," is a defect in a would-be lover *paramours*. While Pandarus may get in an occasional thrust on behalf of "Mars, the god that helmed is of steel" (2. 593), Troilus remains wholly within the bounds of his discretion. By the midpoint of Book 3 this discretion has become a problem. He appeals to Criseyde to teach him "how that I may deserve/Youre thonk" (1293–94), yet refuses, with intuitive delicacy, to "breken youre defence" (1299), until Criseyde at last manages to draw him away from his own vision of fulfillment to perform his role in hers.

At the end of Book 4 Criseyde delivers a two-stanza encomium on Troilus's character that provides an oblique but telling comment on the lovers' relationship at this late stage. It is substituted for a passage in which Boccaccio's Troiolo had enumerated the qualities of beauty and courtliness that caused him to love Criseida. But Criseyde's emphasis is explicitly placed on moral rather than chivalric qualities (1667–72), and as it un-

---

8. Chaucer's language here is in sharp contrast to *Fil.* 4. 117, where the great pressure of grief is emphasized, and Criseida's soul struggles to escape her body.

folds, these qualities somehow come to appear almost as lia-
bilities:

> Ek gentil herte and manhod that ye hadde,
> And that ye hadde, as me thoughte, in despit
> Every thyng that souned into badde,
> As rudenesse and poeplissh appetit,
> And that youre resoun bridlede youre delit. . . .
> [4. 1674–78]

We can see how these qualities must have commended themselves to Criseyde by their intrinsic beauty and their lack of
menace, but we can also see how they circumscribe Troilus's role
as heroic lover and impose a constraint both on his power to act
in resistance to the course of events and on his address to
Criseyde. Moral virtue and the bridling of desire by reason are
admirable in themselves, but they are not the basis for a sexual
relationship; a lover in whom "poeplissh appetit" is wholly absent is not finally a lover Criseyde can feel bound to. She goes on
to defy the power of time and fortune to destroy her attachment
to him, but we can see her setting him at a distance, enshrined
and imprisoned by his virtues, in the very act of praising him.
Burdened by spiritual doubt, moral and chivalric scruple, and
the inevitable failure of physical passion, he is no longer a palpa-
ble presence in her life, and in the end what this speech tells us is
that he has therefore ceased to be wholly real for her.

By the time Criseyde makes the great declaration of loyalty of
which this encomium is the culmination, she has already em-
barked on the course that will lead to her betrayal of Troilus.
The speech is one of a number of means whereby she has managed to control his response to their common situation and to
dictate to him the plan that will allow her to adapt to her new
circumstances with the least possible risk. In effect she has re-
verted from her new alliance with Troilus to the confidential
relationship with Pandarus that lies behind it. For it is Pandarus
who has suggested her course of action to her:

> "Syn ye ben wise, and bothe of oon assent,
> So shapeth how destourbe your goynge,

Or come ayeyn soone after ye be went.
Wommen ben wise in short avysement. . . ."
[4. 933–36]

Pandarus understands how Criseyde operates, and there is a certain tact in the silent shift from "ye" plural to "ye" singular, from a plan the two lovers will devise together ("shapeth" 934) to one that will be Criseyde's own ("wommen ben wise . . ."). We should not be surprised when Criseyde later employs Pandarus's very words in proposing to Troilus that she find means "to come ayeyn, soone after that I go" (1276).[9] As in Book 2 uncle and niece are communicating in a kind of code and seem to understand each other, though neither can foresee what will happen when Criseyde is later forced to make quick decisions with neither Pandarus's advice nor Troilus's anxious devotion to influence her.

Viewed in this perspective the disintegration of Criseyde's love of Troilus in Book 5 is a series of postmortem effects. There is no need to ponder what may be implied in sexual terms by Diomede's having "refte hire of the grete of al hire peyne" (1036), by her gift to him of the "faire baye stede" that had once belonged to Troilus (1038–39), or by the narrator's final admission, half-wistful, half-grumpy, "Men seyn, I not, that she yaf hym hire herte" (1050); nor does it matter how long it was before Criseyde and Diomede actually became lovers.[10] Like Pandarus's intrusion into Criseyde's bed after Troilus's departure in Book 3, these details only confirm the more fundamental betrayal that has already taken place, which indeed is inherent in Criseyde's practical, self-serving, materialistic view of life and

9. Chaucer is surely calling attention to the connection between Criseyde's words and Pandarus's earlier suggestion when he has her preface her proposal with a reference to having been "avysed sodeynly" after the manner of women (1261–62), echoing Pandarus's commendation of women's power of "short avysement" in 936.

10. The narrator makes his last stand on Criseyde's behalf over the absence of any clear testimony on this point (1086–92). See Root, ad loc., who shows that by Benoit's reckoning "between the arrival of Briseida at the Grecian camp and her final acceptance of Diomede there is an interval of *at least* twenty-one months" (emphasis Root's). But by the narrator's own account the process leading to the acceptance "bygan to brede" on the tenth day of her exile, and it can be said to have been in motion from the moment at which Diomede took her "by the reyne" and she lost the reassurance of physical proximity to Troilus.

"felicity." Rather than rebuke Criseyde directly, Chaucer makes
his point by the far more effective means of allowing her in her
final speech to condemn herself, charmingly but decisively, out
of her own mouth. Her priorities are clearly defined by her
opening words, which lament first the loss of her good name
and then the fact of having betrayed Troilus, who, however, is
not named:

> She seyde: "allas! for now is clene ago
> My name of trouthe in love for everemo!
> For I have falsed oon, the gentileste
> That evere was, and oon the worthieste."
>   [5. 1054–57]

The three brief words, "I have falsed," sandwiched incon-
spicuously between lament and encomium, are, we may note,
Criseyde's only direct acknowledgment of wrongdoing in the
entire speech. In the stanza that follows she forsees her fate as a
proverbial figure for falseness, but does not respond, like the
Briseida of Benoit, by confessing "I have done shame to maid-
ens."[11] Instead she concludes on a note of self-pity ("Allas, that
swich a cas me sholde falle!"), and in the next stanza seems
almost to be trying to put her accusers in the wrong:

> "Thei wol seyn, in as much as in me is,
> I have hem don dishonour, weylawey!
> Al be I nat the first that dide amys,
> What helpeth that to don my blame awey?"
>   [5. 1065–68]

Returning to the practical aspect of her situation, she adopts the
language of compromise ("syn I se ther is no bettre way," "to
late," "algate," "syn I no bettre may"), making her famous resolution to be true at least to Diomede and wishing God's blessing
on Troilus. It is hard not to feel compassion for Criseyde as she

---

11. *Roman de Troie* 20259. Criseyde's speech is very loosely imitated from lines
20237–340 of Benoit, but offers nothing like the directness of his Briseida, who
speaks frankly and objectively of her guilt and its causes; of what she stands to
gain, despite her folly, from her alliance with Diomede; and of the strong sense
of remorse that leads her to wish that she could lose all recollection of her past.

pays her final tribute to Troilus's virtues in lines worthy of Malory and is reduced to tears at the thought of his steadfast devotion (1075–78). But she recovers herself magnificently, and the final stanza of her speech is the most Criseydan moment of the poem:

> "And certes, yow ne haten shal I nevere;
> And frendes love, that shal ye han of me,
> And my good word, al myghte I lyven evere.
> And, trewely, I wolde sory be
> For to seen yow in adversitee.
> And gilteles, I woot wel, I yow leve;
> But al shal passe; and thus take I my leve."
>
> [5. 1079–85]

Amid her sorrow Criseyde is sufficiently alert to borrow something of the reflected light of Troilus's virtues. She is at least inspired by them—and no doubt moved by the tender sorrow of her own response to them—to believe, or at least pretend, that a declaration of fidelity on her part could still have meaning. Indeed, if we read this stanza in isolation, it is impossible to tell from it just who has been wronged. It is as though the pious tears of the previous stanza had miraculously cleansed Criseyde of all guilt and entitled her to adopt a tone of charitable good will, almost of forgiveness, toward Troilus. Certainly the fine syntactic and verbal ambiguity of "gilteles, I woot wel, I yow leve" conveys a hint that Criseyde feels *herself* to be guiltless in "leaving" Troilus, that in some irrational way she has managed to reassure herself of her essential innocence. Even the primary meaning of the line—that she "believes" Troilus to be without guilt—is slightly disconcerting. Like her assurance just above that she feels no hatred for Troilus, it enables her to sound magnanimous and somehow fair-minded, even though she is answering a question one would never have thought to ask. And the final "but al shal passe"—so stark in its implications as the poem's final comment on Criseyde's incorrigible worldliness—may also be heard as expressing an almost motherly solicitude toward Troilus in his misery. Thus the ambiguity of the stanza as a whole acts as a kind of linguistic veil, sufficiently opaque to allow Criseyde to leave the stage in some semblance of respectability.

As even Troilus will finally come to sense (5. 1632–34), Criseyde has changed in the course of Book 5. She scarcely attempts to fend off the advances of Diomede; she lies more readily and more grossly than before; and she is even capable of the sheer gratuitous invention of her final letter, which goes so far as to suggest that Troilus has not been faithful to her (1614–15). By this time she is no longer the Criseyde Troilus knows, no longer even the woman who realized too late how seriously she had compromised herself (5. 744–49). Though her desperate need for security is eased by the intervention of Diomede, she continues to use rhetoric and fiction to disguise, and perhaps to deny even to herself, the reality of what has happened to her.

But there are more than sentimental reasons for following the narrator's example and withholding any too strong condemnation of Criseyde in her decline. Though Chaucer makes plain the limitations of her character, he also makes plain the social constraints and precarious circumstances that have compelled her to meet the world on its own terms and to rely so largely on her sexual attractiveness to make her way. Her pursuit of love itself has not been merely idle or sensual; the pleasure she takes in sexual love and the pleasure she gives are indicated in various ways, but she has had more than a beast in view. She has been capable of appreciating Troilus's nobility, and even Diomede, in addition to the sexual prowess on which he prides himself, embodies qualities that, though largely absent in Troilus, are legitimate attributes of the ideal lover foreshadowed by her eagle dream. And Chaucer has taken pains to endow Criseyde with attributes that, in a different world, might have offered her a very different life. Though we take no more seriously than she does the possibility of her pursuing the life of saintly seclusion which she proposes for herself in her first exchange with Pandarus (2. 117–18), the very absurdity of the anachronism and the ease with which Pandarus cajoles her away from such thoughts remind us that such a life is one of many options that are unavailable to her. It may be sentimental to reflect (though Henryson will somehow contrive to make us do so) that Criseyde has lived her life in a world that offers no reward for contrition, and knows nothing of the parable of the one lost sheep or the tradition of the harlot-turned-saint. But it is worth noting that Chaucer makes a surprising number of references to her quasi-religious habit in the scenes in which she first appears. Perhaps it is not going too far to see in this astute, intelligent, and literate woman, who presides over a large female household and who is capable of dealing on equal terms with men in legal and economic matters, one who might have been the prioress of a great religious house. In relation to the more prominent role of Troilus Criseyde is a foil, an image of vain desire and mutable fortune, but she is also a remarkable person in her own right, and there is no more telling illustration of the sober, Boethian moral of Chaucer's poem than the fact that the "real" Criseyde, so circumspect and clear-sighted in her approach to life, should be so much at the mercy of love in charting her course. Though her blindness is neither Troilus's nor Pandarus's, she too is a victim of what the poem will finally identify as "the blynde lust, the which that may nat laste."

No such claims can be made for the narrator of the *Troilus,* whose involvement with his love story makes him ignore repeatedly the evidences of calculation and self-interest in Criseyde's behavior and who is himself a strange combination of the attitudes of Pandarus and Troilus. Though he is deluded by the idealizing euphemisms of his own rhetoric, the narrator's eagerness to bring Troilus and Criseyde together is as clear as Pandarus's, and though, as we have seen, he shows an occasional uneasiness about the means necessary to attain this goal, he is not at all concerned with what may lie beyond. It is only when the consummation has taken place and the lovers are "floating," suspended "bitwixen drede and sikernesse," that he is confronted with the question of what it has all meant.

The narrator, indeed, plays a highly active role in this scene. While the lovers are coming gradually to terms with their new intimacy, he is bothered by a need to justify his presence in some way. Again and again he claims that his language cannot do justice to this sublime moment, but he insists on defending the lovers and the supreme quality of their love against the potentially demoralizing forces of fear, detraction, and the insensitivity of "wrecches." He says nothing that cannot be construed as in some sense affirmative of the lover's bliss, but he seems

incapable of affirming it in a wholly unequivocal way. Like
Troilus, the narrator has felt intense anxiety in looking forward
to this moment; unlike Troilus, he is left deeply unsatisfied by
the consummation of their common desire.

I think we may understand the narrator's difficulty as a failure
to discover in himself the feeling appropriate to the celebration
of the union he has described. In a curiously anticlimactic conclusion to the praise of love in the Proem to Book 3, he appeals
to Venus for "sentement," a capacity to appreciate the "swet-
nesse" of love, and then summons Calliope to help him describe
it in a worthy way:

> For now is nede; sestow nat my destresse,
> How I mot telle anon right the gladness
> Of Troilus, to Venus heryinge?
>   [3. 46–48]

This same "destresse" appears in the narrator's behavior in the
present scene. The moment has arrived toward which all his
faithful service in the cause of love has been directed, and he
must respond in a way that shows that his faith and hope have
been rewarded. Given the desperate, obsessive nature of his
commitment, anything less than total affirmation is unthinkable,
but he cannot, it seems, bring forth such a response.

A hint of the difficulty appears in the final couplet of the
stanza in which the narrator first responds to the consummation:

> That nyght, bitwixen drede and sikernesse,
> They felte in love the grete worthynesse.
>   [3. 1315–16]

It might be argued that "the grete worthinesse" is just the right
phrase, all the more eloquent for its eschewing of any superla-
tive. But I think it is intended rather to sound blunt and vaguely
unsatisfying, whether we hear behind it the more resonant "ultimo valore," or "supreme value" of the corresponding line in
the *Filostrato* (3. 32. 8) or are simply led by the movement of the

stanza itself to expect in the concluding phrase a suggestion of
something unique and supreme. Harder to assess, but again not
so positive as we might expect in its implications, is the placing of
the lovers "bitwixen drede and sikernesse." On the one hand
this phrase reminds us of Troilus's long journey from fatalism
and self-doubt to his present happiness; on the other it hints at
the element of tension, a combination of hope and fear, that is
both part of the emotional pleasure of erotic love and a symptom of its instability. From the perspective of the anxious narrator, the words hint at a falling short, a failure to attain a sure
hold on happiness.

The lovers, of course, feel no such misgivings, and the narrator is left to cope with his own hopes and fears in solitude,
willfully denying the "drede" that continues to haunt him. It is
the effect of this conflict that flaws the attempt at affirmation in
the following stanza, which includes the narrator's wish to have
sold his soul for one night, for the least part, of such joy as he
imagines the lovers to share. The spiritual emptiness of this
quasi-prayer reminds us of the "derknesse," cut off from any
hope of love's joy, in which the narrator had languished at the
opening of Book 1,[12] and when he turns immediately to fend off
"thow foule daunger and thow feere," we can see him beset by
the devils of his own self-doubt.

The impasse at which the narrator has arrived is illustrated
more clearly by his second major intrusion into the scene, an
attack on those whose materialism disqualifies them to appreciate love's virtue. Two of the three stanzas of this diatribe are
closely imitated from the *Filostrato* (3. 38–39); they constitute an
effective rhetorical unit in themselves and end resoundingly
with the wish that God may bring these "wrecches" to grief and
advance all true lovers (1371–72). Their effect is to make the
third stanza, which is wholly Chaucer's, seem like an unpremedi-
tated outburst by the narrator. It merely repeats thoughts al-

12. The effect of the narrator's prayer is very different from the arbitrary
hyperbole of the passage that may have suggested it, *Fil.* 2. 88. 7–8, in which
Troiolo, apostrophizing the absent Criseida in a speech to Pandaro, declares that
if he might spend one winter's night with her he would then willingly spend a
hundred and fifty in hell.

ready expressed in the Boccaccian passage and does so with
what seems an uncalled-for vehemence:

> As wolde god, thise wrecches that dispise
> Servise of love, hadde erys also longe
> As hadde Mida, ful of coveytise,
> And thereto dronken hadde as hoot and stronge
> As Crassus dide for his affectis wronge,
> To techen hem that coveytise is vice,
> And love is vertu, though men holde it nyce.
>
> [3. 1373–79]

That Midas and Crassus are emblems of the sort of punishment
appropriate to covetousness might be sufficient to account for
their appearance here; but the vividness of their evocation in an
otherwise gratuitous passage calls attention to itself and invites
us to consider their possible relevance to the narrator's own
situation. Midas, we should recall, was given his long ears not
because of his greed, but because of the insensitivity that led him
to prefer the song of Pan to that of Apollo.[13] He was also
greedy, of course, and for this greed was punished with the
golden touch, a penalty that included the aurification of food
and drink and thus, though not fatal, resembled the punishment
of Crassus, forced to drink molten gold because of his greed as a
provincial governor.[14] The common element in Midas's twofold
exemplary role is a sensibility so denatured as to be incapable of
distinguishing among the things that attract it: the ass's ears
merely confirm the insensitivity symbolized by his golden touch
and by the fate of Crassus, which reduces all pleasure to a common, chronically unsatisfying materialism.

Chaucer's narrator, though we may cite inexperience in ex-
tenuation of his fault, is guilty of a similar failure of sensibility.
Alienated by his chronic "unlikeliness" from a direct experience
of love, he has tried to appropriate to his own needs the love of

13. Ovid, *Metamorphoses* 11. 146–79.
14. According to Florus and Orosius, the molten gold was poured into
Crassus's mouth only after the Parthians had killed him in battle and sent his
head to their king. But both Dante's and Chaucer's references indicate that they
understood him to have been made to drink it while still alive, and this view is
explicit in John Gower's account of Crassus's death, *Confessio Amantis* 5. 2209–24
(in which Crassus is emperor of Rome).

Troilus and Criseyde, only to find himself excluded from the feast, unable to buy the smallest part of their pleasure. The very imagery of food and commerce suggests the source of his difficulty, the "coveytise" that flaws his idealistic view of love as paradise. Because of this he has preferred Pan to Apollo, failed to appreciate the deeper implications of his own quasi-religious rhetoric or the truly religious attitude of Troilus. As a result he is suspended in an emotional and rhetorical vacuum and expresses his frustration at being unable to participate imaginatively in the love he beholds by attacking Midas and Crassus, whose punishments constitute a perverted image of their materialism and his own.[15]

What the narrator has encountered without realizing it is the finitude of an experience of love in which the impulse to physical consummation has become dominant, so that its emotional intensity is now subject to a desire that ebbs and flows. Three stanzas that conclude the account of the first night's lovemaking express this new reality in terms of the rhetorical problem it poses for the narrator. Two of these stanzas are really two different versions of a single stanza of the *Filostrato* (3. 40); in each the lovers review the history of "wo and feere" that has led to the present happiness. At the end of the first the narrator comments:

> . . . but al that hevynesse,
> I thanke it god, was torned to gladnesse.
> [3. 1385–86]

The second ends with the lovers uniting their efforts

> For to recoveren blisse and ben at eise,
> And passed wo with joie countrepeise.
> [3. 1392–93]

15. Cf. the use of the story of Midas in *Canterbury Tales* D 952–82, where the Wyf of Bath, seeking to derive a different exemplum from it, ends by exposing the chronic materialism that has motivated her own sexual career. Midas and Crassus are both named in the song of the souls being purged of avarice in *Purgatorio* 20. 106, 116–17. We are told that the zeal (*affezion*) of each soul against its own greed determines how loudly it sings (118–20). It is perhaps the *Troilus* narrator's lurking sense of being somehow implicated in his own reference to the "affectis wronge" of Crassus (1391) that makes him speak with such *affezion* in denouncing him.

The nearly identical movement of the two stanzas illustrates the closed circle within which the lovers' emotions now operate. And in the next stanza, which concludes the scene, the narrator can say no more of the night as a whole than that

> It was byset in joie and besynesse
> Of al that souneth into gentilesse.
>   [3. 1399–1400]

As with "the grete worthinesse" a hundred lines earlier, there is a vagueness about the concluding abstract "gentilesse," a diffusion of potential energy in euphemism and generality which sums up the problem that has bedeviled the narrator throughout the scene. At every point at which a strong affirmative phrase has been called for, he has undergone a momentary inability to focus clearly on the lovers' experience and a consequent failure of rhetoric. It all happened, he assures us, yet somehow he "kan nat tellen al," and we may see in the contrast between his suspension in abstractions and the lovers' concrete engagement with one another a parodic resemblance to the way Troilus's scrupulous courtliness had insulated him from the realities of sexual intrigue earlier in Book 3. Disqualified earlier by his insensitivity from doing justice to the lovers' initial raptures, the narrator now appears incapable of reexalting by his powers of idealization a love that has subsided naturally into the rhythm of physical desire.

At this point the narrator steps forward to deliver a two-stanza apology for his role.[16] He has, he declares, presented the gist of his author's meaning, and anything he may have added "at loves reverence" (1405) is subject to correction by those more fortunate than he, who "felyng han in loves art" (1410) and who will thus know how to edit and interpret for themselves what he has

16. The placement of these stanzas at this point is a distinguishing feature of the B text of the poem, which Root considered the most nearly authoritative; editors since Robinson have printed them in a slightly altered form as 1324–37. Charles A. Owen, Jr., defends the B reading, largely on the grounds of dramatic propriety, in "Mimetic Form in the Central Love Scene of *Troilus and Criseyde*," *Modern Philology* 67 (1969–70):132. On the linguistic and metrical superiority of the B text generally, see his "Minor Changes in Chaucer's *Troilus and Criseyde*," in *Chaucer and Middle English Studies in Honor of Rossell Hope Robbins*, ed. Beryl Rowland (London, 1974), pp. 302–19, esp. pp. 314–18.

written. The phrases I have quoted suggest the two separate
levels on which the passage may be understood: it is at once a
rueful confession of the narrator's inadequacy to this task and at
the same time a reminder that the poem has expressed a reverence for love, and an astuteness about the art that love involves,
of which the narrator is almost wholly unaware.[17] What he has
added to Boccaccio's narrative "at loves reverence" ranges from
the invocation of divine love in the Proem of Book 3 to the
ingenuity with which the blissful night is prepared by Pandarus;
it includes the elaboration of Troilus's visionary experience and
the narrator's own less successful attempts at sublimity. In all of
these areas what he has told us goes far beyond his conscious
purposes, and it is his dim awareness of this fact that leads him
to bid his audience to accept his good intentions and "doth ther-
withal right as yourselven leste" (1407).[18] The openness with
which he acknowledges his incapacity resembles the diffidence
of Troilus, who has at one moment "putte al in goddes hond,"
and at another urged Criseyde to guide him lest he do her
"displeasaunce" through his ignorance. But while Troilus is only
confused as to the relation of the sensual and the visionary in his
experience, the narrator, as we have seen, has failed to make
contact with either.

The final and perhaps most striking instance of the narrator's
emotional and rhetorical dilemma is the conclusion of his account of the lovers' second night together, which gave them a
thousand times more pleasure than the first:

> And bothe, ywys, they hadde, and so they wende,
> As muche joie as herte may comprende.
>
> This is no litel thyng of for to seye;
> This passeth every wit for to devyse;
> For eche of hem gan otheres lust obeye;
> Felicite, which that thise clerkes wise
> Comenden so, ne may nat here suffise.

17. See Ida L. Gordon, *The Double Sorrow of Troilus* (Oxford, 1970), pp. 78–80.
18. The line may recall the earlier apology of Pandarus for his role in preparing that night when, as he assures Troilus, "al shal ben right as thi selven liste" (3.
259); Pandarus's misreading of Troilus's intentions exposes the limitations of his
"felyng" as plainly as the present passage exposes those of the narrator's.

This joie may nat writen be with inke;
This passeth al that herte may bythynke.
[3. 1686–94]

This is the narrator's final attempt in the poem to speak of the love as such, and we may note that the stanza just quoted contains four separate declarations of the impossibility of doing so. Indeed the protestation of inadequacy is so overwhelming as almost to obscure the reference to the lovers themselves, which appears rather unclimactically in the third line of the stanza and which defines what is in fact the high point of their love, the point at which their capacity for emotional fulfillment is precisely circumscribed (and, for the moment, satisfied) by the limits of physical pleasure. It is a moment of considerable importance for later developments in the story, but its significance is all but ignored by the narrator at this point. Nothing in the poem better illustrates his "unlikely" relation to love than the remarkable disjunction between the "joie" the lovers experience here, satisfyingly commensurate with their hearts' desire, and the narrator's insistence that this same joy exceeds the heart's power to conceive. As the lovers' pleasure approaches its peak, the narrator is excluded from the sphere of their communion to the point at which his rhetoric ceases to bear any relation to their experience. While they have passed from an initial awe and uncertainty to an increasing appreciation of physical "suffisaunce," he has moved away from his initial desperate attempts to grasp some sense of their pleasure to the point at which he now celebrates a felicity that is wholly of his own imagining.

The dislocation of the narrator at this point is only the first stage of a steady distancing of all the principals in the story from one another. As I will argue in the following chapter, Troilus is essentially alone during the last two books of the poem. Pandarus's manipulative powers diminish rapidly over the course of Book 4, and Criseyde gradually and unobtrusively withdraws into an alert privacy. But this distancing only confirms an essential separateness and an uncertainty of communication which are present from the start. Like their historical and spiritual vision, the power of Chaucer's Trojans to realize one another is severely limited. The misguided idealism of Troilus, Criseyde's conscious or unconscious self-interest, and the lonely desire of Pandarus and the narrator work together to create a social climate in which disinterestedness has no place.

A pattern that expresses the failure of social relations in the poem and may provide an apt conclusion to this discussion of Criseyde and the narrator is the imagery of jewelry that recurs in Book 3. The gift of jewelry is evidently Criseyde's preferred way of expressing her good faith. She tries to allay Troilus's jealousy of Horaste by sending him a special ring (3. 885–89); in bed she exchanges engraved rings with him and pins to his shirt a brooch set with a heart-shaped ruby (1354–58). Her elaborate oath of fidelity on the following morning centers on the declaration that Troilus's image is "graven" deep within her heart (1499), as though by one of those engravers of "small seals" whom Troilus had mentioned a moment earlier and who have some use for that daylight which is so hateful to lovers (1461–62). This last image is almost certainly taken from *Ecclesiasticus*,[19] in which such engravers appear in a catalogue of artisans whose work absorbs all their attention: they work "by night as well as by day," and their work is skillful, but their absorption in it disqualifies them for the pursuit of wisdom and the exercise of political leadership.

The image of Troilus in Criseyde's heart is aptly represented by such a seal—unique and beautiful, but finally negotiable, like the brooch Troilus will give her and she will later give to Diomede. I think we may see this small, hard image at the center not only as pointing to the significance of the highly conventional dawn-song sequence amid which it is set—an intricate ritual with no permanent meaning—but also as an implicit comment on the whole elaborate enterprise that has come to fulfillment in Book 3. It provides the appropriate counterpoise to the narrator's hollow affirmation of felicity, his attempt to assign a transcendent meaning to something that by nature repudiates

19. See Robert E. Kaske, "The Aube in Chaucer's Troilus," in *Chaucer Criticism*, ed. R. J. Schoeck and Jerome Taylor, 2 vols. (Notre Dame, 1960), 2:177, and *Ecclesiasticus* 38. 28. As Kaske notes (p. 179, n. 15), Chaucer's "smale" in 1462 probably corresponds to the diminutive form of the Latin *signaculum*, "seal." Criseyde's use of the engraving image and its context seem to recall *Song of Songs* 8. 6–7, traditionally read as the words of the *sponsus*, which begins "Set me as a seal [*signaculum*] upon thine heart . . ."

transcendence. Troilus and the narrator alike have committed themselves totally to a union that, once realized in physical terms, becomes a mere *signaculum,* a material image of their hopes and ideals. It mocks the narrator's desire like Midas's golden food, and it repays Troilus's genuine devotion with a promise of fidelity that will prove as meaningless as the rings and jewelry with which the lovers have ratified it when larger forces and events—the proper concern of wise men and governors of cities—conspire to dissolve it.

[7]

Troilus Alone

With the falling away of the other characters and the increasing demoralization of the narrator in Books 4 and 5, Troilus comes at last to stand alone. This chapter will trace the major stages of Troilus's experience in the last two books of the poem. From the point at which he first responds to the prospect of losing Criseyde by rehearsing imaginatively a life and afterlife of solitary romantic pathos, he emerges into the practical world only to reveal his utter powerlessness to help or hinder Criseyde in her plan of action. But in the face of the actuality of loss he experiences an emotional and spiritual renewal and recovers his sense of that quality in his love for Criseyde that enables it to withstand loss and betrayal. The strength of feeling which this resiliency demonstrates becomes in effect the power that carries the poem's action forward to its conclusion; Troilus breaks out of the bright world of Troy and meets his fate in an atmosphere of austere heroism for which nothing in the poem's action up to this point has prepared us.

By way of introduction to a consideration of the role of Troilus in the final books of the poem, I would call attention to certain structural features of the transition from Book 3 to Book 4. Though the remainder of Book 3 stresses the happiness of Troilus in love, there is something ominous in the suddenness with which it ends. The shift from a final affirmation of the wonder wrought in Troilus by love (1800–1806) to the dismissal of Venus and the Muses at the end of Book 3 shows Chaucer rearranging material from the *Filostrato* to achieve a very different effect. Boccaccio's third chapter, corresponding to Book 3 of the *Troilus*, ends with the warning note about Fortune that begins Book 4 of the *Troilus*. The stanzas of the *Filostrato* that most nearly correspond to Chaucer's farewell to Venus, signaling the end of the lovers' joy (4. 23–24), occur only after the Trojan parliament has decided to surrender Criseyde to the Greeks.

One function of Chaucer's placement of these farewell stanzas is to remind us once more of the limitations of the narrator's point of view. By dismissing the Muses as well as the god and goddess of love, he points up the narrowness of his conception of the meaning of his poem and of his own role as the poet-servant of the servants of love. Now that the love story has reached its happy climax, he is, as it were, trying to arrest its development. The other side of this desire to leave Troilus suspended "in lust and in quiete" (1819) is the desperate forward lunge in the proem to Book 4, when the narrator, faced with the inevitable, prays to the Furies to bring the whole story, Troilus's life as well as his love, to the quickest possible conclusion.

But the gesture of dismissal here, in addition to what it tells us about the narrator, also has a thematic significance for the later books of the poem. It has the effect of making the ending of the portion of the *Troilus* that is dominated by love into an event wholly separate from the later, public events that are the ostensible cause of the lovers' sorrow. By this adjustment Chaucer points up something that has been implied at several points and that Book 4 will confirm. The love of Troilus and Criseyde has reached its emotional and physical peak; they are suspended in an equipoise from which they must inevitably descend as habit and the ebbing of passion weaken the force of their attraction to each other. It is the existence of this inevitability as something wholly independent of the external operation of Fortune that the ending of Book 3 calls to our attention, and in Book 4 we will see that the alteration of the lovers' feelings and the alteration of the circumstances that have nurtured their love proceed along intersecting but essentially separate paths.

The early portions of Book 4 describe successively a public event, Troilus's private response to that event, and an interview between Troilus and Pandarus, a sequence that is an obvious parallel to the action of Book 1. Chaucer is inviting us to compare Troilus at this crucial stage with his earlier self, and the contrast is striking. Throughout the early stages of Book 4 he shows himself incapable of spontaneous impulse. His feelings, which had earlier fallen instinctively into patterns of articulation derived from the *Roman de la Rose,* Petrarch, and Dante, seem now to have been contaminated by the lugubriousness of the narrator, whose Proem to Book 4 amounts to a total capitulation to the power of Fortune and the Furies. Like the version of Dante's tree simile already discussed,[1] the scene in which Troilus reacts in anticipation to the departure of Criseyde is a strange mixture of pathos, melodrama, and comedy. Once alone in his bedchamber,

> He rist him up, and every dore he shette
> And wyndow ek, and tho this sorwful man
> Upon his beddes syde adown hym sette,
> Ful lik a ded ymage, pale and wan;
> And in his brest the heped wo bygan
> Out breste, and he to werken in this wise
> In his woodnesse, as I shal yow devyse.
>
> [4. 232–38]

The emphasis on deliberate action in the first two lines recalls Troilus's "disposition" to break out in a rage in the tree-simile stanza, which immediately precedes this one. As he sits on the side of his bed, it is as though he were consciously gathering strength for the outburst to follow, and there is a hint of deliberation too in "werken in this wise," which seems almost to contradict the suggestion of an involuntary rush of feeling in "out breste." This hint is reinforced by the narrator's "devyse" in the last line: the verb recurs at 259, after Troilus's initial transport has run its course, and the two occurrences provide a sort of frame or label, identifying Troilus's outburst as a set piece, a grand effect, something demanding artistry to describe.[2] But set

---

1. See ch. 1, pp. 38–41; ch. 5, pp. 173–76.
2. Note the bracketing of Criseyde's lament (736–98) with "devyse" (735) and with the narrator's elaborate apology for his artistic limitations (799–805).

in the middle of the stanza is Troilus's face, with its ghastly pallor "ful like a ded ymage," and the trance into which he falls at the end of his soliloquy can hardly be deliberate.

The juxtaposition of Troilus's behavior with that of Troiolo in the equivalent scene of the *Filostrato* reveals a similar joining of contradictory effects. Troiolo is worn out by weeping to the point at which his speech is reduced to incoherent "wild cries" calling for death and condemning the gods (4. 28. 4–8). Chaucer uses this occasion to show another contradiction: when weeping has "refte" Troilus's speech (249), he can still "unnethes" utter a forceful curse, which Chaucer quotes verbatim (250–52). The comic effect is balanced by the substance of the curse, a condemnation of the day nature brought him into the world, which recalls the self-denying despair of the souls on the shores of Dante's Acheron (*Inf.* 3. 104–6).[3] But in the stanza following, we shift back to comedy, as the passing of Troilus's initial crisis is described in oddly casual terms; whereas Troiolo, still "burning in the fire of suffering," had thrown himself down on his bed without ceasing to weep (*Fil.* 4. 29. 3–5), Troilus seems ready for a nap:

> But after, whan the furie and al the rage
> Which that his herte twiste and faste threste,
> By lengthe of tyme somwhat gan aswage,
> Upon his bed he leyde hym down to reste. . . .
>   [4. 253–56]

The almost absurdly gentle effect of the last two lines rests in unresolved contradiction to the forcefulness of the first two. In his hymn at the close of Book 3 Troilus had called on God to "twist" those cold hearts unacquainted with love and make them acknowledge its value (1769–71). The verb suggests both the dominance of love and its potential violence. Here Troilus's heart is "twisted" by a fury that has made him long for death; the image and diction link his situation with that of the narrator and remind us of his utter subjection to the power of love, but without forestalling the comic effect of the two lines that follow.

---

3. The same passage is recalled more vividly by Troilus's blanket condemnation of the gods and the human condition in 5. 207–10, in a situation closely parallel to the present one.

The long soliloquy on which Troilus now embarks follows
Boccaccio closely (*Fil.* 4. 30–36), but a series of interpolations by
Chaucer enables us to see Troilus as willfully declining into the
role of the conventional abandoned lover. Where Troiolo is angry, Troilus is merely resigned, and from the outset he looks
forward to a future of unvarying misery,

> . . . in which I wol bewaille
> Criseyde, allas, til that the breth me faille.
> [4. 272–73]

From this point he passes on to imagine a merely passive state in
which he will "alwey dye, and nevere fulli sterve" (280), before
commending his soul to Criseyde (302–8, 320–22) and pro-
nouncing a sort of epitaph appealing to happy lovers to remember him, "for I loved ek, though ich unworthi were" (329).

The course of this imaginative descent to the shades is not
unbroken; at its center are two stanzas that balance remembered
happiness against present misery in terms that remind us of the
broader dimensions of Troilus's experience and the more than
conventional lover's sorrow that burdens his imaginings. In the
first he reproaches the god of love for violation of "trouthe":

> Syn ye Criseyde and me han fully brought
> Into your grace, and bothe oure hertes seled,
> How may ye suffre, allas, it be repeled?
> [4. 292–94]

In the second he views the torment of his bereavement as driv-
ing him toward a final darkness:

> Ne nevere wol I seen it shyne or reyne;
> But ende I wol, as Edippe, in derknesse
> My sorwful lif, and dyen in distresse.
> [4. 299–301]

Like the narrator's appeals to the Furies, the introduction of
Oedipus here is startling and disturbing: the grim imaginings of →
the narrator seem to have surfaced in Troilus's own imagination
and overcome his earlier lofty view of love's service. Deprived of
the light essential to his existence as a lover and convinced that

he is at the mercy of an inevitable fate, he is entering the dark world of those "that ben despeired out of loves grace."

But while it is possible to use mythography or psychology to develop a more sustained comparison between Troilus and Oedipus at this point, there is something fundamentally incongruous about the pairing. Oedipus's darkness is the result of far more than a young man's first setback in love. Troilus's comparison is not arbitrary, but it is melodramatic, and it occurs, moreover, in the course of a soliloquy whose fatalistic and increasingly funereal cast creates an impression of unique, irremediable privation that is not justified by his actual situation. In a scant hundred lines he lays out a scenario for the rest of his life, inspired by the willful assumption that the worst is inescapable. Moreover, the crisis Troilus faces exists largely in his own mind, for at this point he has failed even to consider the possibility of resisting or evading the parliament's decree. And of course, he has no idea yet of the full horror of the isolation he will know after he has been betrayed not simply by circumstance, but by the very source of the light that gives his life meaning. In view of all this, juxtaposition with Oedipus tends to diminish rather than enhance Troilus's tragic stature. His imaginings, the narrator suggests, are themselves food for sorrow (339), and it is the collaboration of sorrow with its imaginative rehearsal that reduces Troilus finally to a trance, a state that is at least partly due to genuinely overpowering feelings, but which we must see at the same time as largely of Troilus's own making.

Troilus maintains his posture throughout his interview with Pandarus, who has himself become so upset that "for wo, he nyste what he mente" (349) and who finds himself, for once, "So confus, that he nyste what to seye" when ushered into Troilus's presence. His uncharacteristic confusion and inarticulateness almost seem intended to suggest a response more plausible than Troilus's to their common sorrow. His attempt to rally Troilus's spirits only provokes more elaborate declarations of Troilus's intention to "lyve and sterve" in perfect fidelity:

> But fro my soule shal Criseydes darte
> Out nevere mo; but down with Proserpyne,
> Whan I am dede, I wol go wone in pyne;

And ther I wol eternaly compleyne
My wo, and how that twynned be we tweyne.
                [4. 472–76]

Responding to Pandarus's urging that he take action and steal
Criseyde away, Troilus reveals a capacity for logical argument
which we have not seen previously. From his opening lines there
is an odd formality about his procedure, as he demands an "audience" for the presentation of his case and promises Pandarus
equal opportunity to present his own (544–46). He then takes
up a series of possible lines of action, shows how in each case he
would run the risk of violating Criseyde's honor in some way,
and concludes with an almost syllogistic precision:

> Thus am I lost, for aught that I kan see;
> For certeyn is, syn that I am hire knyght,
> I moste hire honour levere han than me
> In every cas, as lovere ought of right.
> Thus am I with desir and reson twight. . . .
>   [4. 568–72]

Troilus immediately bursts into tears again, but his rationalizing
of his inaction and the dogmatism with which he cites courtly
values as a constraint should arouse our suspicion, as they
arouse that of Pandarus, who tells him, "Devyne nat in resoun ay
so depe, / Ne curteisly . . ." (589–90). But Troilus is unmoved by
Pandarus's increasingly vigorous appeals to his hardihood and
"corage," and the interview ends when Pandarus resolves, with
no apparent encouragement from Troilus, to confer with
Criseyde.

To an extent Troilus is simply overwhelmed by the change in
his fortunes, and we may see the recurring funereal-infernal
emphasis of his lamentings as a genuine response to greater
sorrow than he has known before. But the almost perverse fe-
cundity of these imaginings, and the way they conspire with the
new rational element in his thinking to prevent his attempting
some decisive action, suggest that at an unconscious level they
are the symptom of an alteration in the love that had previously
provided a focus for all his emotional energy. The passion that
had made him descend from idealism into carnal involvement

with Criseyde and that had reached a peak of its own in the later portions of Book 3 has now begun to ebb. The result is a failure of purpose, an irresolution, which he interprets as a constraint imposed on him by fortune.

This irresolution will be made painfully clear in Troilus's long last scene with Criseyde, in which, after a few sporadic and feeble attempts to assert himself, he will finally acquiesce in the plan that will lead directly to his betrayal. Throughout this long episode he will appear very much as "sely Troilus," the victim of his very innocence and virtue, unwavering in his commitment to values and abstractions but powerless to take action in his own behalf and so as vulnerable to the whims of fortune as he has been "subject" to love and blissful Venus throughout the poem. But before introducing the long and emotionally exhausting scene, Chaucer interpolates the famous soliloquy, based on Boethius's discussion of divine foreknowledge and human free will, which serves as a cumbersome but powerful means of expressing in absolute terms Troilus's sense of helplessness.

In the *Consolation,* the prisoner's struggle to deal with the problems of "fixed fate, free will, foreknowledge absolute" is his last attempt to sustain his side of his dialogue with Lady Philosophy. He ends by denying the efficacy of hope, prayer, or virtuous behavior in a world where all is predetermined, and the poem that follows expresses his exasperation with the limits of human knowledge. For Boethius this crisis seems to mark the point at which philosophy begins to require the support of something like religious faith; the arguments with which Lady Philosophy seeks to extend the prisoner's understanding of providence and of the timeless vision of God climax in a series of affirmations which, though beautiful and compelling, elicit no rational response from the prisoner.

For Chaucer, too, the subject of the long speech seems to be a test of the limits of philosophy and, more significantly, a test of the adequacy of pagan "faith" to sustain itself amid the constraints of ignorance and the many temptations to fatalism. But he has also adapted the speech carefully to Troilus's situation. The Troilus who could affirm his sense of divine love with such intensity when the impulse to do so was reinforced by love of a more immediate kind has now been betrayed by that lesser love and subjected to the necessity that governs his own physical and emotional nature. This loss of intensity is paralleled by the "descent" from vision to philosophical argument. The descent is appropriate psychologically as well as symbolically, for Troilus has his own emotional reasons for denying the freedom of his actions. What constitutes a serious rational dilemma for Boethius's prisoner is for Troilus largely the construct of his own self-defeating powers of rationalization.

Thus once again, as at so many points in Book 4, we must recognize Troilus's seriousness in this speech and at the same time keep our distance from it. The setting, a temple in which he invokes the gods while being stalked unawares by Pandarus, suggests both the essential purity of his response to his Boethian predicament and his vulnerability in the absence of a sustaining Lady Philosophy, his liability to succumb to the weakness of his own affirmative powers and the persuasiveness of his worldly friends. We must surely accept as genuine the conviction with which he appeals to the "pitous goddes"

> To doon hym sone out of this world to pace;
> For wel he thoughte ther was non other grace.
>
> [4. 951–52]

But the stanza following, which introduces the soliloquy, undercuts the force of these lines somewhat by reminding us of the rationalizing element in Troilus's outlook:

> He was so fallen in despeir that day,
> That outrely he shop hym for to deye.
> For right thus was his argument alway:
> He seyde he nas but lorn, weylaway!
> "For al that comth, comth by necessitee;
> Thus to be lorn, it is my destinee."
>
> [4. 954–59]

From the despair of the first line we pass to determination ("shop") and an increasingly intrusive sense of "argument" to the point at which we begin to hear Troilus's own voice actively engaged in *proving* the helplessness of his situation. And the emphasis on argumentation, the very fact of Troilus's ability to "dispute" with himself in the midst of his "heaviness" (1083–84), is as much to the point as the sense of helplessness the speech reveals. Unlike Boethius's prisoner, Troilus does not pursue his argument to the point of denying the value of hope and prayer. He begins and ends by appealing to the gods, and the contradiction between this gesture and the burden of his argument makes it plain that he has not engaged at a profound level the problem with which he professes to deal. The causes of Troilus's dilemma are more psychological than circumstantial, and the force of his argument is largely an unconscious response to the need to fill an emotional void.[4] Its validity as a characterization of his situation is further weakened by the fact that Pandarus, entering at its conclusion, immediately and almost effortlessly argues Troilus out of his inactivity (1114–22) and sends him off to commiserate with Criseyde.

The interview that follows is obviously painful for all concerned, but here, too, comedy intrudes, first and most strikingly with Troilus's elaborate reaction to Criseyde's swoon at the outset. Chaucer devotes four stanzas to the sequence of calling her name, probing for signs of life, discovering that she is dead, lamenting her death, and laying out her body. Each gesture is repeated two or three times, and they follow one another in rapid succession like the expressions of alarm, confusion, and chagrin in an early silent movie. Then four stanzas are given to Troilus's desperate resolve and the final speech, delivered with sword in hand, in which he prepares to join Criseyde in death. The speech itself follows Boccaccio closely and is not inherently comic, but the effect of its placement at the end of the elaborate pantomime of Troilus's response to Criseyde's apparent death is to make it seem no more than a further piece of posturing. As such it helps to prepare the wonderful moment that instantly dispels any lingering hint of seriousness in the scene: Troilus, his sword pressed against his heart, is about to commend his spirit to Criseyde, when she, "as god wolde," stirs, sighs, calls his name,

4. On the un-Boethian character of the soliloquy as a whole, see F. Anne Payne, *Chaucer and Menippean Satire* (Madison, Wis., 1981), pp. 125–33. Her argument, however, goes too far in its stress on this aspect.

And he answered: 'lady my Criseyde,
Lyve ye yit?' and leet his swerd down glide.
[4. 1214–15]

When Criseyde is once again sufficiently her alert self so that
her eye strays aside and discovers Troilus's naked sword, the
discovery leads to the delicious shared pleasure of reflecting on
their near brush with death and the greatness of soul that each
would have displayed had it been necessary. Criseyde is so far
carried away as to imagine committing suicide with this very
sword (1240–41), but then, as if recognizing that this was an
overindulgence ("hoo for we han right ynough of this," 1242),
she recalls their present commitment to love and its problems
with a rather disconcerting abruptness:

And lat us rise and streight to bedde go,
And there lat us speken of oure wo.
[1243–44]

In the rest of the scene most of the speaking is Criseyde's;
Troilus listens to her increasingly confident presentation of her
plan of action "with herte and erys spradde" like a faithful dog
(1422) and puts down his own misgivings by resolving to trust
her in any event.

Troilus's trust and Criseyde's course of action carry forward
unbroken into Book 5, but whereas Troilus has appeared almost
foolishly pathetic in the scene just discussed, Criseyde's actual
departure has a gradual but significant effect on him. Confined
within a city that has become a monument to lost love, Troilus
experiences the actuality of loss, which parallels, at a far more
intense level, the sense of betrayal he had felt in the early scenes
of Book 4. There is nothing staged about the fury to which he
gives vent after returning from his embassy, and it is the narrator, rather than Troilus himself, who articulates the "infernal"
element in his ravings (205–12). The nightmares of abandonment which Boccaccio's Troiolo describes to Pandaro (5. 26–27)
are here reported objectively, and Chaucer alters his version so
that the violent bodily quakes and tremors and the sense of

falling from a great height which came over Troiolo in his
dreams become part of Troilus's actual waking experience (253–
59). When he announces his impending death to Pandarus and
issues detailed instructions for his funeral and the disposition of
his effects, though the gesture in itself remains absurd, the precise and literal emphasis gives an impression of conviction which
had been lacking in the death speeches of Book 4.

The power of Troilus's feelings, his conviction that Criseyde's
return is a matter of life and death to him, and his obsessive
need to dwell on her loss come increasingly to govern the movement of this section of the poem. The narrator confesses himself
exhausted by the very thought of Troilus's emotion (270–74).
Even Pandarus is overwhelmed by a "folye" of such force and
can only reflect that

> . . . whoso wol nat trowen red ne loore,
> I kan nat sen in hym no remedie;
> But lat hym worthen with his fantasie.
>
> [4. 327–29]

With no further reason to manipulate Troilus's feelings, Pandarus can only seek to distract him from them, arguing at length
against his preoccupation with his dreams and drawing him for
the first time into society. But Troilus spends his week at the
house of Sarpedon in a "maze" (468), thinking only of Criseyde
when in company and imagining her present when alone.

More important than the dominating influence of Troilus's
obsession in itself is the revival of his power to give expression to
the love that lies behind it. The melodramatic rhetoric of despair
that had predominated in Book 4 is now replaced by something
like the innocent idealism of the earlier books as Troilus, in the
course of expressing his sense of bereavement, affirms the
meaning of what he has lost. The first significant expression of
this renewal of vision appears in the two-stanza apostrophe to
Criseyde's abandoned house (540–53), which in most respects
presents his situation in a highly ironic light. In this passage the
sense of desolation seems at first overwhelming, and the passage
is further burdened by the heavy irony of the sexual implications of his images. The house itself, a finite, material place, is a

monument to the limitations imposed on the lovers by the limited vision of Pandarus, the "architect" of their relationship (1.
1062–71). The lantern to which it is compared is a common
image for chastity, and the irony of the fact that its light is
"queynt" is reinforced by the probably punning significance of
that word. Its characterization as a ring "fro which the ruby is
out falle" recalls Pandarus's use of this image with unmistakable
sexual innuendo in commending the idea of love to Criseyde (3.
585).[5] The first stanza, moreover, is pervaded by the sense of
finality: the light is "queynt"; day has turned to night; the house
is "desolat," "empty," and "disconsolat":

> Wel oughtestow to falle, and I to dye,
> Syn she is went that wont was us to gye!
>
> [5. 545–56]

But in the second stanza, though its tone remains elegiac and
the sense of loss prevails, the language of idealization is beginning to work more actively:

> "O paleis, whilom crowne of houses alle,
> Enlumyned with sonne of alle blisse,
> O ryng, fro which the ruby is out falle,
> O cause of wo, that cause hast ben of lisse,
> Yit, syn I may no bet, fayn wolde I kisse
> Thi colde dores, dorste I for this route;
> And farewel, shryne of which the seynt is oute!"
>
> [5. 547–53]

Here the unconscious sexual emphasis of the previous stanza is
joined with reminders of Troilus's spiritual blindness, culminat-

---

5. On the interplay of sexual and religious meanings in the passage as a whole
see Ida L. Gordon, *The Double Sorrow of Troilus* (Oxford, 1970), pp. 132–38, and
John F. Adams, "Irony in Troilus' Apostrophe to the Vacant House of
Criseyde," *Modern Language Quarterly* 24 (1963):61–65. Gordon's general re-
marks on the passage (p. 138) rightly emphasize the sincerity of Troilus, but like
Adams, she dwells on the irony of his blindness to the sexual significance of his
language in a way that seems to me largely beside the point. Sensible criticisms of
Adams's reading are offered by William Frost, "A Chaucerian Crux," *Yale Review*
66 (1976–77):551–61; Morton Bloomfield, "Troilus' Paraclausythron and Its
Setting," *Neuphilologische Mitteilungen* 73 (1972):23–24.

ing in the bizarre idolatry of the shrine that has been literally abandoned by its mortal saint. And the abortive gesture of affirmation, the kiss Troilus would bestow upon the doors, "dorste I for this route," sums up all the pathetic futility of his attempts to deal with Criseyde's removal. But in this deeply ironic context a line like "Enlumyned with sonne of alle blisse" still glows with the pure devotion of the early stages of Troilus's love. He has known what he has known, and the passage reminds us that his faith in that early vision remains undiminished. When both Pandarus and the narrator have been reduced nearly to silence by their premonitions (468–69, 505–8), Troilus continues to be borne up by the sustaining power of memory, and it is this that comes strongly to the fore in the stanzas that follow his address to the empty palace. Though he immediately succumbs again to the pain of his loss, growing deadly pale and speaking with difficulty, the apostrophe has set in motion a process of recollection, and as he continues to ride through the city, reviewing "his newe sorwe and ek his joies olde" (558), the emphasis on remembered joy becomes steadily greater. He recalls his first sight of Criseyde, her words to him in an affectionate moment, her playfulness and, finally, the place where "my lady first me took unto hire grace" (580–81). As the Black Knight in Chaucer's *Book of the Duchess* is drawn out of a near-fatal lethargy and his spirit renewed by the compulsion to rehearse the history of his love, so Troilus dwells on the memory of Criseyde's voice and manner until they have become so real that he can take pleasure in them undisturbed by the thought of their absence:

> "And at that corner, in the yonder hous,
> Herde I myn alderlevest lady deere
> So wommanly, with vois melodious,
> Syngen so wel, so goodly, and so cleere,
> That in my soule yit me thynketh ich here
> The blisful sown. . . ."
>
> [5. 575–80]

The passage shows us more than the resurgence of Troilus's idealism, of course; it shows us also how utterly vulnerable he still is to "hire mevynge and hire chere," the poise and discreet coquetry with which Criseyde had conquered him in Book 1 (288– 94). It shows us to how great an extent he has been isolated by his fascination with these graces, how they have bred in him a wholly private conception of love with no clear relation to external reality, the character of Criseyde, or even sexual desire. But in the very process of exposing the disorientation of "sely Troilus," the passage points up once again the innocence and reverence that make his love unique and important. Nobody but Troilus himself could intuit the "entente" with which he addresses Cupid in the prayer that follows;[6] when he tells the god "thow woost wel I desire/Thi grace moost of alle lustes leeve" (591–92), he is clearly appealing for a grace that involves the sexual, but involves it only as part of a larger religion of love, the "byleve" in which Troilus is irrevocably bound to live and die (593).

What Troilus wants most of all is a reconfirmation of the meaning he has sensed in love, but what he is actually given is a growing understanding of the terms on which love has been granted. His prayer begins with a beautiful intuition of the uniqueness of his experience, which expresses both his suffering and his dedication:

> "O blisful lord Cupide,
> Whan I the proces have in my memorie;
> How thow me hast werreyed on every syde,
> Men myghte a book make of it, like a storie."
> [5. 583–85]

The oddly moving quality of these lines derives not only from the weary lover's capacity still to claim a meaning for the experience that has defeated him, to rise to the dignity of affirming it as his destiny, but also from the dawning awareness that this destiny has been lived through, that the end is near. In the prayer's final lines he hints at this end. Shifting abruptly from thoughts of his private need, he appeals to the god to withhold from Troy the cruelty that Juno had visited on Thebes, and with

---

6. Chaucer may be pointing to this incommunicability when he tells us that lines 582–602 are "thought" by Troilus (582), meaning perhaps that they are not actually spoken and are hence inaccessible to Pandarus.

this gesture he acknowledges at least the possibility that Troy
and his love are doomed. His acknowledgment is tentative and
highly subjective, for he is no more ready to accept the implication that Criseyde's absence is part of an inevitable course of
events than he will be at a later point to admit the validity of
Cassandre's reading of his dream of the boar. But in spite of his
resistance, his imagination is moving toward the intuition of a
pattern in the events that have affected his love, and he is becoming prepared inwardly for the shock of the discovery of
Criseyde's infidelity.

Troilus withstands this dawning knowledge as best he can. He
still has in reserve the desperate energy of his last direct address
to Criseyde, the letter that reaffirms her role as one uniquely
empowered to save or condemn him; and in the aftermath of his
interview with Cassandre there is a point at which he actually
seems ready to defy the omens that point to his betrayal. Having
cited Alceste in rebuttal of Cassandre's reading of his dream, he
seems for a moment to draw inspiration from her exemplary
spiritual courage:

> Cassandre goth; and he with cruel herte
> Foryat his wo, for angre of hire speche;
> And from his bed al sodeynly he sterte,
> As though al hool hym hadde made a leche.
> And day by day he gan enquere and seche
> A sooth of this, with al his fulle cure. . . .
>
> [5. 1534–39]

There is no precedent in Troilus's experience for the sort of
healing anger to which he responds in these lines. It is tempting
to see his sudden recovery of both health and purpose as a
reintegration of physical and spiritual virtue like that which em-
powers Hercules to pursue Alceste in the face of death. For the
first time, it seems, he is prepared to *act* in response to what he
sees as his fate, to embrace his destiny like a tragic hero.

But the potential significance of this moment of renewal and
seeming reorientation is never realized, and despite Troilus's
initial zeal, his pursuit of truth is curiously unproductive. His
only real action in the course of the next hundred lines is to

write again and again to Criseyde, and his letters are not demands for information but "pitous" appeals for her return. Far
from pursuing knowledge, he makes excuses for Criseyde's absence and goes against his own instincts by refusing to question
the motives of the letter she eventually sends him. The righteous
wrath in which he resolves to seek out the evidence that will
vindicate Criseyde, and in which he appears for a moment the
embodiment of heroic virtue, proves inadequate to overcome his
underlying fear that she cannot be vindicated.

In bringing Troilus's virtue briefly into focus by these elaborate means, only to show it issuing in failure, Chaucer is presenting something comparable, though on a smaller scale, to the
elaborate parody of Dante's *Commedia* at the center of Book 3. As
this had enabled him to balance the intense Dantean vision of
Troilus against the ironies of the dawn-song sequence and the
grotesque parody of Criseyde's morning interview with Pandarus, so the sudden rise and decline of Troilus's heroic virtue
here contrasts the idealism that inspires that virtue with the
reality that betrays it. The real Criseyde is neither a Beatrice nor
an Alceste: the Criseyde Troilus believes in, the quasi-divine
being he invokes as uniquely empowered to save or damn him,
and the woman in defense of whose honor he is here miraculously restored to life exists now entirely in his imagination and
must coexist even there with the suspicion that there is no real
being capable of adequately reciprocating his devotion or justi-
fying his willingness to die on her behalf. Hence, rather than
resulting in heroic action, his virtuous impulses are suspended
by a wholly internal conflict—a need to know the truth and a
terror of discovering it. There can be no positive resolution to
such a crisis. Only after he has irrefutable evidence of his betrayal in the form of his own brooch affixed to Diomede's armor
does he embark upon the final heroic action that leads to his
death at the hands of Achilles. At this point his heroism has
nothing left to affirm; he is powerless to "unlove" Criseyde
(1696–98) or even to wish her ill, and so can never quite abandon himself to that furor to which even Vergil's Aeneas finally
succumbs. Boccaccio's Troiolo had looked forward to vanquish-
ing Diomede as a way of causing pain to Criseida (*Fil.* 8. 16) and
had even called on the heavens to do away with Criseida herself

(8. 18); but Troilus, while eager to meet with Diomede, cannot entertain toward him anything like Troiolo's bloody thoughts (8. 21) and relinquishes to God the office of doing "vengeaunce of this vice" (1708). The necessary condition for Troilus's final display of courage is not madness or hatred, but despair; and the only motive for his "wrath" is the desire to achieve his own death.

Thus it is that in the final stanza of his final speech Troilus makes his one really self-assertive gesture. For the first time in the poem he prepares himself to act on the basis of sure knowledge and toward a definite end:

> "And certeynly, withoute moore speche,
> From hennesforth, as ferforth as I may,
> Myn owen deth in armes wol I seche;
> I recche nat how soone be the day. . . ."
>
> [5. 1716–19]

Even here, however, Troilus spends two lines clearing his throat before coming out with his fatal vow, and even then the vow is followed by a final backward glance:

> "But trewely, Criseyde, swete may,
> Whom I have ay with al my myght yserved,
> That ye thus doon, I have it nat deserved."
>
> [5. 1720–22]

And this wistful note will sound again as the poem moves haltingly toward its conclusion. For Troilus's are only the first in a series of "last words."

After a brief final speech by Pandarus, the narrator steps in to offer a moral that seems at first to have something of the ironic finality of Cassandre's "Wepe if thow wolt, or lef":

> Criseyde loveth the sone of Tideus;
> And Troilus moot wepe in cares colde.
> Swich is this world, whoso it kan byholde;
> In ech estat is litel hertes reste. . . .
>
> [5. 1746–49]

The note of finality in these lines is deceptive, for the narrative resumes immediately, but the lines do mark a stage in the complex articulation of the final phase of Troilus's experience. At this point the love story as such is over, and the remainder of the poem will dramatize the narrator's attempt to bring it to a decorous conclusion.

After two stanzas that show Troilus pursuing Diomede in vain across the battlefield, the narrator steps in to call attention to the new departure that Troilus's rage represents:

> And if I hadde ytaken for to write
> The armes of this ilke worthi man,
> Than wolde ich of his batailles endite.
> But for that I to writen first bigan
> Of his love, I have seyd as I kan. . . .
>   [5. 1765–69]

The fifth line of this stanza, surely as weak and halting a line as Chaucer ever wrote, tells its own story. The narrator's farewell to Venus and the Muses at the end of Book 3 had marked a turning point in his attitude toward his story, and now, after the long, slow decline of the love affair has finally ended, this line represents the exhaustion, the last gasp of the narrator's original inspiration. The energy that moves the poem forward beyond this point is Troilus's desire to compensate his loss on the battlefield. As Troilus breaks through the various rhetorical barriers by which the narrator attempts to impose a formal closure on this story, the narrator is forced to come to terms with his urgent demand for fulfillment and with a growing awareness that he himself has also been left unfulfilled by his experience of Troilus's woe, weal, and loss of joy.

[8]

The Ending of the *Troilus*

I have suggested that it is Troilus whose unfulfilled passion impels the narrator and his story forward in the closing portion of the poem. But perhaps it would be equally appropriate to say that he is guided by providence. I began this essay by comparing the enterprise of the final stanzas to that of Chaucer's *House of Fame*, and at first sight the situation of the *Troilus* narrator at this stage may well seem as hopelessly confused as that of the dreamer in the earlier poem. But his outward confusion is strangely combined with an underlying purpose that, though it is at this point wholly subliminal and is never ratified by any such vivid sign as the Jovian eagle of the *House of Fame*, is far surer in its orientation than the quest of the dreamer. I would like to begin tracing the *Troilus* narrator's providential journey by considering the four stanzas that constitute his first attempt to conclude his poem, a passage that begins with his appeal to "every lady bright of hewe" (5. 1772) and ends with his prayer that his book be understood. Throughout these stanzas he is utterly at sea regarding his own intention in the *Troilus* and yet somehow undergoes a significant transformation that leaves him with a new appreciation of the role and capacities of poetry. Though he seems utterly at the mercy of the cumulative effect of his long-standing delusions, there is in fact no moment in the poem at which he is closer to Dante and the poets of the past. To understand the conclusion of the *Troilus* it is necessary first of all to recognize the effect of the providential instinct that guides the narrator through this crucial transition.

The stanzas in which the narrator seeks to cap the narrative with a moral capable of satisfying both the male and the female portion of his courtly audience show him characteristically evading responsibility for the implications of his story. Other books have told of Criseyde's infidelity (1776), and for his part the narrator finds the falseness of men a more serious issue. With a certain amount of spluttering he manages to convince himself that an appropriate moral for the poem is "Beth war of men," then quickly dismisses the problem by formally offering his completed book to the world. But his ostensible *envoi* brings us not to the end of the poem, but to the threshold of a complete reevaluation of the story of Troilus and his relation to it:

> Go litel book, go litel myn tragedye,
> Ther god thi makere yit, or that he dye,
> So sende mught to make in som comedye!
> [5. 1786–88]

The opposition of tragedy to comedy here is often explained as a balancing of the *Troilus*, now almost complete, against the *Canterbury Tales*, but when these lines are read as part of the conclusion as a whole, they may be seen not as pointing forward to a work still to come, but as referring to the precarious generic status of the *Troilus* itself at this crucial stage in its narrative unfolding.[1] Though the story of Troilus's double sorrow has run its course, his life is not yet complete, and the narrator's discovery of the meaning of "lyf and love yfeere" is only beginning.

In the course of rising to a new awareness of the meaning of his poem, the narrator becomes aware of the relation of his work to that of earlier poets, and, at the same time, of its separate status as a product of his own place, time, and language:

---

1. For the view that the lines look forward to the *Tales*, see Donald Howard, *The Idea of the Canterbury Tales* (Berkeley, 1976), pp. 30–36, 75. The alternative view is discussed by Anne Middleton, "Chaucer's 'New Men' and the Good of Literature in the *Canterbury Tales*," in *Literature and Society*, ed. Edward W. Said, Selected Papers from the English Institute, n.s. 3 (Baltimore, Md., 1980), p. 35.

> But, litel book, no makyng thow nenvie,
> But subgit be to alle poesie;
> And kis the steppes, where as thow seest space
> Virgile, Ovide, Omer, Lucan, and Stace.
>
> [1789–92]

The first stage of this process is the subordination of the narrator's sense of himself as a "maker" to the recognition of his more significant role as a participant in the continuum of poetic experience and poetic tradition. Whether we take "maker" as meaning simply "craftsman," the practitioner of an art, or understand it in a more specific sense as denoting one who writes love verse to the specifications of a courtly audience, Chaucer clearly intends to set this function in contrast to the larger responsibilities of one who would follow the *poetae*.[2] After the insistent repetition of "makere," "make" and "makyng" in 1787–89, the word "poesie" is introduced into the poem for the first time in 1790. Now, also for the first time, references to the tyrannizing book of "myn auctor" and the chimerical Lollius are replaced by the naming of real poets. In bidding his book revere these poets, Chaucer echoes Statius's admonition to his own poem to follow reverently in the footsteps of Vergil (*Theb.* 12. 816–17), and so proclaims both his affinity with Statius and his tentative claim to a place in the canon.

With this gesture, the narrator rids himself once and for all of the "disese" that had led him at a number of points in the story to deny his responsibility for his handling of the love story and that has appeared again in his attempt to explain away the moral implications of his treatment of Criseyde. To pass from "making" to "poesie" means in effect passing from the service of the god of love and a concern with the rhetoric of "sentement" and "loves art" to a concern with universal values and a recognition of the authority of poetic tradition as a repository of these values.[3] Though the narrator's emphasis is clearly on his "subject" status, and he never claims for himself the name of poet, his new

---

2. See above, Introduction, notes 1 and 3.

3. On tradition as "the preserved record of what is constantly meaningful to all men in all times and places," see Robert O. Payne, *The Key of Remembrance* (New Haven, Conn., 1963), p. 84.

position is very different from the hapless subservience in which, overwhelmed by the sorrows of love, he had abandoned himself to the pagan, tragic view of his material earlier in the poem.

In the context of this new departure, the use of the term "poesie" is highly suggestive. Unlike "poetrie," used of "olde clerkes speche" in 1855, "poesie" occurs nowhere else in Chaucer. In using it to make this crucial transition, he may be recalling Dante's sole use of *poesì*, in the opening lines of the *Purgatorio:*

> Ma qui la morta poesì resurga,
>   o sante Muse, poi che vostro sono . . .

> But here let dead poetry rise again, O holy Muses, since I am yours . . . [Purg. 1. 7–8]

Both poets invoke "poesie" as part of a gesture of self-dedication, and for both, its appearance marks the recovery of vital contact with the classical tradition.[4]

But while the discovery of an allegiance to "poesie" is clearly of the utmost importance, it is harder to determine how sure the narrator feels about it. His naming of his *auctores* implies an emerging sense of his own identity, but the literalism with which he bids his book "kis the steppes" where the poets have walked suggests a lingering sense of his own slightly comic ineptitude in comparison with the great masters. In the stanza following, in which he accepts at last the fact of his own responsibility for the language of his poem, his assertion of autonomy is balanced by an anxiety about the ability of his words to survive the process of oral and written transmission—thoughts that are very far from the concluding reflections of Statius and Ovid on the enduring power of art.

Nevertheless, when the narrator discovers simultaneously

---

4. The rhyme scheme of the "poesie" stanza is also unique in the *Troilus* and suggests a further evocation of Dante. A single rhyme is sustained through five lines, and the sequence of "tragedye," "comedye," and "poesie" stands out with the effect of Dante's *terza rima*.

both the nature of his literary indebtedness and the final independence of his own poem, he holds the key to liberation from his inhibiting emotional involvement with the story of Troilus. We can reconcile the significance of the change he is undergoing with his evident uncertainty about it by comparing his experience to that which Dante dramatizes in the later stages of the *Purgatorio*. In both cases we must recognize the peculiarly "poetic" nature of this experience; it can be communicated only through poetry and largely by way of one poet's insights into the work of another.

The symbol of this process is Dante's Statius, and its nature is indicated by Dante's emphasis on the wholly intuitive character of the knowledge vouchsafed to Statius in the course of his transformation from pagan poet to purified Christian soul. The catalyst of his experience of conversion was the language of Vergil, which, by a process compounded of partial misreading and half-conscious translation, came gradually to seem to him "consonant" with the doctrines being proclaimed by Christian preachers (*Purg.* 22. 37–42, 67–81). We cannot analyze this process, nor can we point to clear indications of Statius's further spiritual evolution during the period when his crypto-Christianity was concealed, as he tells us, by an outward paganism (*Purg.* 22. 91).

In Purgatory Statius's knowledge remains wholly intuitive. His account of the unchanging climate of the upper reaches of the mountain of Purgatory is not an explanation, for the phenomenon he is describing cannot be explained in natural terms. There is no alteration here, yet there is change; there is no natural cause for the trembling of the mountain, yet it trembles (*Purg.* 21. 43–45, 55–60). Statius candidly confesses his inability to explain these phenomena, and his bafflement is in keeping with his own experience: for the process of purgation from which Statius has just emerged and which concludes with the shaking of the mountain is imperceptible even by those who undergo it, its only confirmation consisting in the sudden "surprising" of the soul by the newly liberated will (61–63).

By emphasizing the intuitive element in Statius's newfound knowledge and by representing this knowledge as the fulfillment of insights first expressed in Statius's own poem, Dante is calling attention to the special importance of poetry as the medium of Statius's experience. Statius claims that his poetic and religious lives had diverged and that he had maintained an outward paganism and continued to write classical poetry long after receiving Christian baptism (22. 88–91). But this very poetry remains the sole documentary basis for Dante's account of his career, and by his allusive use of Statius's own poems, Dante reminds us that we, too, are almost wholly dependent on intuition in our attempts to gauge the spiritual significance of a poetic text. Any Christian interpretation of Statius must be a matter of intuition, for no single detail of his poetry will yield a clear and unmistakable Christian meaning. The kind of reading needed to bring the *Thebaid* into line with Dante's spiritual biography of its poet is close to the kind of reading that Dante credits Statius with having applied to the poetry of Vergil (*Purg.* 22. 64–73). It depends on our giving a privileged significance to elements in the poetic text that may well have had an altogether different value for the poet himself. By inventing a spiritual-historical context for Statius's own poetic activity and for his revisionist reading of Vergil, Dante is establishing him as an important intermediary between the classical and Christian worlds, between imaginative and spiritual experience, between the great poetry of the ancient world and the poetry of Dante himself.

But if we cannot locate Statius's conversion in time or define it in precise psychological terms, we can see the symptoms of it already in the *Thebaid*. Its most striking foreshadowing, as I have already suggested, is the account of the conversion of Menoeceus, which becomes the basis for Statius's discourse on the soul in Purgatorio 25.[5] In delegating Statius to trace the development of human life from the origin of the natural embryo to its consummation in the soul, Dante is pointing to the presence of a kind of "embryonic" spirituality in the *Thebaid* itself: Statius's intuition of the inner experience of Menoeceus becomes the germ of his own liberation from the psychological chaos of Thebes. Poetry, it would seem, can mean more than it knows, and by inventing the conversion of Statius, Dante is

5. See above, chapter 4, pp. 138–40.

positing a mode of uniquely *poetic* experience, an interaction of literary sensibility and spirituality as impervious to analysis as the image of the transformation of sunlight into wine which climaxes Statius's discourse (*Purg.* 25. 76–78).

One of Dante's boldest acts of invention thus becomes the vehicle of one of his most serious explorations of the capacities of poetry. What the apotheosis of Menoeceus comes to represent in the spiritual career of Statius as "invented" by Dante is what this same act of invention represents for Dante himself. Statius's conversion is finally most important as a symbolic prefiguration of Dante's own growth to spiritual maturity through poetry, a growth that will be illustrated in his encounters with Bonagiunta da Lucca and other poets in the later cantos of the *Purgatorio*. Thus by a series of engagements in which poetic and spiritual experience are indistinguishable, Menoeceus's encounter with Virtus in the *Thebaid* leads directly to that moment in the *Purgatorio* in which Dante will discover himself capable of explaining the inspiration of his own poetry as a response to the in-breathing of divine love:

> "I' mi son un che, quando
> Amor mi spira, noto, e a quel modo
> ch'e' ditta dentro vo significando."

> "I am one who, when Love inspires me, takes note, and goes setting it forth after the fashion which he dictates within me." [*Purg.* 24. 52–54]

This creative process is hardly less mysterious than the infusion of the human soul which Statius will describe in the same imaginative terms in the following canto:

> lo motor primo a lui si volge lieto
> sovra tant' arte di natura, e spira
> spirito novo, di vertù repleto. . . .

> The first Mover turns to [the fully formed foetus] with joy over such art of nature, and breathes into it a new spirit replete with virtue. . . . [*Purg.* 25. 70–72]

In both of these moments of insight there is something essential that defies analysis. We cannot *see* the unfolding of the process that brings about Dante's self-discovery or the animation of the human embryo. In both cases, in Dante's terms, we are *surprised*—as we are surprised by the apotheosis of Menoeceus; as we are surprised by the appearance of Statius in Purgatory and his retrospective unveiling of a history that had been invisible in his own poetry; as the soul is surprised by the sudden liberation of the purified will. And it is as a surprise of the same order that Chaucer's narrator will realize the power to resolve his poem in a new way, such that its completion leads, as in the case of Statius's treatment of Menoeceus, to the discovery of spiritual meaning.

In simplest terms, the narrator of the final dozen stanzas of the *Troilus* bears the same relation to the narrator of the poem up to that point that Dante's Statius bears to the Statius of the *Thebaid*. But Chaucer goes even further than Dante in emphasizing the narrator's subservience to tradition and his inability to appreciate what is happening to him. When he bids farewell to his "litel book," he is clearly unaware that he is soon to gain a new perspective on his story and break free once and for all from his acquiescence in its tragic message. When he "subjects" his poem to poetic tradition, it is hard to find any trace of Dante's implicit confidence in his own power to rival the great poets of antiquity and go beyond them into new areas of experience. Even the lines that urge respect for the poem's language are primarily an expression of anxiety: though they stand in significant contrast to the narrator's earlier disclaimers, their main concern is with the dangers of misconstruction to which the linguistic enterprise of the *Troilus* had rendered him liable. Certainly there is no hint of anything like Dante's pride in his refinement of the mother tongue. If the process through which Dante achieves poetic self-awareness in Purgatory is left obscure, its equivalent in the case of Chaucer's narrator seems to be an impulse that never becomes fully conscious. The intuitive sympathy that had made possible Statius's appropriation of Vergil and Dante's Christianizing of Statius is here reduced to a subliminal instinct, which carries the poet forward almost in spite of himself.

We may begin to understand the contradiction between the narrator's lack of awareness and the poetic purpose being enacted through him if we compare with his situation the circumstances under which "poesie" had first exerted its influence on his great predecessors. Dante at the opening of the *Commedia* is lost in the absence of Beatrice, beset by moral and spiritual doubts to the point that he has been turned back upon himself when he encounters the shade of Vergil, who becomes his guide. Statius, too, tells us that he would have died in pagan blindness and excess if Vergil's words had not shown him his error. In both cases the stabilizing influence of poetic tradition manifests itself at a time when the beneficiary is incapable of self-determination. From the beginning, then, the capacity for "poesie," though it assumes a deep love and respect for ancient poetry, is from the poet's point of view largely fortuitous, a matter of "lucky words," and it comes only gradually to exercise its formative influence on the poet's conscious will.

Again and again in the course of the *Troilus* we have seen the narrator in the position of abandoning all self-awareness in favor of his idolatrous and desperate attachment to his love story, and his futile attempt to conclude the story reflects the implications of this attachment. He is seeking to cut it off at the point at which it threatens to outgrow his sentimental notion of tragedy and challenge him with moral and spiritual questions he feels unable to resolve. So Dante had foundered in *pietà* when confronted with Paolo and Francesca, and so Statius had turned away from the larger concerns of the *Thebaid* and ended his poem by joining in the general lament over the dead. In their several ways all three poets show themselves irresolute in facing the implications of their themes, and it is only the shaping power of "poesie" that renders these themes in a form sufficiently definitive that maturer vision can discern their full significance. We sense, as the Pilgrim of *Inferno* 5 cannot, the importance of his lurking awareness that Paolo and Francesca come forth from the company "where Dido is." We can see ahead, as the historical Statius could not, to the completion of his insight into the death of Menoeceus in his account of the birth of the soul in *Purgatorio* 25. The Dante who conceived the Francesca episode, deeply conditioned by Vergil's account of Dido's fatal passion, reveals that conditioning by inventing a story of fatal passion which inevitably refers us to Dido as its archetype. In the *Purgatorio*, Dante, reading Statius from his own Christian vantage point, revises the *Thebaid* in a way that brings out a potential significance of Statius's poetic rendering of spiritual experience. In both situations, poetry, conceived as a means of giving stable and enduring form to the most serious human experiences, is the essential source of continuity, making possible the creation of new poetry that develops the intuitions of the old, while at the same time ensuring the essential conformity of the new to what is universal in the old.

To be a poet, then, is to participate in a continuum of imaginative experience which transmits the essential truths of human life from one generation to another. The "truth" of poetry consists in its fidelity to its own tradition and its capacity to reveal new meaning in the light of evolving historical and spiritual perspectives on that tradition. It is in terms of such a view of poetry that we must understand the experience of Chaucer's narrator. In reducing him to a virtually unconscious collaborator in the discovery of his true poetic vocation Chaucer is not simply exhibiting his characteristic humility. His purpose is to show by this comic means just how far it is possible to proceed in the direction of spiritual enlightenment under the influence of the "olde clerkes." In the absence of any conscious application of craft or knowledge on the part of the narrator, it is "poesie" itself, the normative influence of poetic tradition, that guides his hand, enabling him to complete his artistic task and give full expression to the implications of Troilus's experience.

The first confirmation of the narrator's new vocation appears in the four stanzas that describe Troilus's death and posthumous vision. With the rendering of the "epic" aspect of Troilus's experience—his final show of valor, death in battle, and ascent to the eighth sphere—the formal and moral demands of "poesie" in its classical aspect will be satisfied. In bringing Troilus's life to completion, the poem will complete itself at a new and deeper level and assume its authentic place in the providential, Dantean economy of the narrator's development as a poet. Thus when the narrator returns abruptly "to purpose of my rather speche" after his remarks on language (1799), both he and his hero are poised for flight. Troilus, like Statius's Menoeceus, is on the threshold of death and a posthumous transcendence of the tragic world in which he has been drawn by his special virtue toward his inevitable end. He ascends through the spheres and comes to see at last the terms on which life is lived in a pagan universe. There can be little doubt that we are intended to see this final vision as a confirmation of the purity and depth of his intuition of the meaning of love.

It would be a mistake, of course, to assign any final meaning to this vision in itself. Despite the richness of Chaucer's account of Troilus's enlightenment, with its echoes of the *Somnium Scipionis* and the *Paradiso,* we must recognize that he is actually suspended in a spiritual void, that there is no category of religious experience to which we can confidently refer his celestial journey.[6] And we must not forget that he ascends to the eighth sphere only to set forth again and vanish with Mercury we know not where. But this final flight, which both fully articulates and finally circumscribes the aspiration of Troilus's spirit, also represents the first exercise of the narrator in his newfound role of *poet.* And like the apotheosis of Menoeceus, viewed in the light of Dante's retrospective account of Statius's career, Troilus's ascent to heaven is finally meaningful only insofar as it foreshadows the poet's transcendence of the world of his poem. True to his resolve to be "subject" to the great poets, the narrator's attitude is hardly distinguishable from Troilus's own as they ascend the spheres, and Troilus speaks for both of them in his sensitive response to the cosmological and spiritual vision of

6. See John W. Conlee, "The Meaning of Troilus' Ascension to the Eighth Sphere," *Chaucer Review* 7 (1972–73): 27–28, who points out that Chaucer's introduction of the celestial journey is not a declaration about the fate of Troilus's soul. Obscurity on this point mars the fascinating study of John M. Steadman, *Disembodied Laughter: Troilus and the Apotheosis Tradition* (Berkeley and Los Angeles, 1972). He notices (pp. 137–42) but does not really deal with the problem that Troilus's life has not been of the sort traditionally rewarded by admission to Elysium. And while lines 1826–27 leave many possibilities open, there is no real basis for Steadman's assertion (p. 167) that they show Troilus attaining "'a perdurable seete' above variableness and shadow of turning—a steadfast good common to both classical and Christian tradition." Ian Bishop (*Chaucer's Troilus and Criseyde: A Critical Study* [Bristol, 1981], pp. 95–96) points to the solitary and intellectual cast of Troilus's experience. Certainly there is nothing congratulatory about the "Swich fyn!" stanza, which follows immediately.

neo-Platonism. Only then, after Troilus's life has come to its imaginative consummation and he has been relegated once and for all to the unknown, does the narrator emerge, suddenly and powerfully, as a Christian poet.

In the final stanzas of the poem the voice we hear is that of a poet who has been finally liberated from the darkness of his long and excessive involvement with the story of Troilus. He is distanced from his "completed" work to the point at which that work can finally assume the status proper to a work of art, an embodiment of aesthetic and human qualities that may be appreciated for themselves and for their exemplary value with no danger that they will be confused with the spiritual values that are now the poet's primary concern. The very structure of the poem's final six stanzas may perhaps be seen as symbolizing the poet's new perspective; they may be read as two triads, each of which begins with an almost frenetic rejection of earthly vanity and pagan folly and each of which ends in religious affirmation.

In the first of these triads the finally abortive love of Troilus is balanced against the love of the young lovers in Chaucer's audience, which is not confined by the tragic world view and which can be matured and refined in the light of inner vision to the point at which it becomes an all-consuming love of God. The three stanzas and the three types or stages of love with which they deal form a sequence like that of Inferno, Purgatory, and Paradise, and in this evolving pattern lies the essential meaning of the poet's emancipation from the world view imposed by his pagan story. He has sent forth his book and commended his poetic fortunes to God, only to have the "litel tragedye" return to him transformed into a divine comedy.

But the transformation of the poet and his distancing from the world of the poem are not so absolute as may appear, and we are reminded that his emancipation has been achieved only at a price: as Troilus, from among the spheres, views the world both harshly ("This wrecched world") and tenderly ("This litel spot of erthe, that with the se / Enbraced is"), the poet, too, is insecure in the face of the story's lingering attraction for him. He vacillates between the need to reject it with harsh moralism and the desire to preserve some bond of appreciative sympathy. Thus the

stanza that begins with the heavy repetition of "Swich fyn!,"
"Swich fyn!," ends with a couplet that traces the arc of Troilus's
experience with no hint of condemnation:

> And thus bigan his lovyng of Criseyde,
> As I have told, and in this wise he deyde.
>
> [5. 1833–34]

These lines have the moral gravity of the preceding exorcism
without the violence. They focus on the sad fact of Troilus's loss
in a way that lends urgency to the following stanza, in which the
poet reminds his young hearers that they, at least, have an alternative to "feyned love." And in a sense it is the very force of the
exorcism that precedes them which, by purging the narrator's
tone of any trace of sentimentality, makes possible their combination of objectivity and compassion. So in the *Thebaid*, as
Statius condemns the dead sons of Oedipus to suffer all the
punishments of hell, he thinks simultaneously of the sad condition of mankind (11. 574–76) and immediately mitigates even
his judgment on the princes themselves with the spectacle of the
mourning of the bereaved father Oedipus, who comes at last to
discover fatherly piety and the power of the bonds of nature (11.
605–9). In both poems the fulfillment of the curse of Tisiphone,
the completion of the story told under her inspiration, releases
in the poet the capacity to express a larger, more humane appreciation of the meaning of that story.

But in the *Troilus* we are made to linger over Troilus's experience by more than compassion. As the emotional force of the
poet's appeal to his young readers derives in large part from the
sadness and finality of the couplet that is his last word on their
love, so there is a significant continuity between the moral content of the lines that appeal to the "yonge fresshe folkes" and
that of Troilus's posthumous vision in the preceding stanzas.
Looking down on the world at the culmination of his celestial
journey, Troilus had recognized and dismissed

> . . . al oure werke that folweth so
> The blynde lust, the which that may nat laste;
> And sholden al oure herte on heven caste. . . .
>
> [1823–25]

Though these lines ostensibly represent Troilus's own final reflections, we should notice the marked shift of emphasis in the
final line and the slight syntactic disjunction ("And sholden . . .")
that sets it apart from the tightly structured lines that precede it.
In fact, we cannot say with certainty who speaks this line, which
seems at first only the completion of Troilus's realization, but
which can perhaps be taken equally well as expressing the narrator's own futile desire to draw Troilus toward the affirmation
that would be the spiritual complement to the *contemptus mundi*
he has already come to feel. Heard in this way, the line would
also represent an involuntary reemergence of the narrator's own
Christian instincts, intruding themselves again as artlessly and
unselfconsciously as in the final stanzas of the Proem to Book 1.
But the significant effect of the ambiguity is to render imperceptible the precise point at which the narrator's insight into
Troilus's experience becomes clearly distinguishable from
Troilus's own. It is almost as though the religious lesson the
narrator goes on to draw from that experience were being
vouchsafed to him by Troilus. This continuity of experience is
reemphasized by a continuity of language: the injunction to
"caste" our hearts on heaven strikes a note that sounds again
when, after condemning the futility of Troilus's love and the
squandering of his nobility in the pursuit of "false worldes bro-
telnesse," the narrator issues his beautiful appeal to the young to
"cast up" their inner vision to God. The point so simply made is
profound: the love that "upgroweth" in Chaucer's young Christian readers has grown as well in Troilus. The difference between his "blynde lust" and their power to attain the vision of
God and Christ is a body of knowledge that the poet then recalls
with paternal simplicity:

> And of youre herte up casteth the visage
> To thilke god that after his ymage
> Yow made, and thynketh al nys but a faire
> This world. . . .
>   [1838–41]

The subtlety of these lines, the unobtrusive artistry with which
their highly Latinate syntax sets off the meanings conveyed by

"herte," "visage," "ymage," is emblematic of the long poetic schooling that has issued in the narrator's recovery of what he now offers as simple truth: we see most truly with the eyes of the spirit; we are made in the image of God; the beauty we behold outwardly will pass away. The absence of such knowledge, so fundamental as to be taken for granted and all but forgotten by the "yonge fresshe" medieval reader, is what caused Troilus to fall short, to worship a deceiving, ephemeral incarnation of that divine presence he had sensed so strongly at the heart of his experience of love.

The final three stanzas of the poem again follow an ascendant, Dantean pattern, moving from an exorcism of the themes and cosmology of classical poetry through the presentation of Chaucer's own text for the scrutiny of learned friends to the final prayer. Here the emphasis has shifted from the implications of the poem to the experience of the poet, and in the first of the three stanzas he balances a vigorous rejection of the pagans and their gods with a couplet that states plainly his debt to the world he is rejecting:

> Lo here, the forme of olde clerkes speche
> In poetrie . . .
>
> [5. 1854–55]

The placement of this couplet in its triad corresponds precisely to the placement of the couplet in which the poet had mentioned Troilus's story for the last time (1833–34), and the parallel is significant. As the earlier couplet conveys a sense of both strong compassion and spiritual distance, the latter implies both the poet's debt to poetic tradition and his new perspective on that tradition. He has finally separated himself from his pagan story and set it in a larger context that transforms its significance, but the "form" around which his spiritual intuition has taken shape is that of a poem in the classical tradition, a poem whose treatment of human experience, like Statius's account of Menoeceus viewed from the perspective of Dante, can now be seen as bearing a typological relation to the narrator's own experience in creating it, an experience that has culminated in the discovery of religious truth.

There is something jarring in the sudden emergence from this last evocation of the literary past into the fourteenth-century reality of the address to Gower and Strode. This has the same practical emphasis as the earlier stanza on the instability of English. Unlike Dante, who presents himself frankly as having realized the truth-telling capacities of his idiom more fully than the older poets he encounters in Purgatory, Chaucer appeals to his friends as one conscious of the danger that he may not have realized his intention, that in seeking to do justice to human love he may have failed to satisfy the demands of truth. We may see these lines, with the earlier stanza on language, as providing a realistic frame for the intuitive and highly symbolic transformation of the poet-narrator's role which takes place in the intervening eight stanzas. They show us a poet who remains humbly aware of the perishability of his medium and of his own precarious status as *auctor*. They remind us, in short, that Chaucer is a writer, setting pen to paper in a particular place and time. Whatever may have happened to the narrator of the *Troilus* under the influence of "poesie," through his responsiveness to "the forme of olde clerkes speche," has happened because Chaucer made it happen, because he invented it, and he in his frailty must accept responsibility for it.

Or have *I* invented it? In claiming for poetry, or in claiming that Chaucer claimed for poetry, the power to guide its subjects to the threshold of spiritual understanding, have I perhaps succumbed to my own need to discover something "important" in the *Troilus*, like the narrator responding to the consummation in Book 3? Has the critic merely taken advantage of the openness and good will of Chaucer and his narrator to make them act out his own idea of how poetic tradition ought to work? I have not been given the run of these handsome pages to engage in such soul-searching, but there is something about the clear air of the Gower-Strode stanza that encourages it, and I too have had learned friends in the back of my mind as I thought about the ending of the poem. *Has* Chaucer rendered the reality and value of poetry so accessible as I have pretended? As my friend Jean Krochalis once remarked, there is a disconcerting sense in which the *Troilus*, for all its appeals and signals to the reader, can seem a curiously private poem, something Chaucer might have written purely for his own satisfaction. At the very least we must acknowledge that much of the significance of whatever continuity he came to sense between his own work and that of the *poetae* is incommunicable, concealed beneath the words of the text like the conversion of Dante's Statius, and that its discovery was for Chaucer the poet largely an end in itself.

Moreover, even if we share, or feel we share, Chaucer's appreciation of the achievement of the *poetae*, is not this appreciation, as Anne Middleton argues, inseparable from a recognition of their remoteness, their powerlessness to speak directly to the living? Poetry in the sense in which Chaucer understood the term can, she declares, "have no real designs upon the world"; it "confers no certain good on the living human community." Still less can the *poetae* help us spiritually: "no work of literature can, by its very nature, have *as a deed* the kind of efficacy that the smallest prayer has."[7]

There is no getting around the fact that it is the combination of Chaucer's largely cryptic suggestions and our own responsiveness as interpreters which accounts for whatever role we understand the *poetae* to play in the *Troilus*. As Middleton further reminds us, there is no verb that can specify in the present tense what the *poetae* did, and thereby bring their intention to bear upon us.[8] But what we can do is to read them, as Chaucer's narrator bids us read, or hear, the *Troilus*, "with a good entencioun" of our own. Perhaps they cannot teach us all we need of charity, and the *telos* of our desire may lie beyond their dreams, but if we bring to our reading of them good will and the capacity for a love that "upgroweth," they can help us achieve moral and psychological integration and purpose. This is what Dante's Pilgrim, mindful all the while of Beatrice, discovers in Vergil:

> "Oh pietosa colei che mi soccorse!
> et te cortese ch'ubidisti tosto
> a le vere parole che ti porse!
> Tu m'hai con disiderio il cor disposto
> sì al venir con le parole tue,
> ch'i' son tornato nel primo proposto."

7. Middleton, "Chaucer's 'New Men,'" pp. 33, 38.
8. Middleton, p. 39.

"Oh, how compassionate was she who helped me, and how
courteous were you, so quick to obey the true words she spoke
to you! By your words you have made me so eager to come
with you that I have returned to my first resolve." [*Inf.* 2.
133–38]

Within barely a hundred lines the Pilgrim will once again lose
this sure sense of his "first resolve," abandoning himself to a
fruitless sympathy with the damned. He must learn the worst
and most painful as well as the noblest truths that poetry has to
teach, and his progress through the Inferno is punctuated by a
series of shocks. The very eloquence of the *poetae*, as we saw in
considering Dante's imitation of Vergil at the end of *Inferno* 3,
has a dangerous power. The unwary imitator is always in danger
of conjuring up demonic forces, as Chaucer's narrator involves
himself unwittingly with Tisiphone. But both the Pilgrim and
Chaucer's narrator are sustained by love, however dimly realized. The Pilgrim is never wholly cut off from the impulse to
honor the lady whom he envisions "in the court of heaven" (*Inf.*
2. 123–32), and the narrator of the *Troilus*, even at his most
disillusioned, preserves subliminally that half-wistful, half-com-
passionate sympathy with all lovers which flowers at last into
charity.

In the *Troilus*, moreover, our sharing of the narrator's ex-
posure to the psychological constraints and spiritual uncertainties of the world of the *poetae* is not controlled by the rigid terms
of the *Inferno*. Though we are given a clear perspective on the
narrator's involvement and made vividly aware of its potential
dangers, the deeper effect of Chaucer's treatment of the ancient
world is to enlarge our sense of human community, even as we
withdraw to the religious distance of the poem's final stages. We
do not need to engage in speculation about the salvation of the
righteous heathen to find value in an experience of poetry
which withholds the final orientation of a religious perspective
until we have been made to see in the condition of Troilus, and
in the lives of the Ovidian victims and Statian heroes with whom
he is compared, the lineaments of the love that upgroweth in
Chaucer's hearers. The motive for such a use of the *poetae* is, I
think, very close to that which will lead Chaucer to create the

violent secular world of the *Canterbury Tales* and seek out the spiritual element in the lives of even its most worldly and tormented inhabitants.

Even the prayer that concludes the *Troilus* conveys something of this sense of human community. There can be no questioning its religious emphasis, and it constitutes the first and sole moment at which we can hear the poet speaking with no direct reference either to the poem itself or to his activity as poet, but there are nonetheless signs that Troilus and his world are within its purview. It is based on the invocation used by those souls in Paradise who await the perfecting sacrament of reunion with their earthly bodies:

> Quell'uno e due e tre che sempre vive
> e regna sempre in tre e 'n due 'n uno,
> non circunscritto, e tutto circunscrive . . .
>   [*Par.* 14. 28–30]

> Thow oon, and two, and thre, eterne on lyve,
> That regnest ay in thre, and two, and oon,
> Uncircumscript, and al maist circumscrive . . .
>   [*Tr.* 5. 1863–65]

The translation is word-perfect, beautiful English that is at the same time a complete rendering of the Italian. There could be no clearer affirmation of the bond Chaucer feels himself to have established with Dante: they speak here with one voice. But Chaucer's allusion may have been prompted by Boccaccio, who echoes Dante's prayer in the second section of the *Filostrato,* making Pandaro declare to Criseida that no soul so perfect as Troiolo's has informed another being "since he who circumscribed the universe made the first man."⁹ The intention of this

---

9.   "poi che colui che 'l mondo circoscrisse
       fece il primo uom, non credo piu perfetta
       anima mai 'n alcun altro venisse
       che quella di colui che t'ama tanto,
       che dir non si potrebbe giammai quanto."

       "Since he who circumscribed the universe made the first
       man, I do not believe that anyone was ever endowed with a
       soul more fine than belongs to him whose love for you passes
       expression." [*Fil.* 2. 41. 4–8]

allusion in Boccaccio is hard to gauge: it is one of many instances in the *Filostrato* in which the appropriation of Dantean rhetoric to the celebration of earthly love seems almost an end in itself. But it is easy to imagine its ironic appeal for Chaucer, who has rendered in so much more depth the sorrow of Troilus's abortive vision. If we can imagine him thinking simultaneously of the fatally circumscribed spirituality of Troilus and of the glory of the bodily regeneration promised to the souls in Paradise, then his use of Dante's lines may be seen as a plea for the reintegration of human life, for the redemption of the imagination and a resolution of that psychological schism that has allowed Troilus to invoke love in the language of Dante's Saint Bernard, praying to Mary at the summit of the *Paradiso*, yet has allowed him also to believe that Paradise is the love of Criseyde.

But of course the allusion is first and last to Dante, and it may be seen both as symbolizing Chaucer's sense of indebtedness and as marking the point at which the two poets part company. Dante allows his disembodied souls a lingering concern with the spiritual well-being of others who had been dear to them in the world, but his emphasis in the prayer as a whole is on the supernatural radiance that the resurrected body will exhibit. Poetry, too, is for Dante only a means; in the *Paradiso* he has already distanced himself immeasurably from the world that poetry can claim to engage. Chaucer never turns so decisively away. His concern is more with aspiration than with transcendence, and to the end of his career he makes us aware of the importance for him of poetry as a mode of vision. He sees deeply into Dante's achievement and makes it the measure of his own achievement in the *Troilus*, but he finally chooses to follow a different path.

Index

Library of Congress Cataloging in Publication Data

Wetherbee, Winthrop, 1938–
Chaucer and the poets.

Includes index.
1. Chaucer, Geoffrey, d. 1400. Troilus and Criseyde.
2. Chaucer, Geoffrey, d. 1400. Troilus and Criseyde—Sources.
3. Chaucer, Geoffrey, d. 1400—Knowledge—Literature.
4. Love in literature. I. Title
PR1896.W48 1984   821'.1   84–7080
ISBN 0–8014–1684–1 (alk. paper)